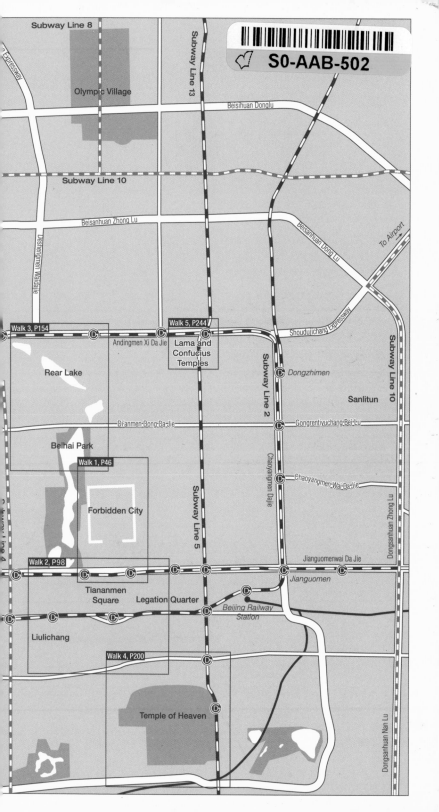

ODYSSEY BOOKS & GUIDES

Odyssey Books & Guides is a division of Airphoto International Ltd.
903, Seaview Commercial Building, 21–24 Connaught Road West
Sheung Wan, Hong Kong
Tel: (852) 2856 3896; Fax: (852) 2565 8004
www.odysseypublications.com

Distribution in the USA by W.W. Norton & Company, Inc.
500 Fifth Avenue, New York, NY 10110, USA
Tel: 800-233-4830; Fax: 800-458-6515
www.wwnorton.com

Distribution in the UK by Cordee Books and Maps
3a De Montfort St. Leicester, UK, LE1 7HD, UK
Tel: 0116-254-3579; Fax: 0116-247-1176
www.cordee.co.uk

Distribution in Australia by Tower Books
Unit 2/17 Rodborough Road, Frenchs Forest, NSW 2086, Australia
Tel: 02-9975-5566; Fax: 02-9975-5599
www.towerbooks.com.au

Beijing Walks—Exploring the Heritage
ISBN: 978-962-217-762-8
Copyright © 2008 Airphoto International Ltd.
Library of Congress Catalog Card Number has been requested.

Managing Editor: Paul Mooney
Assistant Editor: Helen Northey
Captions: Paul Mooney with Neil Art
Design: Alex Ng & Au-Yeung Chui Kwai
Maps: On The Road Cartography

Nineteenth century photos courtesy of Dennis George Crow
Contemporary photography by Magnus Bartlett
Forbidden City in Winter photograph by William Lindesay

Production by Twin Age Ltd, Hong Kong, email: twinage@netvigator.com
Manufactured in Hong Kong

Right: *Bronze Lion, an ornament found on large vats placed*
throughout the Forbidden City, see page 51

Above: *Interior, Hall of Supreme Harmony, Forbidden City*
Right: *The Thousand Year Pavilion in the northwest section of the Forbidden City*
(both pictures Walk One)

"A Chinese proclamation" The Illustrated London News, November 1878

BEIJING WALKS

DON J COHN

Dong Jiao Min Xiang runs past the former US Legation and barracks
shortly before ending at these steps which lead down to Tiananmen Square

Selling the Four Treasures of the Studio, Liulichang West (both pictures Walk Two)

Above: *A stone pagoda, the Botanical Garden, Beihai Park*
Left: *The White Dagoba, Hortensia Island, Beihai Park (both pictures Walk Three)*

Author's Dedication:

*In memoriam Josef Marx (1913–1978) whose
oboe first enticed me on the Way to Peking.
And with gratitude to Saeko Shibayama
for continuing the journey.*

Acknowledgements

Grateful acknowledgement is is made to the following authors and publishers:

John Murray Publishers Ltd for *The Book of Ser Marco Polo* by Sir Henry Yule

Les Editions Nagel for *Nagel's Encyclopedia Guide: China*

Derk Bodde *for Peking Diary: 1948–49, A Year of Revolution.*

Henri Vetch for *In Search of Old Peking* by L.C. Arlington and
William Lewisohn (Peking 1935). Reprinted with an introduction
by Geremie Barme. Oxford University Press 1987.

Peking by Juliet Bredon, first published by Kelly and Walsh, Shanghai
1919. Reprinted from the 1931 edition with an introduction by H.J.
Lethbridge. Oxford University Press 1982.

The Moon Year by Juliet Bredon and Igor Mitrophanow, first published by
Kelly and Walsh, Shanghai, 1927. Reprinted by Oxford University Press 1982.

The Adventures of Wu by H.Y. Lowe, first published by the The Peking
Chronicle Press in 1940 and 1941.

Excerpt from *The Soul of China* by Richard Wilhelm, copyright 1928 by
Harcourt Brace Jovanovich Inc., and renewed 1956 by John Jolroyd Reece.

Photographer's Dedication:

For Tabitha Storm, David Tang

&

Yan Yan,

Left: *The five-hundred-year old pagoda tree (Sophora Japonica) in the grounds
of the Divine Music Bureau, the Temple of Heaven (Walk Four)*

Curiosity Street, Pekin. The Illustrated London News, February 16, 1861.

PRELUDE

As we near the capital the stream of life becomes continuous. Mule-litters and sedan-chairs, though less frequent, add their touch of quaintness to the scene; and strings of solemn, silent-footed camels occasionally block the roads—each tied by a string through the nose to the tail of its foregoer. From the shaggy neck of the leader jangles a deep-toned, not unmelodious bell; and on its back a Mongol nods and sways half asleep, his purple robe and yellow sash adding a note of color to the dingy humps he bestrides.

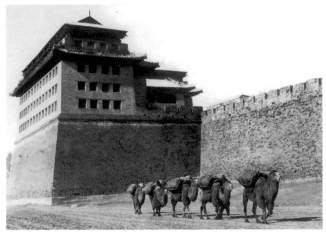

"Camel caravan, this is frequently seen going from and coming to the city. It does a great deal in the transportation of coal from the hills near Peiping and also of local produce of the farmers" from A Guide to Peking *published by* The Leader *in 1931, price thirty cents*

The scene is a fascinating one for the new arrival, whether from over seas or over land: the tinkle and clang of mule and camel bells; the cries of the drivers; the grunting sing-song of the barrow coolies; the strange, blue-coated, bronze-featured throng, all working out their existence unconscious of any world beyond a radius of a few li. And yet so civilized! To our polite "Chieh Kuang!" (jie guang: Lend me your light!) they make way at once, showing no rude surprise at our sudden appearance, incongruous and travel-stained. Often the conventional "Shang na'rh?" is asked in return—a "Whither bound?" to which we are at last able to reply, not to such-and-such a village or mountain-pass, but "Chin Ch'eng!" (jin cheng: To town!).[1:1]

(1:1) Archibald R. Colquhoun *The "Overland" to China* (London and New York: Harper & Brothers, 1900). p. 157.

CONTENTS

MAPS:

A pailou (ornamental archway), one of three at the entrance to the Lama Temple (Walk Five)

INTRODUCTION

The city of Beijing is probably as old as Chinese civilization itself, as Peking Man inhabited the caves at Zhoukoudian in the suburbs some 500,000 years ago. Written records attest to local settlements dating from around 1000 BCE, and for all but a few of the last 800 years, Beijing has been the capital of the empire—be it Mongol, Han Chinese, Manchu, republican or communist. Ever since Marco Polo reported on the splendor of Cambaluc, as he referred to the 13th century Mongol capital Khanbaligh, Peking has captured the Western imagination like few other ancient cities.

The contents of the vast curiosity shop known as Old Peking, stocked with the customs, manners, language and material culture of centuries of inhabitants, remained remarkably undisturbed by the ravages of time until the beginning of the 20th century. But the collapse of the Qing dynasty in 1911, the Japanese occupation (1937–45) and the subsequent communist takeover in 1949 took their toll on some of the more fragile contents of the shop and its gentle proprietors. In the 1950s the communists had little trouble transforming the city in their own image, developing a proletarian sprawl relieved occasionally by pockets of imperial pomp and socialist privilege.

The transformation of Old Peking into New Beijing had actually begun at the beginning of the 20th century, but the 1950s and 1960s saw the completion of a number of monumental projects that changed certain aspects of the city beyond recognition. Perhaps the most heartbreaking of these changes, for those who knew Old Peking, was the demolition of the vast city walls and gate towers, which dated in part from the Ming, a project that was completed by the early 1960s, supposedly in the interest of traffic flow. Secondly, the clearing of a vast space in the heart of the city to create Tiananmen Square—lined by the Soviet-inspired hulks of the Great Hall of the

Near the East Palace Gate, one of several lions dating from the Qianlong period, the Summer Palace (Walk Six)

"The Wall of Pekin from a sketch by our specialist artist in China".
The Illustrated London News, February 1873

People and the National Museum of China, and spiked in the center by the Monument to the People's Heroes—destroyed the symmetry inherent in all ancient Chinese capitals. And finally, the closing of dozens of Buddhist and Taoist temples, imperial palaces and gardens, and Manchu princes' mansions, all formerly open to the public, had a deleterious effect on the cultural life of the people.

After studying China and Chinese for a decade, I first arrived in Beijing in 1979 as a tour guide, a cultural shock broker. One of the qualities of the city that required the lengthiest acclimation was the pace. Beijing's shop assistants, telephone system, taxi drivers, traffic lights, petty bureaucrats, restaurant kitchens, even the teenagers, moved at the wound-down pace of a single-speed bicycle, and with the harmony and uniformity of a blue cotton Mao jacket. Life was suspended in the mid-20th century at a pace of ten miles/16 kilometers per hour, and any exertion by anyone beyond that particular gentle velocity seemed futile, art-less and gauche, anti-social and even counter-revolutionary.

In summer the choruses of cicadas crying out in the trees drowned out the polite ring of bicycle bells in the streets below, and everyone put on their short sleeve shirts on the same day in May. No one initiated the transformation, and there was no end in sight. The entire city, including the 60 taxi drivers (who turned off their engines 200 feet before every red light and glided to a halt, to save fuel) in the entire municipality of 10 million souls and the elderly street sweepers with their broad corn straw brooms, straw hats and face masks, siesta'd from around 12:30 pm to 2:00 pm, as no business was ever too pressing to pre-empt sleep. Today, only the traffic jams on the Avenue of Heavenly Peace near Tiananmen Square and the Second and Third Ring Roads can yank me back to the bicycle reality of those softer, dreamlike years.

The Chinese dragon whose head is Beijing has shed its skin several times, changing color with each molting. It's a cliché that when you return to Beijing after a two-month absence the city is unrecognizable. The cliché is true to a degree—in terms of new buildings, denser traffic, more McDonalds and Starbucks, and another all-night tongue-piercing parlor. But it is not true for the author, and hopefully not for the readers of this book.

In recent years, the tourism industry in Beijing and China has flipped many somersaults and continues to perform vigorously. Beijing is one of the most popular destinations for tourists in China, no matter where they come from.

Firstly, the positive side; to accommodate the great influx of visitors generated by the 2008 Olympics, major sites have been upgraded, renovated, reinforced and protected, while formerly closed temples and gardens have been opened to accommodate the army of visitors. The number of good hotels and restaurants has increased, and it is relatively easy to book accommodations in advance online or by phone and to dine well and cheaply without knowing more than a few words of Chinese. The number of flights, trains, taxis and buses to, from and within Beijing has shot up, as well as the number of roads, making it easier to get to and around the city.

As for the downside, oceans of tourists from every corner of the earth (including China) make enjoying, studying and even getting a decent glimpse of the prime sites in Beijing difficult. There is no crowd control on the broad patio in front of the main throne room (The Hall of Great Harmony) in the Forbidden City. As in so many other situations in China, the supply of throne views cannot meet the demand, and thus visitors are forced to dive into the sea of bodies to get a peek at the emperor's chair.

A few means of getting around these obstacles is discussed in the General Information chapter, namely by picking the right season to come, by staying out of rush hour traffic, by using the subway (Beijing underground) occasionally and by choosing the location of your hotel based on the length of your stay.

These considerations aside, Beijing remains the Greatest Show on Earth for the Chinese government and people, and in the many-ringed circus that is Chinese culture. Shanghai, Xi'an, Hong

Circular Street, and the Arrow Tower. The Illustrated London News (Walk Two)

Kong and Taipei all have their respective virtues, but they lack the script that tells the grand story of China over the past 1,000 years. As for where China, or Beijing, is going next, or next year, this is less a matter of *how* the chameleon changes its color, but *what* the chameleon thinks.

Despite these changes, some of them the inevitable consequences of modernization, the visitor to today's Beijing can experience much of the former grandeur of the palaces, temples and gardens of Old Peking equipped with a modicum of history, folklore and imagination. *Beijing Walks* was written to provide a stimulus for such visions.

Rather than dwelling on the sins of the past, this guide provides clues to help the visitor rekindle the aura that once surrounded Old Peking. There are maps and detailed instructions of where to go and what to see, as well as enough fact, legend and rumor to forge some of the missing links between the past and the present. In the chapter on the Forbidden City, for example, some curious details of the emperors' private lives are included, while the description of the former Legation Quarter quotes the strikingly candid observations of a Dutch diplomat from the turn of the 20th century. Our approach has been eclectic and our intent to inform as well as to entertain.

We would have liked this book to have been twice as long, given the wealth of available information, but then it would be a book for sitting with rather than walking. Beijing is an elusive city, where the dreamlike is constantly clashing with the everyday. Much of what matters still takes place behind walls, with the fate of more than a billion people balancing in the hands of the secretive party leadership. Given this quirk of history, the true personality of the city will not reveal itself readily to the uninformed. *Beijing Walks* encourages the visitor to break down the intimidating walls, to look behind the millions of bricks encircling the Forbidden City, to bask in the sunset over the Western Hills, and to weather the spring dust storms blowing through Tiananmen Square. Beijing presents a challenge to all, but a challenge worth taking, for sooner or later, the city touches all who come close to her.

As I write and as you read, the destruction and reconstruction of the capital proceeds on in an insomniac frenzy. More and more of Old Peking is crumbling into the dust from which it came. At the same time, the publication of this book can be viewed as an assertion of confidence in the notion that what is abandoned and forgotten can be recalled and revived, if only we sit back and let our imaginations wander, perhaps over the pages of this book.

Read *Beijing Walks*, then, in the spirit of rebirth.

Don J. Cohn, Beijing, November 2007

From the front-cover of the Illustrated London News, February 1861

HISTORICAL AND CULTURAL BACKGROUND

W hat's in a Name? Pekin? Peking? Peiping? Beijing? Beiping? The world remains divided on this sticky issue. Some see the *pinyin* "Beijing"–pronounced like "paging" with a "b" instead of "p"–as a pedantic intrusion into the domestic affairs of the English language. But no matter how you spell it, the present name of the city means "northern capital". In 1935, seven years after the capital had been relocated in Nanjing (southern capital) and Beijing renamed Peiping (northern plain, or peace), a guidebook published by the *Peiping Chronicle* devoted an entire page and bold face type to this issue:

Why "Guide to Peking" when this is Peiping? Because:

1. The average tourist is not so much interested in the city of today, which is Peiping, as he is in the city of the past–Peking.
2. Peiping is so new a name that many of the tourists still feel more familiar with the name Peking, and are more apt to buy a *Guide to Peking* than a *Guide to Peiping*.
3. What's in a name, anyway?

British literatus Osbert Sitwell was also fixated upon the name Peking, as he wrote in the Preface to his dreamy *Escape with Me! An Oriental Sketchbook*, based on four months he spent in the city in the 1930s:

> *I shall, too, continue to call it Peking, and neither Pekin nor the modern Peiping, for it is as Peking that I have always thought of it since I first read its magic name in childhood upon the program of a pantomime.*[1:2]

(1:2) p. xvi.

Borrowing this logic, in this book "Peking" will be used to designate the city of the past and "Beijing" to indicate the present-day capital.

Dynasties and Republics

Several dynasties and imperial reigns figure prominently in the city's history. The bone structure of Beijing is predominantly Ming, laid over a Yuan blueprint; most of the vital architectural organs are Qing; the city's complexion today, warts and beauty marks included, is Republican and People's Republican.

From about 1000 BCE, a series of small states made the area around Beijing their capital. While the emperors of the Han, Tang and Song dynasties built their capitals in central and eastern China, Beijing was under barbarian rule or served as a northern outpost of the empire. In the 10th century, the Khitans, a non-Chinese horde, founded the Liao dynasty and established their capital Yanjing here; in the 12th century, the Jurchen Tartars conquered the Liao and named their Jin dynasty capital Zhongdu (central metropolis). The Mongols sacked Zhongdu in 1215, and in 1260 Kublai Khan established the capital of the Yuan dynasty on the same site, calling it Khanbaligh, or Dadu (big metropolis). This was the Cambaluc Marco Polo so lavishly described in his famous travel book. Oddly enough no mention of the Venetian or anyone like him appears in contemporary Chinese records.

In 1368, the Ming dynasty, a Chinese house, succeeded the Yuan and built its capital at Nanjing in south China. And in 1403, Zhu Di, one of the sons of the founding emperor, Zhu Yuanzhang, unseated his nephew, the second Ming emperor, from the throne. Ruling as the Yongle emperor, Zhu Di then began to build his greatly expanded capital Beijing—so named for the first time—on the ruins of Khanbaligh. Yongle's masterpiece, ·completed in 1420, provided the city with the stately geometric pattern that remains little changed today, and in that year the city was formally named Jingshi, or Capital City, a designation that survived until 1912.

Traveling in China–the mid-day halt as seen by an artist commissioned by the Illustrated London News in 1859

The Qing, or Manchu dynasty (1644–1911), embellished their Ming inheritance by building grand gardens in the western suburbs and erecting a number of splendid mansions, Lamaist temples and dagobas throughout the capital. No expense was spared in the elaboration of the imperial properties, which were off limits to all but members of the imperial clan, officials attending audiences and the thousands of maidens and eunuchs who served the Son of Heaven and his concubines high and low. The most creative Manchus were Kangxi, Qianlong and the notorious, kitschy Empress Dowager Cixi.

During the Republican period (1911–49) scattered attempts were made to create a style of modern Chinese architecture that combined Chinese essence with Western permanence. Examples of this can be seen at Tsinghua (Qinghua) and Peking (Beijing) universities. The Kuomintang (KMT), or Nationalist Party, moved the capital to Nanjing in 1928, and when the war with Japan broke out in 1937, Peking, then renamed Peiping, entered into a twilight period of decline.

The People's Liberation Army "peacefully liberated" Peiping from the Nationalists in 1949, and established it as Beijing, the capital of the People's Republic of China. Post-liberation architecture from the 1950s is a hodgepodge of Soviet wedding cake fantasies, such as the Beijing Exhibition Hall near the zoo, Stalinist neo-classical piles, like the Great Hall of the People, The National Museum of China and Beijing Railway Station, and kitschy Chinese flavored buildings like the Friendship Hotel, which was criticized for the high cost of its glazed tile roofs.

During the 1960s, cheap pre-fabricated housing blocks, bland to the eye and depressing to inhabit, went up to accommodate the population explosion, and many of these eyesores dot the main avenues of the city. More fallout shelters and underground tunnels than buildings seem to have been created during the decade of the Cultural Revolution (1966–76).

Beginning in the late 1970s, a slight improvement could be seen in the design of apartment buildings and offices, although no building of character was built at this time. One notable exception was I.M. Pei's remotely-located Fragrant Hills Hotel, which incorporates elements of Suzhou gardens in the hotel's forest setting. Only in the mid-1980s, once the many joint venture hotels and office towers had come on stream, did the authorities in Beijing permit architects to dabble in international styles. The People's Bank of China building, shaped like a traditional Chinese silver "shoe" ingot, is an essay in cuteness, but no one can claim it is not Chinese.

The Beijing headquarters of the Bank of China, like its sister in Hong Kong, is designed by I.M. Pei, who seems to have trouble refusing major Chinese commissions, while continuing to complain about his bosses. Pei's latest venture in China is the new Suzhou Museum, which he calls his last.

Since the early 1990s, Beijing has engaged in a construction boom unprecedented in its history. Commercial residences, offices and shopping centers continue to mushroom at dizzying speed and in claustrophobic proximity to each other, while virtually every ministry in Beijing has a new glitzy headquarters, many of them sited along the prestigious Chang'an Avenue. A Central Business District has emerged, but the CBD lies in the eastern part of the city in the Chaoyang District near the China World Trade Center, several miles from the traditional heart of Beijing, Tiananmen Square.

A new generation of Western architects has been called upon to confer internationality upon China. Nowhere is this more evident than in the pompous parade of new high rises, banks and commercial centers that line Chang'an Avenue for several miles to the east and west of Tiananmen Square.

Cast of Characters

The following figures have made significant contributions to Peking, and are referred to frequently in the text. Each represents an age.

Yongle: (reigned 1402–24) Third Ming emperor who usurped the throne from his nephew and laid down the pattern of Beijing as it

"The Chinese Imperial Marriage at Pekin: Procession from the Imperial Palace to the bride's residence on the wedding day", the Illustrated London News December 1872

basically stands today. Yongle also restored the Grand Canal to supply the capital with grain and cloth from the south. He dispatched the great Moslem eunuch admiral, Zheng He, on seven expeditions to the Indian Ocean, thus establishing China's naval supremacy in Asia for the only time in history; he also forced the Japanese into vassal status for the first time, and exacted tribute from as far away as Africa.

Kangxi: (reigned 1661–1722) Son of the first Qing emperor, Kangxi was second emperor of the Qing dynasty. He built gardens in the western suburbs and a summer palace at Jehol (now Chengde), patronized scholarship and the arts, and assigned foreign Jesuits to the Board of Astronomy. He fathered 20 sons and eight daughters who grew to maturity.

Qianlong: (reigned 1736–96) Kangxi's grandson and the fourth Qing emperor. Successful in military affairs, prolific poet and writer, patron of the arts and garden builder, he launched a literary inquisition, rejected England's petition for relaxing trade restrictions, and tolerated Jesuits in his court. He had 17 sons and 10 daughters, and joined a military campaign at the age of 85.

Cixi: (1835–1908) whose name looks, and nearly is, unpronounceable, was the virtual ruler of China from about 1865 to her death. The old spelling, Tz'u Hsi, is of little help for the uninitiated. Try the "ts" as in "bits" for Ci and "she" for "xi". Cixi was the:

—concubine of the Xianfeng emperor (reigned 1850–61)
—mother of the Tongzhi emperor (reigned 1861–74)
—aunt and regent of the Guangxu emperor (reigned 1874–1908) from 1874 to 1888; Guangxu was three years old when he became the emperor in 1874, but only married and began his reign in 1888.

Mao Zedong: (1894–1976) The great helmsman of the People's Republic who condemned the city walls and ensconced himself and his cronies in imperial palaces. Mao, who was 13 when Cixi died and 16 when the Qing dynasty fell, spawned the Cultural

Revolution (1966–76) that ended with his death. The official verdict on Mao and his contributions to modern China is that he did 70 per cent good and 30 per cent bad.

The Four Cities of Peking

The names of the four contiguous walled cities date from the Qing dynasty and Republican period. The only "city" standing today is the Forbidden City, the walls of which are intact. The four "cities" during the Qing dynasty and early Republican period were:

The Four Cities of Beijing in the Ming and Qing Dynasties

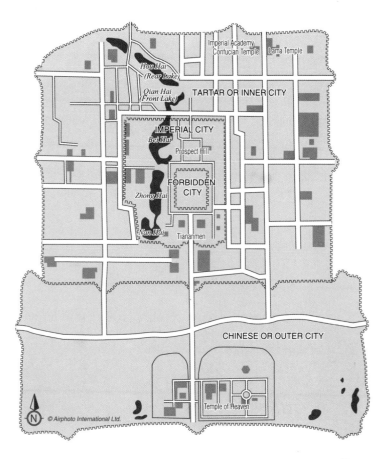

THE FOUR CITIES

Tartar (Manchu or Inner) City, includes the Forbidden and imperial cities:
Residence was restricted to the imperial troops and the bannermen, who were originally Manchu, Mongol and Han Chinese soldiers organized into eight groups represented by different colored banners.

Imperial City:
Home to the members of the imperial clan. Today a portion of the Qing-dynasty Imperial City wall surrounds the south and west borders of Zhongnanhai.

Forbidden City:
The palace itself, inhabited by the emperor, his female entourage, and thousands of eunuchs.

Chinese (or outer) City:
Chinese residential area and principal urban commercial and entertainment district.

Fengshui

Fengshui (wind and water), or geomancy, is as scientific, in the modern sense, as astrology. But the history of city planning and architectural design in China cannot be understood without reference to this ancient art. *Fengshui* experts investigate the shapes of bodies of water, hill configurations, and nearby structures to determine the ideal location, size and orientation of a building (or grave, bank, fish tank or parking lot) with the aim of enhancing the welfare of its inhabitants. Negative influences that cannot be modified, such as mountains or skyscrapers, can be mollified just as positive influences can be reinforced.

The layout of Peking demonstrates several basic principles of *fengshui*. The major buildings in the Forbidden City rest on a north-south axis that forms the backbone of Beijing. Because evil influences emanate from the north, all of these buildings face south. Prospect Hill (Jingshan, or Coal Hill), the artificial mound that stands immediately north of the Forbidden City, prevents these evil influences from infiltrating and polluting the palace. According to legend, when the Yongle emperor was planning his new capital in the early 15th century, a geomancer presented him with an anatomical blueprint according to which key locations in the Forbidden and imperial cities corresponded with the vital organs of a mythical being named Nozha. Like Chairman Mao's embalmed corpse in his mausoleum in Tiananmen Square, Nozha's imaginary head lies to the south with his feet pointing north. Thus, according to contemporary geomancy, Nozha's *membrum virile* corresponds to the Memorial to the People's Martyrs.

Hutongs

Pronounced with an "r" after the "o", accent on the second syllable, *hu-torng* is a Chinese transcription of a Mongol word, *hotlog*, which means "water well." Many Beijing hutongs have colorful names with interesting historical connotations, though in recent decades some of these names have been purged of their "feudal" content.

The worst historical abuses in this regard were perpetrated during the Cultural Revolution (1966–76), when lanes and alleys took on names like Red-to-the-End Road, Great Leap Street and People's Commune Street. Some street names changed many times during this decade.

Altogether some 600 streets and hutongs were renamed after 1949. One reason for this was to avoid duplication. According to a 1944 street guide, Beijing had 16 Shoulder Pole (*Biandan*) *Hutongs*, 14 Well (*Jing'er*) *Hutongs*, 11 Flower Blossom (*Huazhi*) *Hutongs* and seven Arrow Shaft (*Jian'gan*) *Hutongs*. There were also a good number of *hutongs* with names that the local inhabitants found objectionable. Stinking Skin (*Choupi*) *Hutong* became Longevity (*Shoubi*) *Hutong*; Pants Crotch (*Kudang*) *Hutong* became Warehouse (*Kucang*) *Hutong*; Hang-up-and-beat (*Diaoda*) *Hutong* became Perfect Filial Piety (*Xiaoda*) *Hutong*. A small sampling of present-day names suggests their variety: Fried Beans, Bean Sprouts, Split Beans, Big Stone Tiger, Iron Bird, Sheepskin Market, Sesame Seeds, Tea Leaves, Antique Cash, Lamp Wick, Soldiers and Horses, Sound the Drum, Sweet Well, Dog Tail, Big Ears and New Fur Warehouse.

Ethnology

Beijingers, or Pekinese, like most Northern Chinese, are a great mixture of ethnic types. Though most locals identify with the Han majority, their taller-than-average (in China) stature and facial features common in Northern China attest to early intermixture with Mongols, Manchus and other Central and Northern Asian peoples. Beijing has a large population of Moslems (Hui), some of whom are physically indistinguishable from the Chinese, some with more prominent noses and deep sunk eyes. The distinctly Caucasian men selling *shish* kabob in the street are Uighurs, most of whom come from the Xinjiang Autonomous Region.

Chinese Architectural Features

Lion-dogs: These playful creatures, always in pairs, guard entrances to important buildings. Lions are not native to China, but Han-dynasty (206 BCE–220 CE) annals record emperors receiving lions as tribute offerings from Parthian and other Central Asian missions to China. The king of beasts has been considerably domesticated over the years after numerous incarnations in bronze and stone. The female (with mouth closed) is always shown with her cub; the male (roaring, or perhaps yawning) is playing with a ball, perhaps representing the sun or the earth. Legend has it that mother lions feed their cubs milk through their paw, and that the ball is a storage place for milk, which can be extracted and used by humans as medicine.

Marble terraces: Following a tradition at least 3,000 years old, all major religious and ceremonial buildings and the residences of the emperor and imperial clan are built on marble terraces, with the height of the terrace indicating the importance of the building. The tallest terrace in Beijing is the foundation of the Three Great Halls in the Forbidden City, 7.12 meters (23.3 feet); the tallest circular terrace in the Temple of Heaven is nearly two meters (six feet) shorter. The Round Altar in the Temple of Heaven is an example of a terrace that is a building in itself. The Chinese name of these structures is "Mt. Sumeru terraces" (*Xumizuo*); according to Indian and Buddhist mythology, Mt. Sumeru (or Mt. Meru, associated with the actual Mt. Kailash) is located at the center of the universe and is trillions of feet in height.

Pailous: Freestanding multi-roofed gateways or arches of wood or stone erected in streets or on the axis of a temple, tomb, or palace. Peking had several dozen street *pailous* in 1949; only a handful remain. On our walks, *pailous* can be seen in Beihai Park, the Summer Palace, on Guozijian Street, and in the Guozijian and Lama Temple. Some scholars suggest that the design of the *pailou* is of Indian origin. Compare the ornate stone *toran* (or *torana*) arched gateways at the early Buddhist temples at Sanchi with the pailou immediately to the north of the Round Altar in the Temple of Heaven.

Roof creatures: Examples of glazed ceramic roof creatures guarding the eaves of important buildings are plentiful in the Forbidden City, where they appear in groups of as many as ten. Often the first "creature" in the queue is a man mounted on a phoenix. This is Prince Min of the Warring States period (475–221 BCE), who was rescued from his death by the giant bird on which he is seated. The other animals are auspicious: the dragon and phoenix symbolize harmony and nobility, male and female; the lion, ferocity and majesty; the heavenly horse and sea horse, good fortune; the two mythological lion-like creatures, justice; a member of the dragon family wards off fire; a monkey-like creature with wings brings up the rear. The large dragon-head figures at each end of the ridge of the roof are the offspring of the dragon, responsible for controlling ocean waves and rain.

Roof Tiles The colour of roof tiles indicates the status of the buildings. Yellow was reserved solely for imperial ceremonial buildings and dwellings. After imperial yellow, the pecking order descends as follows: blue, green, black, unglazed.

Staircases: In imperial buildings, all of which face south, the terraces usually have three sets of staircases corresponding to the three openings in gate towers. The central staircase, like the central opening, was reserved exclusively for the emperor; looking north, the left (western) staircase was for military officials, the right (eastern) for civil officials. The central imperial staircase was again divided into three sections. The emperor was carried in a sedan chair over the long marble slope, set between two staircases, elaborately carved with the imperial symbols of dragon and phoenix disporting in the waves and clouds. The sedan chair bearers ascended the staircases to the side. Strange though it may seem, the carved marble slope was often covered with a rug on ceremonial occasions.

In describing the marble slope, or "imperial path" leading up through the three terraces of the Hall of Prayer for a Good Harvest in the Temple of Heaven, the French writer Pierre Loti explained after his visit in 1900 the function of the carved slab in what seems like an entirely fanciful, if not physically precarious manner:

> *An "imperial path" is an inclined plane, usually an enormous monolith of marble placed at an easy angle, upon which the five-clawed dragon is sculptured in bas-relief; the scales of the great heraldic animal, its coils and its nails, serve to sustain the Emperor's steps and to prevent his feet, dressed in silk, from slipping on the strange path reserved for Him alone, on which no Chinese would dare to tread.*[1:3]

Lake Tai stones (Taihu shi): The Chinese term for large chunks of limestone that are placed on the bed of a lake or stream to be eroded by the flow of water and time. A crucial decorative element in every classical Chinese garden, these miniature mountains were produced in the Yangzi delta area and traveled north as an exotic luxury. Before they were shipped to Peking on Grand Canal barges, Taihu stones were covered in mud which, when dry, gave them a protective husk. The preference for the

---

[1:3] Pierre Loti *The Last Days of Pekin*, p. 78.

gnarled, irregular, grotesque shapes of these stones derives from an aesthetic that cherishes the old and wizened, the wild and the "natural." The elaborate man-made mountain for viewing the moon in the northern corner of the Imperial Garden in the Forbidden City, composed of hundreds of chunks of Lake Tai stone glued together to form a many-storied maze, is one of the largest conglomerations of the rocks in northern China. One courtyard in the Lion's Garden (*Shizi Lin*) in Suzhou is filled entirely with a vast maze, all made of these uncomfortable looking rocks.

Osbert Sitwell attempts to explain the Chinese reverence for these odd shapes:

> *They must be crags grotesque or sinister, worthy of exhibition in the surrealist museum, natural objects with a kink, born with a likeness to something else, to a mountain, to a man or a thing he has fashioned, to an animal, an insect, even; and the more fantasy the stones betray, the more complicated and extravagant their resemblance to, let us say, an ant-eater, a microscope or a motor-car, the more they esteem and wonder at it....*[1:4]

Walls: In his book on Chinese architecture, D.G. Mirams wrote: "The Chinese wall is not only a wall but a design. It protects and at the same time it embellishes." The Chinese word for wall, *cheng*, has "city" as its secondary meaning. Walls divided the city from the country in traditional China, just as the Great Wall was built to protect the agricultural settlements of the Han from the nomadic barbarians. The height of a wall indicates the status of those who live within, but in Peking even the most humble *hutong* hovels had their walls.

(1:4) Osbert Sitwell *Escape with Me! An Oriental Sketch-book*, p. 273

Looking north towards a fanciful and distinctly understated Forbidden City in the 1870s, the Illustrated London News

Chinese Dynasties

Traditional Spelling	Pinyin	Dates
Hsia	Xia	2070–1600 BCE
Shang	Shang	1600–1027 BCE
Western Chou	Xi Zhou	1027–771 BCE
Eastern Chou	Dong Zhou	770–256 BCE
Spring and Autumn	Chun Qiu	770–476 BCE
Warring States	Zhan Guo	475–221 BCE
Ch'in	Qin	221–206 BCE
Western Han	Xi Han	206 BCE–25 CE
Eastern Han	Dong Han	25–220
Three Kingdoms	San Guo	220–280
Western Jin	Xi Jin	265–316
Eastern Jin	Dong Jin	317–439
(Including Sixteen Kingdoms)		
Southern and Northern Dynasties	Nan Bei Chao	420–589
Sui	Sui	581–618
T'ang	Tang	618–907
Five Dynasties	Wu Dai	907–960
Liao (Khitan)	Liao	916–1125
Northern Sung	Bei Song	960–1127
Southern Sung	Nan Song	1127–1279
Chin (Jurchen)	Jin	1115–1234
Western Hsia (Tangut)	Xi Xia	1038–1227
Yuan (Mongol)	Yuan	1279–1368
Ming	Ming	1368–1644
Ch'ing (Manchu)	Qing	1644–1911
Republic of China	Min Guo	1911–1949
People's Republic of China	Zhonghua Renmin Gongheguo	1949–

Ming and Qing Emperors and PRC leaders

Ming Dynasty (1368–1644)

Traditional Spelling	Pinyin	Reigned
Hung-wu	Hongwu	1368–1399
Chien-wen	Jianwen	1399–1403
Yung-lo	Yongle	1403–1425
Hung-hsi	Hongxi	1425–1426
Hsüan-te	Xuande	1426–1436
Cheng-t'ung	Zhengtong	1436–1450

Ching-t'ai	Jingtai	1450–1457
T'ien-shun	Tianshun	1457–1464
Ch'eng-hua	Chenghua	1465–1487
Hung-chih	Hongzhi	1488–1505
Cheng-te	Zhengde	1506–1521
Chia-ching	Jiajing	1522–1566
Lung-ch'ing	Longqing	1567–1572
Wan-li	Wanli	1573–1619
T'ai-ch'ang	Taichang	1620
T'ien-ch'i	Tianqi	1621–1627
Ch'ung-cheng	Chongzhen	1628–1643

Qing (Ch'ing) Dynasty (1644–1911)

Traditional Spelling	Pinyin	Reigned
Shun-chih	Shunzhi	1644–1661
K'ang-hsi	Kangxi	1662–1722
Yung-cheng	Yongzheng	1723–1735
Ch'ien-lung	Qianlong	1736–1795
Chia-ch'ing	Jiaqing	1796–1820
Tao-kuang	Daoguang	1821–1850
Hsien-feng	Xianfeng	1851–1861
T'ung-chih	Tongzhi	1862–1873
Kuang-hsü	Guangxu	1874-1908
Hsüan-t'ung (Puyi)	Xuantong	1908–1912

The Republic of China (1912–1949)

(Due to the complexity of power shifts during this period, with its many local warlord leaders, only the three main actors are listed.)

Yuan Shikai:1913–1916; president until his death.

Sun Yat-sen: 1921–1925; KMT leader until his death.

Chiang Kai-shek:1926–1975; Led the KMT army, fled to Taiwan in 1949, remained president of the "Republic of China" there until his death in 1975.

People's Republic of China (1949–)

(Generally, these dates reflect the perceived period of leadership rather than the possession of official titles)

Mao Zedong: 1949–1976

Hua Guofeng: 1976–1978

Deng Xiaoping:1978–1993

Jiang Zemin: 1993–2003

Hu Jintao: 2003–

WALK · 1

THE FORBIDDEN CITY

Duration: Approximately 3.5 hours

Starting Point: This walk starts at The Gate of Heavenly Peace on Chang'an Boulevard, at the southern entrance of the Forbidden City, *aka* the **Palace Museum**, and takes you into the Forbidden City, arguably the world's largest imperial palace, in terms of building space. But the grounds at Versailles are more spacious.

Hours: The visiting hours of the Forbidden City, open daily but rarely closed without notice, are as follows:
November–March: 8:30 am–4:30 pm (last entry at 3:30 pm);
April–October 15: 8:30 am–5:00 pm (last entry at 4:00 pm).

How to Get There: Taxis cannot stop just anywhere near the Forbidden City. You can be let off on either the east or west side of Tiananmen Square. Bus routes T1, T5, 1, 2, 4, 5, 9,10, 22, 44, 47, 48, 53, 52, 57, 59, 101, 103, 109, 111 and 116 stop near the square. If you take the east-west Line 1 of the Beijing underground get off at Tiananmen Dong (east) or Tiananmen Xi (west).

How to Leave: Bus routes 101, 103, 109, 111 stop near the rear (north) gate of the Forbidden City. A number of taxi drivers hang out in front of the north gate but avoid getting a taxi there. These drivers will often try not to use the meter and will ask for unreasonable fares. The best place to catch a taxi is at Jingshan Dong Jie or Jingshan Xi Jie, about 200 meters east/west of the north gate.

Websites:The Palace Museum's website lists current events and provides information on opening and closing hours and special exhibitions. www.dpm.org.cn/english/default.asp

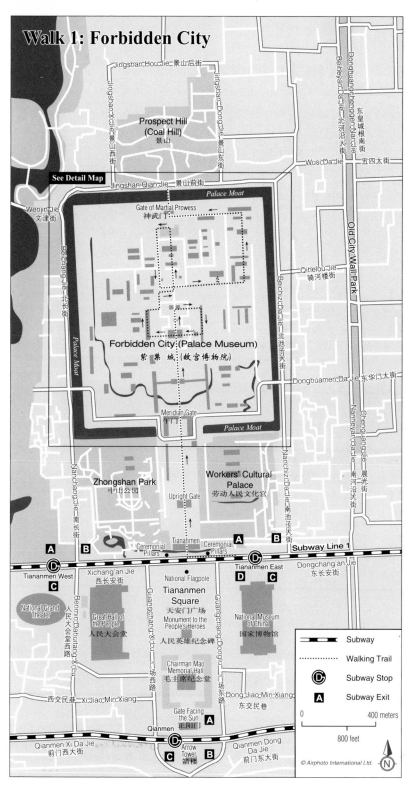

Walk 1: Forbidden City

Jingshan-Hou-Jie 景山后街

Jingshan-Xi-Jie 景山西街
Jingshan-Dong-Jie 景山东街
Jingshan-Qian-Jie 景山前街

Beiheyan-Da-Jie 北河沿大街
Donghuangchenggen-Nan-Jie

东皇城根南街

Wusi-Da-Jie 五四大街

Prospect Hill
(Coal Hill)
景山

See Detail Map

Wenjin Jie
文津街

Beichang-Jie 北长街

Palace Moat

Gate of Martial Prowess
神武门

Palace Moat

Qihelou-Jie 骑河楼街

Old City Wall Park

Beichizi-Da-Jie 北池子大街

Forbidden City (Palace Museum)
紫禁城 (故宫博物院)

Palace Moat

Donghuamen-Da-Jie 东华门大街

Meridian Gate
午门

Palace Moat

Nanchizi-Da-Jie 南池子大街

Nanheyan-Da-Jie 南河沿大街

Chenguang-Jie 晨光街

Nanchang-Jie 南长街

Zhongshan Park
中山公园

Workers' Cultural
Palace
劳动人民文化宫

Upright Gate

Tiananmen

Ceremonial
Pillars

Ceremonial
Pillars

A

B

Subway Line 1

A

Tiananmen East

Dongchang'an Jie
东长安街

A

Tiananmen West

B

Xichang'an Jie
西长安街

C

National Grand
Theater

Renmin-Dahuitang-Xi-Lu 人民大会堂西路

Great Hall of
the People
人民大会堂

Guangchang-Xi-Lu 广场西路

National Flagpole

Tiananmen
Square
天安门广场

Monument to the
People's Heroes
人民英雄纪念碑

Guangchang-Dong-Lu 广场东路

D

C

National Museum
of China
国家博物馆

Chairman Mao
Memorial Hall
毛主席纪念堂

Xi-Jiao-Min-Xiang 西交民巷

Dong-Jiao-Min-Xiang
东交民巷

Gate Facing
the Sun
正阳门

A

Qianmen

D

Qianmen Xi Da Jie
前门西大街

Arrow
Tower
箭楼

C

B

Qianmen Dong
Da Jie
前门东大街

	Subway
	Walking Trail
D	Subway Stop
A	Subway Exit

0 ⸻ 400 meters

800 feet

© Airphoto International Ltd.

N

FORBIDDEN CITY

THE FORBIDDEN CITY

Only about one third of the buildings in the Forbidden City are now open to the public, many fewer than in the 1930s. Entry for tourists is through the **Meridian Gate** (*Wumen*) in the south part of the complex, or the **Gate of Martial Prowess** (*Shenwumen*) in the north.

The Forbidden City served as both residence and court for 24 Ming and Qing emperors over the course of five centuries, from its grand opening in 1421 until 1924, when Puyi, the deposed last emperor who in 1912 had relinquished the imperial throne, was impolitely removed from his own ancestral court-home-and-palace by Feng Yuxiang, a warlord known as the Christian General. Portions of the palace were converted into a public art museum in 1914 to display a small selection of objects from the former imperial collections, and the **Palace Museum** (*Gugong Bowuyuan*), which comprises both the palace and the art collections, formally opened in 1926.

"Reception of the Foreign Ministers and consuls by the (new) Emperor of China at Pekin".
The Illustrated London News, September 1873

Right: *Glorious yellow roofs,*
the Pavilion of Everlasting Reign situated in the Imperial Garden

On the eve of the Japanese occupation in 1937, the most valuable works of Chinese art were crated and transported to Nanjing and Shanghai for safekeeping. When these cities were on the verge of falling to the Japanese, the crates were shipped further west to the inland provinces of Sichuan and Guizhou. In the late 1940s they were returned to Peiping, as the city was then called, and in 1948, as Chiang Kai-shek retreated from the mainland with the remnants of the Kuomintang troops and thousands of civilians, a total of 2,972 creates of the finest jades, bronzes and paintings were transported by military planes and ships to the island of Taiwan, They now make up the bulk of the magnificent collection of the fortress-like Palace Museum, built into the side of a mountain in the suburbs of Taipei. In Chinese political parlance, and echoing the promise made to Hong Kong by Deng Xiaoping before the former British colony returned to Chinese sovereignty, "One country, two systems," the situation with the Palace Museum can be described as "One museum, two collections."

Beginning in 1952, the People's Government, carried out a major palace-cleaning, during which 250,000 cubic meters of rubbish was discarded. During the Cultural Revolution (1966–76) Zhou Enlai is credited with having extended his personal protection to the Forbidden City when the Red Guards threatened to destroy it and its feudal contents.

Inside the Hall of Supreme Harmony

The Beijing Palace Museum still has one of the largest collections of Chinese art in the world, and has replenished its earlier depleted holdings with donations from China and overseas as well as through purchases, donations and acts of "liberation" from

The huge bronze and iron vats placed throughout the palace were kept filled with water, as a fire prevention measure

"reactionary" private collections during the Cultural Revolution. Until recently, countless items in the Palace Museum collection remained uncatalogued, among them some 150,000 paintings and tons of precious Qing-dynasty documents in Manchu, a language understood by only a small handful of scholars in China. In the 1990s, the Palace Museum built a state of the art underground storage area to safeguard the bulk of the collection. In recent years, the quality of the displays has improved markedly, reversing the situation in which no new electric wiring was permitted in the palace out of a well-founded fear of fire.

Pyrophobia is nothing new in the Forbidden City; large sections of the palace went up in flames in the Ming, Qing and Republican periods. The worst fire in modern times took place in 1923 and resulted in the loss of many valuable antiques. The former last emperor, Puyi, had ordered his eunuchs to make an inventory of the works of art in the Palace of Establishing Happiness (*Jianfu gong*) in the northwest section of the palace. A number of these devious non-men, who had been spiriting away priceless treasures from this palace over the years, panicked when they received their orders and set the fire to destroy all evidence of their transgressions. The conflagration was extinguished by soldiers from the Italian legation guard only after extensive damage had been done. At the suggestion of Puyi's English tutor,

Reginald Johnston, a tennis court was built in the freshly cleared rectangle. Henry (the English name Johnston conferred on Puyi) and his younger brother William (Pujie) also learned to ride a bicycle here, and had some of the original high thresholds in the Inner Court removed or provided with ramps to facilitate their movements.

The **Palace of Establishing Happiness** was rebuilt from scratch over the course of six years, beginning in 2000, and formally opened in a private ceremony in the fall of 2005 (attended by former president George Bush Senior and former Chinese foreign minister Qian Qichen) as a reception center for visiting dignitaries and a showcase of Chinese architecture, with contemporary interior spaces for private exhibitions. Whether the hoi polloi, or general visitors to the Forbidden City, will be admitted to these buildings is unclear as of this writing. The project was undertaken by the Hong Kong based China Heritage Fund, which invested US$5 million in the project. If this sort of complicity between overseas wealth and power and Beijing cultural officials results in the creation of exclusive venues that sanctify "Chinese culture" for the benefit of the privileged, the money has been wrongly spent and a poor precedent established. The China Heritage Fund is also footing the bill for the reconstruction of the Zhongzheng Dian, or Hall of Rectitude, a Tibetan Buddhist temple, also consumed in the flames in 1923. The project is scheduled for completion before 2009.

But the palace's present-day overseers didn't stop there. In 2003, they signed an agreement with the World Monuments Fund to restore—using US$3.3 million of the Fund's funds—the adjacent Lodge of Retirement belonging to the 18th century emperor Qianlong. In March 2005, the Fund designated another $10 million for the restoration of the entire Qianlong garden, which has remained baren of flora, fauna, columns, walls and roofs since 1923. The Palace Museum will contribute $5 million to the project. While most of the popularly visited sites in the palace have been restored for the Beijing Olympics, the entire overhaul of the Forbidden City is not scheduled to be completed until 2020, the 600th anniversary of the palace.

A pool within the Six Eastern Palaces (1982)

Reduced to its basic components, the Forbidden City is a network of walled courtyards within walled courtyards. Once inside the palace, the only communication with the outside world is upwards, through the sky. As Harold Acton wrote, "For once the sky was part of the architectural design."[1:5] All distant views within the palace are severed by walls with the discipline of an insidious geometry that breeds myopia, self-absorption, introspection, defensiveness and, by extension, xenophobia.

Once inside the palace, the only communication with the outside world is upwards

The Forbidden City is the epitome of Chinese exclusiveness. It was designed both to keep strangers out and the emperor in. The English literary critic William Empson, who lived in Peking and taught at Peking University (1937–39, 1947–53), described it as "a biological device for ruling the world."[1:6] Like Chairmen Mao and Deng, who occupied their own imperial quarters in the "sea palaces" in nearby Zhongnanhai, the Chinese emperors before them often grew restless from being constrained for so long in a brick and stone spider web and would head off to their summer palaces or visit the capital's red-light districts incognito.

On his world tour in the 1930s, Osbert Sitwell envisioned critical aspects of China's political future as he viewed the palace from his hotel window:

> ... the Forbidden City showed in the foreground great halls, that, for all their gaily glistening eaves and shining tiles, were, in their lines and sentiment, as solemn and forbidding and grand as any in Moscow (just as Russia has in it something of China, so has China of Russia)....[1:7]

(1:5) Harold Action *Memoirs of an Aesthete* (London: Methuen 1948), p. 276.
(1:5) William Willetts *Chinese Art*, II, p. 679.
(1:5) Osbert Sitwell *Escape with Me! An Oriental Sketch-book*, p. 159.

Aerial view of the Forbidden City in the 1930s, seen from the north axis, Prospect Hill in the foreground

The Hall of Supreme Harmony and its vast courtyard

At the center of the Forbidden City sat the **Son of Heaven**, theoretically the possessor, quite literally, of All Under Heaven, the world, for heaven (sky) and the walls of the palace were all he could see from his limited perspective. Compare Versailles, with its endless views, playful fountains and forests, and vanishing perspectives. The vast ceremonial courtyards of the Forbidden City, flat and bare as a monk's shaven head, had no trees where a sniper might conceal himself; or perhaps trees would somehow diminish the grandeur of the buildings. The chilling courtyards of the Forbidden City can be likened to the drained swimming pools of Atlantis, an archaic expression of empire.

Abel Bonnard (1883–1968) was intrigued by the "order" he found in the palace. After ascending to the top of Coal Hill, immediately to the north of the Forbidden City, he observed:

> Straight before me was a rectilinear enclosure which contains the Forbidden City.... These enclosures are orientated with a complete exactitude; each of their faces looking towards a cardinal point, and no other city in the world is constructed so obviously and patently according to the ordinance which rules the universe. The palaces which rise up closely pressed together in the Imperial City have the same rigorous orientation. They face each other and respond to each other. There is some relation to the fields of agriculture in their great simple forms, and their glorious yellow roofs are dazzling like fields of ripe corn, and seem to be lifting a symbol of the fecundity of the imperial soil up into the sky.... The Imperial City stands alone. All this is around it is as nothing.... The order reigning here is very different from that which we are accustomed to; instead of encouraging man to develop and carry forward new order, it fixes man to the spot, binds him with unbreakable bonds and effaces him.[1:8]

(1:8) Abel Bonnard *In China 1920–1921*, p. 10.

onnard, a French poet and novelist whose fascist views developed in the 1930s, a decade after his trip to China, gained the post of minister of National Education during the Vichy regime (1942–44). Nicknamed "la Gestapette" due to his homosexuality, Bonnard was expelled from the prestigious French Academy after World War II for collaborating with Germany and was condemned in absentia to death. He obtained political asylum in Spain under the Franco government. Retried for his crimes in France in 1960, he received a symbolic sentence of 10 years banishment to "begin" in 1945, but in dismay at the guilty verdict, he returned to Spain where he died in 1968. (www.wikipedia.org, incidentally, this site is sometimes inaccessible in China).

Moat and corner tower

The grand rectangular maze of rectangles would have had an overwhelming effect on the visitor—most of them Chinese officials attending business at court—entering the palace from the south. As William Willets wrote about an observer entering the Imperial City from that direction:

> From the moment he crossed the outer moat he would have been forced into a sort of automatic dance, its rhythm set by the changing masses and spaces of each successive stage over which he made his way.... One can well imagine the growing bewilderment and disquiet of such a person as he passed through one blank wall and beneath one brooding gate-house after another, to find beyond it only a featureless avenue leading to yet another wall and gate. Reality was softening into a dream. His mind, so long attentive to a distant goal somewhere ahead in this labyrinth of straight lines, so long expecting a climax that never seemed to come, must at least have refused to record and memorize the minor differences in scale, proportion and decorative detail of the buildings that were the only landmarks of his progress. As he pressed forward into a world of emptiness and of deadening silence, dream must have intensified into a nightmare of déjà

vu. Whatever self-possession he may have had at the outset must long since have drained away when, crossing Wu Men [Meridian Gate], he finally entered the precinct of the Forbidden City.... And, however ineffectually it may have regulated its own internal affairs, there can be little doubt of its capacity to reduce outsiders to a state of supplicatory awe.[1:9]

An extreme form of male chauvinism was practiced in the imperial palaces. With a few temporary exceptions the emperor was the only biologically functional male of the species among thousands of court ladies, concubines, maids and eunuchs—the latter wonderfully described by Harold Action as "a bustling and cackling intermediate sex with the disadvantages of both." There are records of eunuchs in the palace during the Han dynasty (206 BCE–220 CE). Their numbers and baleful influence reached a peak in the Ming (20,000–30,000), but by the Qing the total was less than 10,000. The grand eunuch Li Lianying served as the Empress Dowager Cixi's right hand "man" in bringing about the decline and fall of the Qing dynasty in the late 19th century. Li, incidentally, must have been one of the wealthiest men in China in his day; as chief eunuch and thus the ultimate concierge of the Forbidden City *and* Summer Palaces, he was able to accumulate an estate consisting of several *tons* of gold.

The general formula of Chinese imperial palace design was set down in the Zhou dynasty (1027–256 BCE.): looking south: left, ancestors; right, earth; front, court; rear, marketplace. For the most part, the Yongle emperor followed this plan when he built the Forbidden City in the early 15th century. To the southeast of the palace stood the Ancestral Temple of the emperors, now the **Workers' Cultural Palace**; to the southwest was the **Altar of Land and Grain**, a site of imperial sacrifices, today **Zhongshan Park**. The southern half of the palace was devoted to court functions; but the rule of the rear markets was not applied as it was in the Summer Palace. The northern section of the palace contains the residential quarters of the emperor and his empress, consorts and concubines, with attached gardens and temples.

(1:9) William Willetts *Chinese Art*, II, pp. 678–9.

Construction: A Ming historian claimed that 100,000 artisans and one million unskilled coolies participated in the construction of the palace over the course of 16 years, 1406–21. The principal building materials are wood, stone, brick and glazed tiles. In the Ming, timber was shipped to Peking from the southwestern provinces of Sichuan, Yunnan, Guangdong and Guizhou via the Yangtze River and the Grand Canal. Shipments from southwestern China would take as long as four years to reach the capital. During the Qing dynasty, the forests of northeast China were the major source of wood used in repairing and extending the palace. The same Ming source quoted above says: "For every thousand men that went into the mountains (to cut timber), only five hundred returned."

Today, according to UNESCO, the Palace Museum, or Forbidden City, has 1,300 employees, approximately one third of whom are security guards and one fifth of whom are researchers.

The rectangular floral porcelain vents set into the burnt madder walls of buildings directly beneath visible bracket systems are there to prevent the concealed wooden columns that support the building from rotting.

The principal building materials are wood, stone, brick and glazed tiles

The River of Golden Water with its white marble balustrades

The white marble used for decorative and structural purposes in the palace was quarried in Fangshan, some 50 kilometers (32 miles) southwest of Beijing. The roof tiles and bricks paving the courtyards were fired locally and in Shandong province and Suzhou. During the Ming dynasty glazed roof tiles were fired in Liulichang, in the southern part of the city.

The statistics concerning Beijing bricks are mind-boggling: 12 million bricks were laid in the wall surrounding the Forbidden City; 20 million in the courtyards and interior walls of the palace; 80 million in the Peking city walls. As these bricks weighed an average of 24 kilograms (almost 53 pounds) each, it has been estimated that, in the early Ming dynasty, 1.93 million metric tons of bricks were fired to build the new capital.

The massive rehabilitation project leading up to the 2008 Beijing Olympics, part of a 20-year project scheduled to end in 2020, includes replacing the tiles on the roofs of the huge Gate and Hall of Supreme Harmony. The new paint jobs these critical buildings are receiving appear bright and harsh and glossy, as glitzy and tasteless as the nail polish on the toes of a floozy. Yet this vulgar makeup may actually reflect a historically sanctioned habit of painting the palaces as brightly and cheerfully as possible, as the contractors and craftsmen knew that the cold impersonal surfaces would mellow in a few years, and would require a makeover in less than a decade. Considering the

The new paint jobs these critical buildings are receiving appear bright and harsh, but Beijing's climate will dull the colors quickly enough

worsening air pollution and increased flow of visitors to the Forbidden City, a thick coat of lacquer and gloss may be the best prescription for protecting the ancient structures from present-day depredations.

The broad defensive moat that surrounds the palace freezes in winter and so it was formerly used for recreational skating. In the old days, sleds pulled by coolies provided local transportation around the circumference of the Forbidden City. The mud dredged to form this moat was piled up to the north of the Forbidden City to form Prospect Hill (*Jingshan*), also known as Coal Hill. So fertile was this mud that beginning in the 17th century, a crop of lotus was planted in the moat to supply the imperial kitchens with fresh lotus root. In the 18th and 19th centuries, as much as one third of the area of the moat was profitably rented out to tenant farmers expert in lotus cultivation.

The huge bronze and iron vats placed throughout the palace, some of them gilded, were kept filled with water drawn from the **River of Golden Water** that flowed through the palace, as a fire prevention measure. In the winter, eunuchs would keep the vats wrapped in padded cotton cosies and set burning charcoal braziers underneath them (note the space left for these in the marble bases) to prevent the water from freezing. Japanese troops

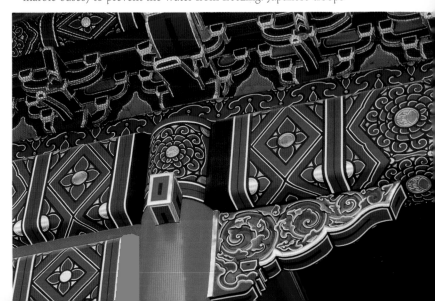

removed and destroyed many of the vats during their occupation of Peking (1937-45).

The first electric lights in Peking shone for the Empress Dowager Cixi in 1888, when a foreign company installed a 5,000-watt generator in the palace. Otherwise oil lamps were used indoors, and standing oil lamps lit up the courtyards and exterior corridors at night.

Two methods were used to heat the palace. In some of the residential quarters, a system of underground flues warmed the floors and built-in brick beds (*kang*) that were a common feature in homes in north China. In the other buildings, charcoal braziers were placed about the ceremonial and other residential halls. Rank determined the amount of charcoal allotted to each palace resident. Daily quotas in the Qianlong period, in catties (one catty equals about 500 grams or 1.1 pounds), reveal an interesting pecking order:

120–Empress Dowager	30–Princess
110–Empress	20–Prince
90–Imperial Consort	10–Imperial grandson
75–Consort	

The charcoal used to heat the palaces and for cooking was of such high quality that it was entirely smokeless. This explains why there are no chimneys or smokestacks in the Forbidden City.

China's emperors had no designated place to go to the toilet. When the need arose, a eunuch would be summoned with the

Considering the worsening air pollution and increased flow of visitors to the Forbidden City, a thick coat of lacquer and gloss may be the best prescription for protecting the ancient structures from present-day depredations

imperial potty, a simple platinum bowl with a cover set in a wooden frame with a horse-shoe shaped seat upholstered in yellow silk. The palace eunuchs and maidens used more conventional chamber pots. With such a dense population, did the Forbidden City stink like a latrine? Not at all.

旅游星级厕所　STAR—RATED TOILET

★ ★ ★ ★

北 京 市 旅 游 局 颁 发
ISSUED BY BEIJING TOURISM ADMINISTRATION

Improved toilet arrangements

The super fine ash from the charcoal burnt in the palace was placed in every potty and night pot to absorb the noxious odors. Young eunuchs washed the chamber pots out after every use, and the accumulated waste was removed from the palace at regular times each day.

As usual, Cixi was a cut above the rest in this regard. Her personal potty was filled with the fine sawdust of fragrant wood, which reputedly emitted the same delicious scent both before and after it was used. A nice bit of panoply accompanied Cixi's evacuations. A specially designated eunuch would carry her carved sandalwood potty, covered with a cozy of yellow imperial silk, and a palace maiden would set it down on a square of oil cloth next to the dowager. Toilet paper was placed in the mouth of the carved wooden gecko that clung to the outside of the potty. When she was finished, this little ritual was repeated in reverse. Cixi probably suffered from hyperthyroid, and had a ravenous appetite. This made it difficult for her to control her bowel movements, and thus this little entr'acte had to be reenacted many times each day.

In the early Ming (14th–15th centuries), large sheets of toilet paper were manufactured in the palace using tribute hemp from Sichuan, though the emperor had his own personal brand, in imperial yellow, each piece measuring only 7 x 9 centimeters (2.7 x 3.5 inches). From the Ming Wanli period on, imperial toilet paper was imported from Hangzhou. Cixi's own brand had a high cotton content, and was folded neatly and ironed flat by her attendants.

Like toilets, there were no designated dining rooms in the palace. The Son of Heaven called for his meal whenever and wherever he pleased. He took most of his meals alone, attended solely by eunuch servers and tasters: elaborate procedures and the intervention of the Household Affairs Department were required to make it possible for his palace ladies to sup with him in the palace. Sharing a sea cucumber with a concubine was much more convenient in the summer palaces and gardens where the rules governing access to His Presence were less rigid.

Ensuring hygienic safety was a top priority in the emperor's diet. A silver plaque was inserted into each of the dozens of dishes served at each meal, as silver would blacken if it came into contact with a poisonous substance such as arsenic. A eunuch taster sampled a mouthful of every dish placed before the emperor, providing a second level of security. Palace regulations also forbade the emperor to take more than two bites of any dish, lest his culinary preferences provide a clue for a potential poisoner. A eunuch stood next to the emperor while he ate. His job was to warn the Son of Heaven sternly if his chopsticks hovered over the same plate for a third time. For the same reason, the emperor could not request to be served any particular food, and his servants were not allowed to recommend any dish or ingredient, even a particular seasonal vegetable or fruit. And thus all the imperial menus were set by the imperial kitchen, where strict discipline also prevailed.

In the late Qing dynasty, one of the larger kitchens in the palace (*Shoushan fang*) had 100 stoves with three persons attending each of them; a chef, a food cutter and a helper, or scullion. The stoves were numbered, and precise records were kept of the names of the people who washed, cut and cooked each dish each day, in order to be able to trace the guilty party should something go amiss.

Palace records are similarly fastidious in reference to the shipment of fresh lychees to North China from the south. Every Chinese high school pupil learns the story of how the Xuanzong emperor of the Tang dynasty had lychees transported to the capital of Chang'an (present day Xi'an) by means of the imperial pony express system, to satisfy the cravings of the famed pudgy concubine Yang Guifei. In the Qing dynasty, advanced naval technology made it possible for entire lychee trees to be placed on boats in the coastal province of Fujian and shipped by sea to Peking. Palace documents detail the number of boats dispatched, the number of trees on each boat, and the number of lychees growing on each tree. The records also tell us how many lychees were consumed in the palace each day, as well as the number of lychees the emperor presented to each concubine and minister, all of whom are named. These statistics provide historians with a tool for determining which concubines and officials were enjoying the emperor's favor at any particular time.

D rinking water for the palace was drawn from a spring in **Jade Spring Mountain** (*Yuquan Shan*) in the north-western suburbs [玉泉山] (see pages 295, 319) and was transported to the palace daily. Water used for sanitation, fire prevention and construction in the palace was supplied by the **River of Golden Water** (*Jinshui He*) that runs along the western wall of the palace and through the courtyard in front of the **Gate of Supreme Harmony** (*Taihe Men*).

Notes on the Walk: You need not fear getting lost in the Forbidden City, as its symmetrical layout facilitates a quick escape to the exits. But it can be very distressing to lose track of a traveling companion in the maze of buildings, especially if both parties lack cell phones. If you enter the palace from the south, be sure to agree on an emergency meeting place, such as the tall man-made mountain in the Imperial Garden at the north end of the palace near the exit, in case a member of your party gets lost.

Our walk will take us from south to north, proceeding through the **Tiananmen**, **Duanmen** and **Wumen** gates, the **Three Harmony Halls**, the chronological art displays and other temporary venues for exhibitions, and then the residential section in the north of the complex with its several thematic art collections. We conclude by climbing **Prospect Hill**, aka **Coal Hill**, to the north of the palace, although only on clear days is the view from the summit worth the climb.

Forbidden City in Detail

Beichizi Da Jie 北池子大街

Prospect Hill (Coal Hill) 景山

Jingshan Qian Jie 景山前街

Palace Moat

Palace Moat

Palace Moat

Gate of Martial Prowess 神武门

Imperial Garden 御花园

Gate of Earthly Tranquility 坤宁门

Palace of Earthly Tranquility 坤宁宫

Hall of Union 交泰殿

Palace of Heavenly Purity 乾清宫

Gate of Heavenly Purity 乾清门

Well of the Pearl Concubine 珍妃井

Pavilion of Peace and Harmony in Old Age 颐和轩

Hall for Joy in Old Age 乐寿堂

Pavilion of Pleasant Sounds 畅音阁

Hall for Nourishing Heavenly Nature 养性殿

Palace of a Peaceful Old Age 宁寿宫

Hall of Imperial Supremacy 皇极殿

Hall of Imperial Treasures 珍宝馆

Nine Dragon Wall 九龙壁

Hall of Ancestral Worship 奉先殿

Six Eastern Palaces 东六宫

Palace of Concentrated Beauty 储秀宫

Palace of Eternal Spring 长春宫

Hall of Mental Cultivation 养心殿

Grand Council 军机处

Six Western Palaces 西六宫

Hall of Preservation 保和殿

Forbidden City (Palace Museum) 紫禁城 (故宫博物院)

FORBIDDEN CITY

Nanchizi Da Jie 南池子大街

Palace Moat

East Flowery Gate 东华门

Palace Moat 筒子河

Chronological Display of Chinese Art 历代艺术馆

Hall of Complete 中和殿 Harmony

Hall of Supreme 太和殿 Harmony

Chronological Display of Chinese Paintings 绘画馆

Gate of Supreme 太和门 Harmony

River of Golden Water 金水河

Meridian Gate 午门

Hall of Martial Heroism 武英殿

Xihuamen Da Jie 西华门大街

Palace Moat 筒子河

West Flowery Gate 西华门

Xihuamen Da Jie 西华门大街

Palace Moat

Beichang Jie 北长街

·········· Walking Trail

Ⓝ N

0   400 feet

0   200 meters

© Airphoto International Ltd.

Chairman Mao, Tiannanmen

The Walk

Cross one of the seven white marble bridges over the stream to the south of **Tiananmen**, the Gate of Heavenly Peace [天安门], which stands at the front entrance of the Imperial City.

Open-mouthed lion, Forbidden City

Ironically, the landmark pointing to the entrance to the Forbidden City is Mao Zedong's much-reproduced portrait, occupying what must be the prime bit of wall space in China. However, the portrait was not always a permanent fixture here. In the early 1950s Mao's visage was only hung there on 1 October, China's National Day, and 1 May, International Labor Day. In the early years of the Republican Period (1911–49), the spot had been occupied by a blue and white (the Kuomintang colors) portrait of Sun Yat-sen, and later by one of Chiang Kai-shek. The portrait, depicting Mao around the age of 60, perhaps before he launched the Cultural Revolution, is well maintained today and is replaced from time to time.

There are two pairs of elaborately carved marble **ceremonial pillars** (*huabiao*) here, one standing inside and the other outside the gate. As the story goes, the lions, or lion dogs that face away from the palace have their mouths open because it is their job to inform the emperor of any wrongdoing committed by palace officials during his absence from the palace. The creatures facing the palace have their mouths closed to remind anyone who knows that the emperor has left the palace in disguise to remain silent about it. The emperors passed through Tiananmen only several times a year on their way to major sacrifices, imperial weddings and military campaigns.

Imperial trials for serious crimes were held in front of Tiananmen, and when the death sentence was handed down, a red tick was penned next to the guilty man's name on an official document, as it is still done today on public execution notices. In the Qing dynasty, imperial edicts were attached to the mouth of a carved golden phoenix that was lowered from the top of the gate onto a tray held by officials from the Board of Ceremonies. In the Ming, such documents were attached to a carved dragon's head suspended from the end of a pole by a colored cord.

Continuing north, pass through a long, narrow courtyard interrupted at its north end by the **Upright Gate** (*Duanmen*) [端门], which served a defensive rather than ceremonial purpose and was never mounted by the emperor. Troops guarding the palace would gather here on summer nights to gamble and occasionally a high official would join them for a round. Continue north in this long rectangular corridor until you come to the next structure, the U-shaped **Meridian Gate** (*Wumen*) [午门], the large formal entrance of the Forbidden City. This gate can be thought of as a set of dragon jaws ready to snatch up whoever comes near them and deliver them into the maw of the palace.

Tickets are sold from windows on the east side of the plaza in front of the Meridian Gate. A single RMB60 ticket covers admission to all the open buildings and exhibitions in the Forbidden City, although special exhibition halls, such as the Hall of Clocks and the Hall of Treasures, require an extra ticket selling for RMB10.

In imperial times, officials awaiting an audience in the palace would gather at the Meridian Gate at about 3:00 am. A number of snack sellers set up their stands near the gate to provide the early risers with a hot breakfast. Once every three years, the emperor would mount the Meridian Gate tower and announce the names of the successful candidates in the triennial palace examinations, the most important in the vast system of civil service examinations. As usual the central entrance in this gate was reserved for the emperor alone, but exceptions were made for the three top-scoring candidates in the examinations, one of them possibly destined for a prime-ministership, as well as for the emperor's fiancée, who was carried into the palace on a sedan chair. The structure over the central gate tower housed a throne; the side towers, a drum and a bell respectively. The bell was struck every time the emperor passed through the gate, and the drum beaten when the sacrifice to the ancestors was held in the Ancestral Temple. In the Ming dynasty, the emperors held banquets here for high officials, during which the Son of Heaven would compose poems along with his guests. In the Qing dynasty, the emperor would issue the new calendar prepared by his astrologers from here each year, and inspect freshly captured prisoners of war.

Passing through the arched passageway, we come to the first broad courtyard of the palace with its five marble bridges spanning the **River of Golden Water** (*Jinshui He*) [金水河]. The river, fed from a sluice gate in the northwest corner of the Forbidden City moat, follows the contours of a hunting bow symbolic of military prowess. Its entire course within the palace also resembles the human digestive tract.

At this early point in the walk, it is possible to interrupt the northward passage to visit two recently opened parts of the palace where superb exhibitions are held. The **Meridian Gate** (*Wumen*) holds temporary exhibitions. You gain access to it by a staircase that ascends to the top on the huge structure's west side.

An even more dramatic venue for displays of objects in the Palace Museum collection is the **Hall of Martial Heroism** (*Wuying Dian*) [武英殿], which stands directly to the west of the **Gate of Supreme Harmony** (*Taihe Men*) [太和门]. A visit here is highly recommended. Access is through the large gate on the western flank of the first courtyard in the palace, through which runs the River of Golden Water. Temporary exhibitions held here often relate to the former imperial collections of books and other printed matter that were produced here in the early Qing dynasty. The European style building to the west of the Hall of Martial Heroism, the **Hall of Preservation** (*Baoyun Lou*) [宝蕴楼], was built as recently as 1914 by Yuan Shikai. It stands on the former Qing dynasty site of a school for Manchu princes.

The gate before you, the **Gate of Supreme Harmony** (*Taihe Men*) [太和门], is guarded by a pair of bronze lions and leads to the vast courtyard that contains the **Three Harmony Halls** (Supreme, Complete and Preserving Harmony). The Ming emperors held audiences in the tower of this gate, and when imperial audiences were moved into the Hall of Supreme Harmony, the gate continued to be used as a depot where the emperor changed from his palace palanquin to a larger sedan chair when setting off on sacrifices outside the palace. The Gate of Supreme Harmony burnt down in a huge fire in 1888 and was reconstructed the next year.

The fire was viewed as particularly inauspicious. It took place only one month before the day selected for the wedding of the Guangxu emperor, and this gate was to play an important role in the ceremonies for the grand occasion. As it was impossible to change the astrologically auspicious date, something had to be done about restoring the Gate of Supreme Harmony.

The solution was to rebuild the gate entirely in wood, with every detail, including the glazed tile roof, crafted to resemble the original structure. A contemporary document recorded that "even people who had served in the Inner Court for years were unable to distinguish it from the original," with its tile roof and brick walls. The present Gate of Supreme Harmony dates from 1889, one year after Guangxu's marriage.

The low buildings on the east side of the courtyard were in the Qing dynasty the offices of a department that tracked the progress of imperial orders, and of another office that handled official appointments and honorary tiles. During the Ming, the buildings on the west housed a school for imperial princes. During the Qing, they became the offices of a Manchu-Chinese translation bureau, and of a secretariat that kept fastidious records of the emperor's movements and pronouncements.

Passing through the Gate of Supreme Harmony we come to a second spacious and empty courtyard, the largest in the palace. According to legend, fifteen layers of bricks, seven laid flat and eight placed upright, pave the ground here to prevent intruders from burrowing their way into the sacred precincts of the palace from the outside. The buildings to the side were storage rooms for the imperial family's leather and furs, silk, armor, saddles, ceramics, gold and silver, tea and clothing. On ceremonial occasions this courtyard was filled with the vast panoply of officials, guards and eunuchs in gorgeous dress, creatively evoked in the 1987 Bernardo Bertolucci film, *The Last Emperor*.

A small hue and cry arose after the shooting of this film. It came from a choir of cultural conservatives who decried the commercial exploitation of the ancient palace as a sellout to

The Meridian Gate, looking south across the
River of Golden Water from the Gate of Supreme Harmony

foreign interests. A similar hue and cry was heard when Starbucks hung its round green shingle in a dull corner of a palace thoroughfare; the shingle was removed, but this was not enough to calm nationalist feelings, and their coffee stopped flowing in July 2007 when Starbucks was forced to abandon the Fobidden City. And perhaps yet another cry and hue will be heard in the land when it is learned that the notorious **Palace of Establishing Happiness** (*Jianfu Gong*), destroyed by arson by palace eunuchs in 1923 and rebuilt in 2006 by Hong Kong philanthropy, is locked away to all but "visiting dignitaries."

The **Three Harmony Halls**, so called because the word "harmony" appears in each of their names, and because dissonance has no place in a location like this, stand on a three-tiered marble terrace over 7 meters (23 feet) tall, decorated with elaborately carved balustrades and a total of 1,142 dragon heads whose mouths function as drains when it rains. One art historian with an eye for the macabre wrote that the balustrades here produce a very complicated and restless effect, which from certain viewpoints is not unlike a modern graveyard.[1:10] The 18 bronze incense burners on the steps of the terrace, cast in the Ming dynasty, represent the 18 provinces of the Qing empire, and served several functions. First, the burning sandalwood raised a smokescreen of anonymity for the emperor, for on windless days the smoke would obscure the entire hall. Second, the incense neutralized the noxious odors of the eunuchs, whose sanitary habits were notorious. Foreigners in the 19th century complained that the poorly cured fur garments worn by Manchus in the winter smelled like dead animals. One also wonders if any voices could be heard over the din produced by the strident wind and percussion instruments played during the ceremonies held in the halls.

The **Hall of Supreme Harmony** (*Taihe Dian*) [太和殿], the first and largest of the Three Harmony Halls, was first built in the early 15th century but was twice destroyed by fire in the Ming dynasty (1420 and 1557) and once again in the Qing

(1:10) D.G. Mirams *A Brief History of Chinese Architecture*, p. 79.

dynasty. The present hall, one of the largest of its type in China, dates from 1695, although it has been refurbished several times. Here the emperor would take part in lavish ceremonies on the first day of the Chinese New Year, at the winter solstice and on his birthday. Other rites included the announcement of a new reign period, interviews with the top candidates in the imperial examinations, and the commissioning of high-ranking military officials who were about to set out on major campaigns. During the Ming and early Qing dynasties, the final round of the imperial examination system was administered here. The following description of the panoply in this hall dates from the 1860s:

> . . . [The Emperor] sits on a high throne in the center of the vast and gloomy hall, facing the south, while about fifty attendants of high rank [chiefly Manchus] stand on each side. These constitute the Emperor's suite, and they enter the temple by side-paths and side-doors, the Emperor himself entering by a central raised path, several feet higher than that by which his attendants enter. In front of the hall, south of the front balustrades, is the space appropriated to the nobility and officers who come to perform the act of prostration. They are arranged in eighteen double rows; the civil officers are on the east side, and the military on the west. Nearest to the hall steps, and upon them, are the princes of first and second degree; with the [two] Manchu ranks. . . ; followed by the five orders of Chinese nobility. . . . These make in all nine. Then come the mandarins of nine grades. Stones are fixed in the pavement to mark their positions, and over these stones are placed copper covers shaped like mountains. Here they perform the immemorial ceremony of the nine prostrations before the unseen emperor, who, deep in the recesses of the hall, is concealed still more completely by a cloud of incense.[1:11]

The objects now displayed on the south terrace are a sundial and a bronze grain measure, the latter a symbol of the emperor's fairness and incorruptibility. What resembles a swastika on its base is actually an inside-out swastika, an ancient Indian Buddhist symbol of good fortune that means "ten thousand" in Chinese.

(1:11) Joseph Edkins *Peking*; in Alexander Williamson, *Journeys in North China, Manchuria, and Eastern Mongolia; with Some Account of Corea*, p. 325.

The much-rubbed crane and tortoise incense burners are traditional symbols of longevity. When the Xuantong emperor, Puyi (1906–67), was placed on the throne in this hall in 1908 at the age of three, he is reported to have cried throughout the ceremony. The throne on view today dates only from the 1950s. In 1915, the president of the Republic of China, Yuan Shikai, removed a throne dating back to the 18th century Qianlong reign, and replaced it with a Western-style chair better suited to his bandy legs. The present throne is a reconstruction based on a 1900 photograph. It was assembled using bits and pieces of an undated throne found in a palace warehouse.

The large elegantly named "golden bricks" paving the interior as well as in most of the other ceremonial and residential halls were for the most part made in Suzhou. After being fired for 130 days, they were marinated slowly in tung oil and polished until they glistened.

The next hall on the north-south axis is the square **Hall of Complete Harmony**, or **Middle Harmony**, (*Zhonghe Dian*) [中和殿]. The smallest of the Three Harmony Halls, this is where the

The Hall of Supreme Harmony, September 2006

Hall of Complete Harmony, the smallest and most exquisite of the Three Harmony Halls, September 1978

emperor would prepare for important rituals to be performed in the Hall of Supreme Harmony, or inspect the seeds and farm implements to be used in the important sacrifice at the Temple of Agriculture. Here also the emperor would confer titles of honor upon the empress, and compile the imperial family genealogical records. The two sedan chairs placed inside are of Qing vintage and were carried by eight bearers. Like the other two Harmony Halls, the Hall of Complete Harmony also contains a throne.

In the **Hall of Preserving Harmony** (*Baohe Dian*) [保和殿], the next building on the axis, the Ming emperors would change their robes before and after attending ceremonies elsewhere in the palace, and occasionally hold banquets for high officials. Here also the emperors feted the Mongol nobility and delegations from other tributary states. Beginning in the Qianlong period and up to the first years of the 20th century, the palace examinations were held here every three years. The emperor would preside over ceremonies held at the start and completion of the exams. In 1795, a Dutch mission was invited to a banquet here. The diarist Van Braam recorded that they were served enough mutton to "disgust a man with [it] for the rest of his life."

This is a convenient point to make a detour to see two displays of Chinese art in the low buildings that run alongside the Three Harmony Halls. The section on the west side of the halls contains a superb selection of Chinese painting and calligraphy, which is changed every few months.

Emerging into the sunlight from the darkened cabinets of cultural relics, make your way north towards the courtyard beneath you at the rear of the Hall of Preserving Harmony, and examine the large stairway that leads down from the center of the terrace. The largest of the three slabs of carved marble set in the middle of the two staircases is 15.2 meters (50 feet) long, 3.3 meters (11 feet) wide and weighs 200 tons. It was installed here around 1420, when the palace was first built, but some of the carving on its surface dates from the Qianlong period, more than 300 years later. The stone, quarried in Fangshan, near Beijing, was transported to the palace in winter by harnessing to it over 1,000 horses and mules that hauled it over a sheet of ice formed by spreading water on the road from wells dug along the way. Only recently was it suggested that this huge slab (obviously deserving of a place in the *Guinness World Records*) is actually two pieces of marble that dovetail perfectly in a joint hidden under the curved contours of the cloud whorls.

In imperial times the wide rectangular courtyard before you was a sanctum sanctorum, off limits to all but the highest-ranking officials and those having special appointments with the emperor, who lived with his empresses and concubines in the apartments to the north. Underlings accompanying officials on imperial business were forbidden from coming within 50 meters (164 feet) of the side gates.

In the northwest corner of this courtyard—in recent times the location of a fast-food venue—stood the office of the **Grand Council** (*Junji Chu*) [军机处]. Founded in 1729 as a command center for military campaigns being waged at the time in northwest China, it evolved into the office responsible for issuing imperial decrees. The peace of this precinct was shattered one day in 1813, when a band of bold peasants broke in and got as far as the Hall of Mental Cultivation, the courtyards to the north of here. The Jiaqing emperor was away from the palace at the time, and though the trespassers were swiftly arrested, the emperor was so terrified by the incident that he cancelled his birthday celebration that year.

The low gate on the central axis, the **Gate of Heavenly Purity** (*Qianqing Men*) [乾清门], serves as the main entrance to the north section of the palace, known as the **Inner Court**. The buildings in the first large rectangular courtyard inside the gate stand on a raised marble terrace, and in terms of overall layout resemble the Three Harmony Halls in miniature. In the early years of the Qing dynasty, the emperor would hold regular audiences seated on a throne situated immediately inside this gate, with his subordinates arranged on the stairs before him.

The Palace of Heavenly Purity (*Qianqing Gong*) [乾清宫], the first building in this complex, was the emperor's living quarters during the Ming and early Qing dynasties. It was here in 1542 that one of the Jiajing emperor's concubines led a contingent of more than a dozen palace women in an attempt to strangle the emperor in his sleep, but the knot in the noose they had brought along slipped. For their pains, the gang was executed in public à la Peking duck, by having their throats cut and the flesh of their limbs sliced off. Following this incident, the Jiajing emperor spent 20 years "cultivating his mind" in solitude in a palace in what is now Zhongnanhai, only returning to the Hall of Heavenly Purity one day before his death. The Ming Wanli emperor, the man who built this palace in the early 15th century, passed away in the small room on the west side of the Hall of Heaven Purity, and his son, the Taichang emperor, only remained on the throne for a month before he died in the hall itself after taking a double dose of a mysterious medicine.

*Prospect Hill, as seen from beneath the **Gate of Martial Prowess** (Shenwumen), the principle north gate of the Forbidden City. Buses and taxis stop close by*

The Qing dynasty emperors also slept and attended daily affairs in the Palace of Heavenly Purity, though after the death of Kangxi most official business was transacted in the **Hall of Mental Cultivation** (*Yangxin Dian*) [养心殿], in the courtyard to the north of the Grand Council. From that time on, the Palace of Heavenly Purity was used for court rituals, banquets, and meetings with foreign missions and high officials. It was here that on several occasions Kangxi and Qianlong invited men aged 60 or over to lavish feasts to celebrate their own longevity; one such feast was attended by 3,000 venerables. During the Qing dynasty this hall was also used as the first resting place of the emperors upon their demise, no matter where they had died. The emperors' remains were then removed to a hall behind **Prospect Hill** (also called **Coal Hill**, to the north of the Forbidden City), and then interred in the **Eastern** or **Western Qing Tombs**. The Tongzhi emperor died of smallpox in the Palace of Heavenly Purity in 1874.

The plaque inscribed by the first Qing emperor, Shunzhi, which hangs over the throne in the hall, reads "Upright, Great, Brilliant, and Lucid," enumerating with modesty the virtues an ideal Son of Heaven should possess. Beginning in the Qianlong reign, the name of the successor to the throne was not announced publicly, as it had been previously, but was written on two pieces of paper, one kept in a pouch on the emperor's person throughout his reign, and the other placed in a small strongbox that was stored behind this plaque. The box was opened when the emperor "mounted the dragon," or, as it were, caught the last palanquin to heaven.

A venerable cypress in the Six Western Palaces complex

The buildings that line the east and west sides of the courtyard of this complex contained at various times over the centuries a Confucian shrine, a Qianlong-period clepsydra (water clock), stores of incense and imperial stationery, a wardrobe full of the emperor's gowns and other accessories, the office of the Hanlin secretariat, a study where the emperor reviewed documents, the headquarters of four literary men who advised the emperor on poetry, and the office of eunuch affairs.

To the north of the Palace of Heavenly Purity is the **Hall of Union** (*Jiaotai Dian*) [交泰殿], the living quarters of the empress in the Ming, and the place where Qing empresses would receive obeisance from the high-ranking civil and military officials on their birthdays. From Qianlong times, this hall was used to store a collection of imperial seals, the oldest of which was said to belong to Qin Shihuangdi, first emperor of the Qin dynasty (third century BCE).

Behind the Hall of Union is the **Palace of Earthly Tranquility** (*Kunning Gong*) [坤宁宫], a *yin* (earthly, feminine) counterpart of the *yang* (heavenly, masculine) Palace of Heaven Purity. In the Ming, this hall was the sleeping quarters of the empresses. It continued to bear this name during the Qing, though in fact the empresses did not stay here. In the Qing dynasty, the Palace of Earthly Tranquility was rebuilt so that its entrance stood at the east end of the south side of the hall rather than in the center, as was the general rule in the Forbidden City. This feature, and the presence of heated beds (*kang*) inside, can be explained by the fact that during the Qing dynasty the palace was used as a shrine for private Manchu shamanistic practices. There was a daily ritual sacrifice to some 15 gods, including Sakyamuni Buddha and a number of Mongolian deities. Four pigs were offered in sacrifice each day, while at major rituals in the spring and autumn personally attended by the emperor and empress, 39 swine went up in smoke. Several of the Qing emperors and empresses lodged in the east "heated chamber" attached to this hall on their three-day honeymoon. The buildings behind the hall to the north housed the imperial medical clinic and pharmacy.

In the northeastern corner of the courtyard, behind the Palace of Earthly Tranquility, is a small display of European and Chinese toys from the 18th and 19th centuries. It should not be missed.

Passing north through the **Gate of Earthly Tranquility** (*Kunning Men*) [坤宁门] we come to the **Imperial Garden** (*Yuhua Yuan*) [御花园], parts of which date back to the Ming. This garden was only one of the many retreats the emperors had at their disposal in Peking, but in spite of its proximity they tended to spend less time here than in the vast grounds of the garden palaces at Zhongnanhai, the western suburbs (in the Yuanming Yuan, Yihe Yuan and Yuquan Shan) and Chengde (formerly Jehol or Rehe, home to the Mountain Retreat for Avoiding Heat). In this palace garden a vast array of disparate architectural elements is crowded into a small space, yet it still gives the impression of spaciousness compared to the more claustrophobic nearby residential courtyards. The paths are decorated with charming mosaic designs of auspicious plants and animals. The rockery hill in the north part of the garden dates from the Ming Wanli period. The emperor and his consorts would climb to the top of this man-made mountain on several occasions during the year: when the paths of the constellations called the Herding Boy and Weaving Girl crossed in the heavens for their annual assignation; on the Mid-autumn Festival to gain a fine view of the full moon; and on the ninth day of the ninth month, the Double-Ninth Festival, when it was customary to climb to a high place (*denggao*). These occasions were also celebrated by the general populace. Reginald Johnston, Puyi's English-language teacher, lived for a time in an apartment in the southwest section of this garden, now a small shop.

The maze-like traffic pattern of the Forbidden City makes it necessary for us to backtrack a bit here. Or use this opportunity to break up your visit by leaving the Forbidden City through the **Gate of Martial Prowess** (*Shenwumen*) [神武门], which stands immediately to the north of the Imperial Garden. If you divide the visit into two sessions, you can enter the Forbidden City from this rear gate on your second session.

Heading south from the Imperial Garden, we return to the open courtyard that separates the Inner and Outer Courts via either of two routes:

1. by following the corridor to the east of the **Palace of Heavenly Purity** complex to the specialized collections of bronzes, ceramics and arts and crafts in the contiguous courtyards known as the **Six Eastern Palaces**, all former residences;

2. by taking the corridor to the west to the **Six Western Palaces**, residences of the Qing emperors and empresses. It was here that Cixi (when she was not otherwise in the Summer Palace, Beihai or Zhongnanhai) lived during the bulk of her lengthy career, from 1865 to her death in 1908.

We will proceed down the west corridor. It was in the north chamber of the **Palace of Concentrated Beauty** (*Chuxiu Gong*) [储秀宫] that Cixi gave birth in 1856 to the boy (Zai Chun) who was to become the Tongzhi emperor (reigned 1861–75). The interior of this hall has been restored to the way it looked on the Empress Dowager Cixi's 50th birthday in 1885, according to a description found in the imperial archives, and what remains here in the way of décor can best be described as frowzy kitsch. Some of the gates in these courtyards, as well as those in the Six Eastern Palaces, have elegantly exaggerated names appropriate for the hatchery of the imperial brood, such as One Hundred Sons and One Thousand Infants, for this is where the concubines favored by the imperial presence lived. Evidently the names worked: Qianlong sired 35 sons by his various consorts, though only 17 grew to maturity. For the most part the interiors here have been restored to the style of the early 19th century.

Faded imperial trim within the Western Palaces area

The **Palace of Eternal Spring** (*Changchun Gong*) [长春宫] to the southwest on the next north-south axis contains a small theater, one of several in the palace where the Empress Dowager would watch Chinese opera performed by the palace's own troupe. It was here that she celebrated her 50th birthday with long hours of opera-going.

The most important building in the Western Palaces area is the **Hall of Mental Cultivation** (*Yangxin Dian*) [养心殿], the living quarters of the Qing sovereigns beginning with Yongzheng in the 1730s. Yongzheng moved here from the Palace of Heavenly Purity after the death of his father, Kangxi, who had lived in the latter for 60 years. From the early 18th century to the end of the Qing dynasty the emperors handled the most important affairs of state in the Hall of Mental Cultivation. Here too is where Puyi, the last emperor, abdicated the throne in February 1912.

This courtyard, like the Forbidden City itself, is divided into two sections, the ceremonial in front (or south) and the living quarters in the rear. In the east "heated chamber" of the front section, the Empress Dowager Cixi famously and literally ruled the empire "from behind a curtain"—a literary expression for a regency under female supervision. She would sit on the larger (easternmost) of the two thrones here that are separated by a hanging curtain, while the young Tongzhi and Guangxu emperors held audiences from their smaller thrones; Guangxi died of suspicious causes in this hall in 1908, only one day before Cixi joined him in the sky.

Ceramic panel within the Western Palaces area

The residential chambers have an intimacy and charm not found in the rest of the palace. The east "heated chamber" was the emperor's bedroom; the west "heated chamber" served as a Buddhist chapel. In the room in the northeast corner the emperor would disport nocturnally with his highest-ranking concubine. The northwest-corner chamber served as the duty room for lesser concubines waiting on the emperor. Eunuchs reportedly carried the concubines into the imperial boudoir wrapped up in a rug, and they were never more than a few steps away from the emperor, day or night, even while he was in bed. The Son of Heaven's most intimate retainers would stand on the far side of a screen while he made love to his palace ladies, and shout warnings such as "Preserve your Imperial body, Sire!" during the course of the encounter.

Court astrologers determined the optimum hours for the emperor to be intimate with his ladies, based on calendrical cycles of *yin* and *yang*. The emperors practiced yogic techniques of *coitus interruptus*, saving up their vital essence for moonless *yang* nights,

Glazed decorative plaque within the Western Palaces area

while working their way up the hierarchical ladder of concubines. If the timing was right and the *yang* was in the ascendant, they figured, a union with a high-ranking concubine would result in the birth of a brilliant dragon boy who would eventually triumph over all the competition and win the assignment for the throne. The fact that most of the emperors had dozens of sons (and daughters) to choose from for their successors makes the contribution of the astrologers seem like so much hocus pocus.

South of the Hall of Mental Cultivation is the former site of the **Imperial Kitchen**. The Qing emperors usually took two main meals a day, breakfast at around 6:30 am and lunch at 12:30 pm, with lighter repasts in the afternoon and evening. Each formal meal consisted of as many as 108 dishes served on plates of gold, silver, jade, enamel and porcelain (some of which is on display in the **Hall of Treasures**, [珍宝馆] see pages 66, 89) set on several dozen tables, many well out of the emperor's reach, as well as out of sight. As a result, many were not replaced at every meal and within a few days grew quite stale. Several restaurants near the Forbidden City did a vigorous trade in palace leftovers spirited out of the palace by the men who worked in the kitchen, not all of whom were eunuchs. While no rooms were specifically designated as dining rooms in the Forbidden City, as mentioned above, most imperial repasts were served in the familiar surroundings of the Palace of Heavenly Purity and the Hall of Mental Cultivation.

This would be the time to see the specialized collections of jade, porcelain and bronzes displayed in the halls off the north-south alley directly east of the Palace of Heavenly Purity.

To continue the walk: Leaving the courtyard that separates the ceremonial and residential quarters, walk east through the raised gate, go down the incline and bear left into the courtyard where the hall contains a wonderful collection of Chinese and European clocks, some of the cherished playthings of the Qing emperors. This is the **Hall of Ancestral Worship** (*Fengxian Dian*)

[奉先殿], where the spirit tablets of the deceased Qing emperors and empresses were kept.

From here we visit the large group of buildings in the northeast corner of the Forbidden City, the **Palace of a Peaceful Old Age** (*Ningshou Gong*) [宁寿宫], which now houses extraordinary collections of exquisite gold and silver objects, dragon robes made with precious stones, an emperor's saddle—actually a selection of the household effects and personal sacred objects belonging to the Qing rulers. This part of the palace was originally built to accommodate the emperor's parents, as well as the empress and the highest-ranking concubines.

The Palace of a Peaceful Old Age is a near replica in terms of layout of the Palace of Heavenly Purity. Here Kangxi refurbished a number of Ming halls and named the palace in honor of his mother's 60th birthday.

In the 37th year of his reign, Qianlong began to convert these buildings into a retirement home that he planned to move into upon completing 60 years of rule, a full 23 years away. He chose the number 60 in deference to his grandfather Kangxi, who had ruled China for 61 years. The palaces and the garden in the east half of the compound were completed in four years, but according to some sources, Qianlong never lived in them. When he was 85, Qianlong held a grand banquet for old men here, with a guest list of over 5,000 venerables. Cixi later chose the Palace of Peaceful Old Age as her own place of "retirement" when the Guangxu emperor attained his majority in 1889.

The vestibular courtyard to the south of the palace contains a **Nine Dragon Wall** (*Jiulong Bi*) [九龙壁], one of two in Beijing (the other is in Beihai Park on the north shore of the lake). The dragon symbolizes the celestial potency of the emperor, as well as controls wind and rain. The number nine is the most auspicious *yang* (male, active) number. As there are nine types of dragons in the world, this wall represents all the dragons in the world, and hence functions as a sort of insurance policy offering broad coverage for the inhabitants of the palace.

A lovely day, azure sky, architrctural detail and ancient trees adjacent to Shenwumen

A legend tells that when the dragon wall was being built, the eunuch supervisor of the project was working against a tight deadline. Threatened with losing his head if the wall was not completed on the auspiciously chosen day, a crisis emerged when a particular piece of a glazed tile porcelain dragon fragmented upon delivery to the site. In order to complete the wall on time, the supervisor had a replacement part quickly carved out of wood. That piece of wood remains in the wall today. Try to find it.

Heading north through the gate opposite the Dragon Wall, we come to a large courtyard empty except for some grand old cypress trees, the occasional vintage crow, and a pair of bronze lions. Beyond the second gate is the **Hall of Imperial Supremacy** (*Huangji Dian*) [皇极殿], a near replica of the Palace of Heavenly Purity. Here Cixi held her final audience before fleeing Peking for Xi'an following the Boxer Uprising in the summer of 1900. Her coffin was also stored here for a year before burial. Today the corridors lining this courtyard house exhibitions of palace treasures, precious stones and jewelry. The hall to the north is the actual **Hall of Treasures** (*Zhenbao Guan*) [珍寶館], with its lavish collection of practical, ceremonial and religious *objects d'art*. There are mountain dioramas of carved jade, solid gold dishes, a large mat woven of ivory splinters, imperial robes, Lamaist reliquaries and other objects characteristic of the extravagant tastes of the Manchu emperors. The state-of-the-art displays here are always packed with visitors, but it is worth nudging and waiting to get a glimpse of the extraordinary objects on display.

In a courtyard to the northeast of the Palace of a Peaceful Old Age is a tall three-tiered opera stage, the **Pavilion of Pleasant Sounds** (*Changyin Ge*) [畅音阁], complete with stage traps and hand-operated pumps for on-stage fountains. The pavilion is a clone of the Garden of Harmonious Virtue (*Dehe Yuan*) in the Summer Palace, where Cixi frequently held command performances, particularly on her birthday. The building to the north that faces the stage, where the court denizens would sit during performances, contains an interesting collection of Peking-opera costumes and props.

Emerging from the Pavilion of Pleasant Sounds, cross the courtyard to the **Garden of the Palace of a Peaceful Old Age** (*Ningshou Gong Huayuan*) [宁寿宫花园], also known as the **Qianlong Garden** [乾隆花园]. This lovely secluded corner of the palace contains many of the elements found in traditional gardens in Suzhou: Lake Taihu stones piled up to form screen walls, a huge maze set around a building; man-made hills; pavilions in different styles; and winding paths that direct the visitor to a series of ever changing views. The layout produces claustrophobia and seems appropriate for an old emperor with myopia.

The **Pavilion for Seeking Pleasure** (*Xishang Ting*), near the southern entrance of the garden, has in its floor a winding channel approximately 10 centimeters (four inches) deep called the "Cup Floating Channel." The original idea for this amusing design is drawn from a famous essay, the *Preface to the Orchid Pavilion*, by the fourth-century writer and calligrapher, Wang Xizhi. In the pavilion, scholars and palace ladies floated their wine cups on the surface of the miniature stream which was supplied with water from a large urn placed nearby. While the cups bobbed along the channel, the participants challenged each other to improvise poems before a cup reached the end. The punishment for procrastinating was to drink the wine in the cup.

Passing out of the northern section of the Qianlong Garden, you find yourself in a courtyard that has three halls now being used to display a large collection of Ming and Qing household furniture. From south to north, the three halls are named the **Hall of Nourishing Heavenly Nature** (*Yangxing Dian*) [养性殿], where Qianlong lived upon his retirement; the **Hall for Joy in Old Age** (*Leshou Tang*) [乐寿堂], formerly a library; and the **Pavilion of Peace and Harmony In Old Age** (*Yihe Xuan*) [颐和轩], where Qianlong came to read and relax in his later years.

The courtyards to the northwest of here that you will pass through on your way out of the palace have a charmingly run-down and authentic look about them, and one fears that if they were repaired and painted, they would lose their character.

Finally, don't forget to pay your last respects at the **Well of the Pearl Concubine** (*Zhen Fei Jing*) [珍妃井] located in a narrow corridor in the very northeast corner of the palace behind the Hall of Treasures. The sad demise of this young woman, Guangxu's favorite, took place the very same day Cixi fled Peking in the aftermath of the Boxer Uprising in 1900. There are at least two versions of this bleak tragedy. According to the first, Cixi had the girl thrown down the well after she had begged the Empress Dowager to leave Guangxu behind in Peking to help resolve the political crisis that had befallen the dynasty. The second version, based on the account of a eunuch who claimed to have witnessed it, tells how Cixi had ordered the concubine to commit suicide, but when she voiced her protest, Cixi ordered another eunuch to force her down the well.

To exit from the Forbidden City, walk west to the **Gate of Martial Prowess** (*Shenwumen*) [神武门], the principle north gate of the Forbidden City, where you can get a bus or taxi. The gate

tower houses an excellent exhibition of traditional Chinese
architecture with blueprints and tools used in the building of the
Forbidden City. The huge gate tower, the view from it, and the
objects on display, make a visit worthwhile (extra ticket required).
If you still have the energy, it is recommended to climb **Prospect
Hill** (*Jing Shan*) [景山], also popularly known as **Coal Hill** (*Mei
Shan*) [煤山]. The five pavilions on the hill, each (once upon a
time) sheltering its own bronze Buddha, date from the time of
Qianlong.

To get to Prospect Hill cross the road (***Jing Shan Qian Jie***) [景
山前街] to Jing Shan Park and buy a ticket at the ticket window to
the right of the entrance. This road is a modern imposition upon
former imperial property, and dates from the 1920s.

The customary route up Prospect Hill is via the east slope.
At the foot of the hill you will pass a scholar-tree (also called a
locust or sophora) with a sign commemorating the spot where the
last emperor of the Ming dynasty supposedly hung himself as the
capital fell to the invading Manchus. The chains that had once
been hung from the tree, to remind passersby of the emperor's
heroic unwillingness to be captured by the enemy, or to accuse it
of complicity in the emperor's death, are said to have been
removed by the Allied Armies in 1900. The original scholar-tree,
called the Guilty Scholar-tree, was deracinated by Red Guards in
the Cultural Revolution. A substitute tree was planted in 1981,
but it is unlikely that it has much of a conscience.

We close this chapter with Abel Bonnard's bitter-sweet and
sour meditation on Chinese versus Western art and taste,
which takes place on a sunny day in the Forbidden City.

> *There is no question then, of the heights of art in which the
> soul of China is set free. On the contrary, in the Imperial
> [Forbidden] City you can only contemplate the great ordered
> China where everything is strictly in its place. I pause at
> midday in the shelter of a narrow patch of shade at the edge
> of immense courts which seem to fill up and block out the vast
> brilliancy of light....*

Bronze lions are grimacing violently on their plinths at the foot of these grandiose buildings which are almost monotonous in their exactitude and perfect correctness, and if I would examine the wall decorations of their halls and chambers I should find the serpentine wriggle of the dragons everywhere.

Here then, we find that convulsion has been made to stand in contrast with absolute rigorous, self-control; and it seems as if all the monsters of Delirium had been set as guards over the palaces of Order.

But just as this architecture is uninventive, so is this appalling animal Chinoiserie unimaginative. We must conclude that a vast gulf yawns in this august and gloomy combination, between the principles of invariable wisdom and the tangled coils of a limited imagination. Contemplating the gulf the Occidental mind struggles to discover a personal affirmation of what the Orient means by it. But in vain. The proud palaces of the Imperial City enclose a vast absence. There is no reply.[1:12]

(1:12) Abel Bonnard *In China 1920–1921*, pp. 62–63.

Above: *Mythical bronze beast in the Six Western Palaces complex*

Right: *Looking south from Prospect Hill: "Walled courtyard within walled courtyard"... the northern entry and exit of the Forbidden City, the Gate of Martial Prowess*

"General Frey, his staff and the French detachment entering the Imperial Palace (Forbidden City) by the north gate". The Illustrated London News, November 1900

WALK · 2

THE FORMER LEGATION QUARTER, TIANANMEN SQUARE, DAZHALAN AND LIULICHANG

DURATION

At least four hours.

Begin with a stroll through the **Former Legation Quarter**, an evanescent semi-European ghost town, explore Tiananmen Square, continue through some of the bustling, winding *hutongs* of the old Chinese City in the **Dazhalan district** and conclude in Liulichang Street, a renovated and re-renovated shopping area that has been a marketplace for Chinese books, scholarly stationery, antiques and curios for more than 300 years.

Note: As of this writing, an alarmingly massive destruction and reconstruction project is taking place in the Dazhalan district. Whole swaths of buildings in the area described in the middle section of this walk are being fenced off and demolished, and not even the long term residents and merchants in the area know the fate of their homes and places of business. A handwritten, yet undated, sign on one of the old heritage emporiums, the Qian Xing Yi Silk Store, which according to the brass plate near the entrance is "one of the ancient China's main contributions to world civilization," noted with apologies that the shop would be closed for two years. At the time of this writing, a uniformed official said that the buildings on the north side of one of the *hutongs*, or lanes, included in this walk, **Langfang Ertiao**, were being demolished, while those on the south side of the lane were to be spared the wrecking ball. Thus visitors to this area should be prepared to detour around the obstacles formed by the work

Not spared the wrecking ball–Dazhalan district, and in the distance the Arrow Tower

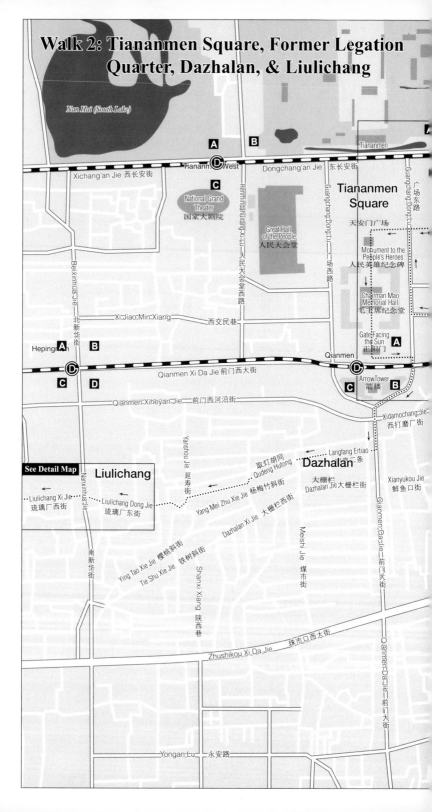

Walk 2: Tiananmen Square, Former Legation Quarter, Dazhalan, & Liulichang

Nan Hai (South Lake)

A **B**

Tiananmen

Xichang'an Jie 西长安街 Tiananmen West Dongchang'an Jie 东长安街

Guangchang Dong Lu 广场东路

C

National Grand Theater 国家大剧院

Tiananmen Square
天安门广场

Renmindahuitang Xi Lu 人民大会堂西路

Great Hall of the People 人民大会堂

Monument to the People's Heroes 人民英雄纪念碑

Guangchang Dong Lu 广场东路

Xi Jiao Min Xiang 西交民巷

Chairman Mao Memorial Hall 毛主席纪念堂

Gate Facing the Sun 正阳门 **A**

Beixinhua Jie 北新华街

A Hepingmen **B**

Qianmen

Qianmen Xi Da Jie 前门西大街

C **D**

Arrow Tower 箭楼 **C** **B**

Qianmen Xiheyan Jie 前门西河沿街

Xidamochang Jie 西打磨厂街

Yanshou Jie 延寿街

Langfang Ertiao 廊房二条

Qudeng Hutong 取灯胡同

Dazhalan 大栅栏一条

Nanxinhua Jie 南新华街

Liulichang

See Detail Map

Liulichang Xi Jie 琉璃厂西街

Liulichang Dong Jie 琉璃厂东街

大栅栏
Dazhalan Jie 大栅栏街

Xianyukou Jie 鲜鱼口街

Yang Mei Zhu Xie Jie 杨梅竹斜街

Dazhalan Xi Jie 大栅栏西街

Meishi Jie 煤市街

Qianmen Da Jie 前门大街

Ying Tao Xie Jie 樱桃斜街

Tie Shu Xie Jie 铁树斜街

Shanxi Xiang 陕西巷

Zhushikou Xi Da Jie 珠市口西大街

Qianmen Da Jie 前门大街

Yongan Lu 永安路

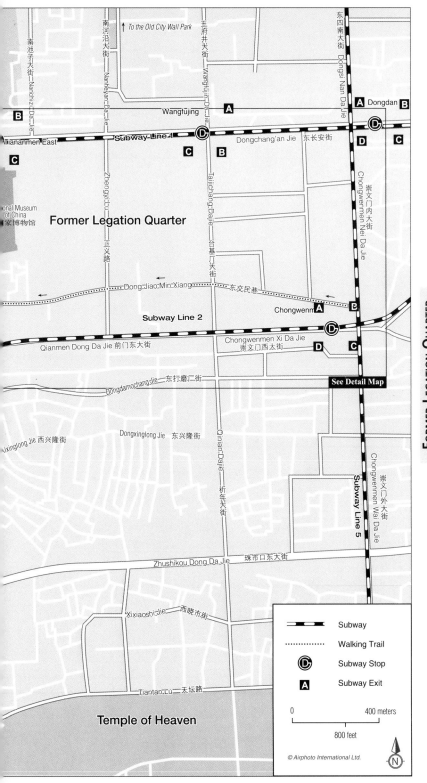

FORMER LEGATION QUARTER

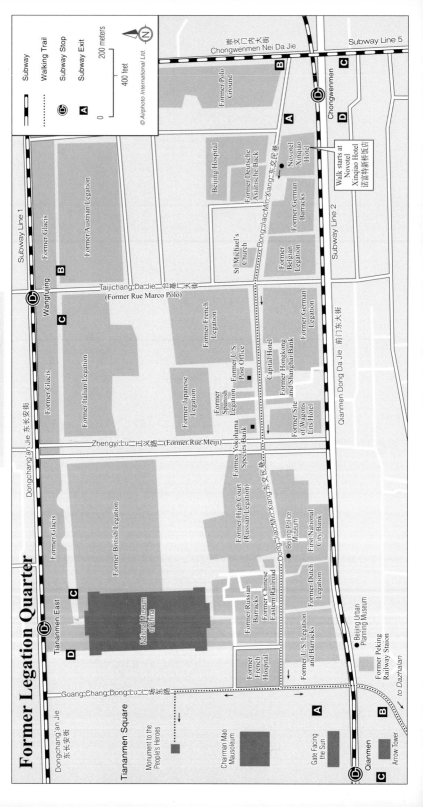

Former Legation Quarter

FORMER LEGATION QUARTER

Tiananmen Square

Monument to the People's Heroes

Chairman Mao Mausoleum

Gate Facing the Sun

Qianmen

Arrow Tower

to Dazhalan

Former Peking Railway Station

Beijing Urban Planning Museum

Former U.S. Legation and Barracks

Former French Hospital

Former Russian Barracks

Former Chinese Eastern Railroad

Former Dutch Legation

Beijing Police Museum

First National City Bank

Former High Court (Russian Legation)

National Museum of China

Former British Legation

Former Glacis

Dongchang'an Jie 东长安街

Dong-Jiao-Min-Xiang 东交民巷

Former Yokohama Species Bank

Zhengyi Lu 正义路 (Former Rue Meiji)

Former Japanese Legation

Former Italian Legation

Former Glacis

Wangfujing

Taijichang Da Jie 台基厂大街 (Former Rue Marco Polo)

Former Spanish Legation

Former U.S. Post Office

Former French Legation

Former Site of Wagons Lits Hotel

Former Hongkong and Shanghai Bank

Capital Hotel

Former German Legation

St. Michael's Church

Former Belgian Legation

Former German Barracks

Former Deutsche Asiatische Bank

Beijing Hospital

Former Austrian Legation

Former Glacis

Subway Line 1

Subway Line 2

Chongwenmen Nei Da Jie 崇文门内大街

Subway Line 5

Former Polo Ground

Chongwenmen

Novotel Xinqiao Hotel 诺富特新侨饭店

Walk starts at Novotel Xinqiao Hotel

Qianmen Dong Da Jie 前门东大街

Guang Chang Dong Lu 广场东路

Dongchang'an Jie 东长安街

Tiananmen East

Legend

Subway

Walking Trail

Subway Stop

Subway Exit

0   200 meters
0   400 feet

© Airphoto International Ltd.

The Imperial Canal looking northward from a point close to the intersection between Legation Street (Dong Jiao Min Xiang) and Rue Meiji (Zhengyi Lu). The building to the left is part of the British Legation and was the house of the First Secretary

in progress, or to discover a new, and most likely sterile, part of Old Peking as they explore one of the historically most important sections of the city.

A *New York Times* article published in July 2006 described the (as usual) cloud of disinformation and obfuscation that hangs about the project, which will result in Qianmen Da Jie, the extension of the central axis of the city of Peking that runs south from Tiananmen Square, being transformed into a pedestrian mall lined with shops confabulated to emulate Old Peking, but which in fact can and will be little more than a Potemkin-like shopping-amusement park. The humble hovels that made up the fabric of this quintessential quarter of Peking are to be replaced by brand new courtyard houses selling for US$1.3 million and up, while the hapless former residents will be lucky if they are given enough money to move to a tiny apartment in a new high rise building outside the Fifth Ring Road . The commercial and practical success of the widened Wangfujing pedestrian shopping mall, which was not essentially a residential area to begin with, is unlikely to be duplicated on the smaller, more intimate scale characteristic of the hutong type of neighborhood near Qianmen. More likely it will resemble Liulichang (see page 141 of this walk), with its brilliantly decorated faux 19th-century shop fronts concealing stodgy state-owned antiques and trinkets shops, or the contiguous Dazhalan Jie (see pages 97, 134 of this walk), which it will intersect, still home to a half dozen of the most famous traditional shops in Old Peking that barely manage to maintain the dignity of their appearances while their immediate neighbors blast mindless rock music into the street to promote their discount blue jeans and year-long summer sales. These classic outlets include emporiums noted for their fine cloth shoes (*Neilian Sheng*), traditional Chinese medicine (*Tongrentang*), tea (*Zhang Yi Yuan*), with upstart Taiwanese competitor Tian Fu right across the way), and silk (*Rui Fu Xiang*). Here too is a rebuilt version of China's first movie theater, with a small museum of the Chinese cinema.

Liulichang with one of its many brilliantly decorated shop-fronts

THE FORMER LEGATION QUARTER

STARTING POINT

Behind the Novotel Xinqiao Hotel in Dong Jiao Min Xiang [东交民巷].

HOW TO GET THERE

Buses 3,on 9, 32, 44, 60, 103, 104, 111, 201, 204, and 209 stop at
Chongwenmen. Or take the Beijing underground train to the
Chongwenmen Station, walk one block north and turn left
heading west behind the hotel. You can also walk through the
main door of the Novotel Xinqiao Hotel and exit the small door
on the back side of the hotel, which will bring you to Dong Jiao
Min Xiang.

HOW TO GET AWAY

Buses 14, 15, 25, 45 and 66 stop near Liulichang. By walking a
few minutes to the north on Xinhua Nan Jie, you can get on the
Beijing underground (metro) at **Hepingmen Station**, immediately
next to Quanjude, the world's largest Peking duck restaurant
(sometimes called the **Wall Street Duck**, as one of the Peking city
walls once ran east-west through the parking lot).

HISTORY OF THE LEGATION QUARTER

The street known today as **Dong Jiao Min Xiang** (Eastern lane
where the people mingle) was formerly called **Dong Jiang Mi
Xiang** (Eastern glutinous-rice lane), and from 1900 through the
1940s in English as Legation Street. This was the location for
several decades of most of China's foreign embassies and
consulates. Today it is a somewhat depressing hodgepodge of
crumbling, rehabilitated and new buildings, barely breathing its last
as a historical site. Yet with its lovely tree-lined tunnel of shade in
summer it offers the visitor sufficient vignettes of the Peking past
and some pleasant surprises to make it worthwhile visiting.

In the 13th century, imperial hydraulic engineers connected
the Grand Canal to the urban waterway system of the Yuan
dynasty capital of Dadu, making it possible for rice, textile and
luxury goods shipments from the south to travel by water
without transshipment to the imperial granaries and warehouses

of the capital. A market for the rice trade grew up in the vicinity of present-day Dong Jiao Min Xiang, the main thoroughfare of which was named *Jiang Mi Xiang*, or the "Lane of Glutinous Rice from the South." This name stuck throughout the ensuing Ming and most of the Qing dynasty, although by Ming times ocean transport had developed to the point that the Grand Canal ceased to be the main means for grain transport. The name *Dong Jiao Min Xiang*, Eastern Lane Where the People Mingle, dates from the later part of the Qing dynasty, and for many decades the two nearly homonymous names were used alternatively. Dong Jiao Min Xiang still refers to the entire former Legation Quarter as well as to the street itself.

During the Ming and early Qing dynasties, the large rectangular area southeast of the Forbidden City was home to the Six Boards, or six ministries, of the imperial government. The first embassy from a "foreign" nation in China, as opposed to tributary states such as Burma, Annam, Korea and Mongolia (which also established their missions here) was that of Russia, which was built on the future site of Legation Street in 1727. More than a century passed before France and Great Britain

British Legation Police, as depicted in the Illustrated London News in 1860

Former German barracks and the former Belgian Legation are on Qianmen Dong Da Jie

became the first European countries to establish their diplomatic presence here, after their troops destroyed the Yuanming yuan (the Old Summer Palace) in 1860.

The next lurch in the evolution of this quarter can be credited to Empress Dowager Cixi, who in 1900 succeeded in unleashing the furor of the peasant secret society of practitioners of the martial arts known popularly as the Boxers, or "Righteous and Harmonious Fists," against foreigners and Chinese Christians in Peking.

On one occasion, the Empress Dowager personally witnessed a demonstration of the Boxers' magical invulnerability to bullets and was so impressed by what she saw that she ordered her court attendants and palace ladies to practice the martial arts. In early 1900, the Boxers, with the support of the court, began to destroy rail and telegraph lines in northern China as a symbolic attack on foreign influence in China. Yet it was with rifles and torches rather than fists that they, reinforced by regular Chinese troops, took over the Legation Quarter of Peking on a sweltering mid-June day that year, and held captive some 900 foreigners from 12 countries and

2,300 Chinese Christians for 55 days. The miraculous survival of the majority of those besieged was due to the fact that the Manchu Rong-lu, who was in charge of the Beiyang (Northern Warlord) Army, was unsympathetic to the Boxers, and only carried out symbolic attacks on the legations. The harsh retaliation delivered by the 18,000-strong relief forces composed of soldiers from Britain, the United States, Japan, Russia, France and Germany led to the signing of the Peace Protocol of 1901, which gave foreign governments the right to establish legations in Peking. A wall was built around the newly-built quarter, and an open area (the glacis) outside the walls was provided for foreign troops to perform military exercises and play polo. As most of the buildings in the area had been burnt to the ground by the Boxers during the siege, the few remaining early structures here date from the first decade of the 20th century.

In the immediate aftermath of this humiliating blow to imperial prestige, the Empress Dowager Cixi, the emperor Guangxu, and the court chose the most expedient path to safety: they fled Peking for two years, traveling west to Xi'an. Upon her

A lovely tree-lined tunnel of shade down Dong Jiao Min Xiang, formerly Legation Street

*Taijichang Da Jie–formerly Rue Marco Polo–looking north across Legation Street,
St. Michael's Church is out of frame, to the bottom right hand side, c. 1900*

return to Peking in 1902, Cixi discovered to her great dismay that
those who held power in the court during her absence had
granted the right of extraterritoriality to the eight countries whose
armies had retaliated against the Boxer punch. Unlike the
situation in the Shanghai international settlements, wrested from
China by the terms of unequal treaties from 1842 to 1860, Chinese
people were not permitted to live in the Peking Legation Quarter.

When Chiang Kai-shek moved the capital of the Republic of
China from Peking to Nanking (Nanjing) in 1928 (Nanking
had briefly been the Ming capital in the mid-14th century) the
foreign embassies followed suit, after which the foreign legations
in Peiping (as Peking was renamed at the time) continued to
maintain *de facto* extraterritoriality until they were taken over by
the People's Government in 1949. In 1948 the eastern section of
the legation quarter, part-glacis, part-polo-ground, was converted
into an emergency airfield by General Fu Zuoyi, but it was little
used. Today this section of the quarter is taken up by Dongdan
Park and Dongdan Stadium.

In the early 1950s, most Western countries withdrew their
embassies from Beijing and set up shop in Taiwan, only to return

to the mainland in the 1970s after China was recognized as a member of the United Nations and Taiwan was excluded. In the interim decades, the buildings on Legation Street were assigned to countries friendly to China: Bulgaria, Hungary, Burma, East Germany and India. In the 1950s, the Soviets moved their legation to the spacious grounds of the 18th-century Russian Orthodox Church mission in the northeastern corner of the old city, which today serves as the Embassy of Russia in China. In the early 1980s, before Perestroika, foreign residents in Beijing were regularly invited here to enjoy Russian champagne and caviar served by conspicuously muscular young Russian gentlemen at complimentary Friday night showings of healthy Russian films. All you had to do was phone the embassy and advise them your nationality, local address and status in China (tourist, diplomat, businessmen, "foreign expert," or journalist), and the number of people coming in your car or taxi—they never asked for names.

No Beijing map available to the public today identifies accurately the numerous high-status government organizations now located in the former Legation Quarter, which include the Supreme Court, Fire Department, Beijing Municipal Government and Municipal Party Committee, Beijing Public Security Bureau, and the Association for Friendship with Foreign Countries. In the northern part of the quarter, east of the Museum of Chinese History, are the ministries of Public Security and State Security. Some of these "work units" have signs with their names on them. Following the old Soviet model, however, buildings without signs in China are assumed to belong to either the military or the police, or to none of your business.

18th century Russian Orthodox Church

THE WALK

The rather stogy 1960s edition of Nagels' *Guide* to China describes the quarter at that time, with a *soupçon* of French disdain:

> *It has nothing Chinese about it. The European houses combine all the styles in fashion at the beginning of the 20th century: mock gothic, mock baroque, mock Empire, modern style, with all the bad taste of the European nations and America put together.*[(2:1)]

Sadly there is less and less to mock here, as some of long-neglected buildings have been torn down and replaced by new office blocks and hotels. And while the former Legation Quarter extends north as far as East Chang'an Street, few of the buildings in the northern section retain their original aspect, or if they do, they are concealed by walls impenetrable by curious civilians. Thus we shall confine our walk to Dong Jiao Min Xiang.

M. Henri Borel, "Official Chinese Interpreter in the Dutch East Indies," visited Peking around 1909 and recorded his opinion of the quarter as follows:

> *What I, as an artist, cannot forgive my white brethren is that they have made this European Ghetto in Peking so ugly and commonplace... The entire Gesandschafts-Viertel [Legation Quarter] in Peking is a wretched crowd of dull buildings trying to look fine, all scrolls and bays and trivialities, all in that vile conventional modern style which causes the new portions of all European capitals to look exactly like each other. A dull, crude common-place city of barbarians, shapeless, colorless, lacking in distinction, huddled in the midst of the exquisite old Chinese architecture which makes Peking a magnificent dream.*[(2:2)]

Start your walk at the **Novotel Xinqiao Hotel**, located at the east end of Dong Jiao Min Xiang [东交民巷] where it meets Chongwenmen Nei Da Jie [崇文门内大街]. The Novotel Xinqiao

---

(2:1) *Nagel's Encyclopedia Guide to China* (Geneva, Nagels Verlag, 1980) p. 531.

(2:2) Henri Borel *The New China: A Traveller's Impressions* (London, Fisher Unwin, 1912) p. 42.

dates back to the 1950s when, as the Xinqiao Hotel, friendship still bridged the ideological gap between the Chinese and Soviet peoples for a decade or so. But since the Accor hotel management group took over in the 1990s, the hotel has operated on a strictly commercial basis. On the north side of the street at the first corner once stood the Deutsche Asiatische Bank, now occupied by a spanking new police station. To the north of this once stood the German hospital, now swallowed up by two huge Chinese hospitals, Beijing Hospital and Tongren Hospital. Patients in hospital pajamas can be seen walking about the neighborhood.

At the next crossing, where Dong Jiao Min Xang meets Taijichang, the church on the north side of the street, **St. Michael's**, was built by the French Vincentians in 1902 and once housed an excellent organ, which unfortunately is no longer found inside, having been replaced by an upright piano. It is prim and clean, neat and modest inside, painted a rich crimson like the walls of the Forbidden City, and is open for mass daily (Monday–Saturday at 6:30 am and 7:00 am in Chinese, Sunday at 7:00 am in Latin, 8:00 am in Chinese, 10:30 am in Korean, 6:00 pm in

St. Michael's Church

Chinese) and for occasional weddings under the name of the Dong Jiao Min Xiang Catholic Church. The impressive red building on the south side of the street was the **Belgian Embassy**, modeled after a villa in Brussels that belonged to King Leopold II (1835–1909). After 1949 it became the Burmese Embassy. Today, it is one of the several buildings comprising the Ruijin Hotel, which is run by the State Council.

Cross Taijichang, formerly Rue Marco Polo (one of the many pre-1949 foreign street names that might be restored, since Marco has contributed more free propaganda for China over the centuries than any other foreign devil, despite the fact he may have never been here). The large, walled and perpetually guarded compound #**15** on the north side of the street, with its impressive fortress-like gate, the former site of the French Legation (confirmed by a Chinese sign on the wall), is now a private guarded state guesthouse where Prince Sihanouk of Cambodia stayed on his visits to Beijing. This compound, like that of the former British Legation, or *fu*, was at first a Manchu prince's mansion in the 1860s before financial troubles forced its owners to rent it out to the foreigners. The buildings in the compound were nearly totally destroyed during the Boxer catastrophe and have been rebuilt in fortress style.

The British Legation, Pekin. The Illustrated London News, March 15, 1873

Adjacent to the guesthouse, also on the north side of the street, is another imposing gate, marked #**17**, concealing three mansions reserved for the likes of the mayor of Beijing (who lived there in the 1960s and 1970s) and members of the all-powerful Politburo. Next to this compound, at #**19-1**, is the former site of the French Post Office (under the system of extraterritorialty, each country had its own post office), which

Legation Street in the aftermath of the siege, looking northwest from the top of the city wall, September 1900

delivered its last letter in the 1920s. The building is today a Sichuan restaurant.

Heading west, the large hotel that looms up on the south side of the street, the Capital Hotel, is run by the State Council, and stands on the site of the former German Legation. Next door to it is the Hongdu Tailors, #28, known for years as the place China's top leaders and other pretenders to the throne had their immaculate Mao suits (in Chinese, Sun Yat-sen jackets) bespoken for. Jardine Matheson, the famous Hong Kong traders of Scottish origins, once had an office in this block. Somewhat beyond it, on the second-to-last plot on this block, there once stood a general store called Keirulf's, the earliest shop for foreigners in Peking, which served several of the functions fulfilled by the Friendship Store until about 1990, when other major department stores drew away most customers. The classic 1930s guidebook, *In Search of Old Peking*, informs us amusingly that:

> The Chinese strongly opposed [Keirulf's] opening in the early [eighteen] nineties on the ground that Peking was not a Treaty Port and therefore foreign trade forbidden, but finally gave way to the argument that the members of the Legations required a shop where they could buy the necessities of life. . . . As a matter of fact, it was not the Diplomatic Body. . .that

The former site of the American Legation, while being prepared for upscale shopping, dining and entertainment as the... Legation Quarter

made the fortune of Keirulf's store, but the Manchu and Mongol princes who right up to the time of the 1911 Revolution could be seen almost any day wandering through the shop, accompanied by a bevy of concubines and their retainers, selecting every and any kind of foreign toy that happened to strike their fancy. [2:3]

On the right at the intersection of Zhengyi Road [正义路] (formerly Rue Meiji, named after the Japanese emperor who ruled from 1868–1911), the handsome well-preserved building on the corner is the former Yokohama Species Bank, now a Chinese finance corporation. The southern corner at the intersection was the site of one of Old Peking's best-known hotels, the Grand Hotel des Wagons-Lits. Our Dutch sinophile correspondent Borel stayed there briefly about 96 years ago and described the contents of his room:

"A trim English bed with silk eiderdowns, lace curtains, a large wardrobe with mirror, electric light bulbs, a lavatory with taps for hot and cold water, a little lamp with red silk shade on a small table by the bed, a comfortable easy-chair—everything in the best modern style. Did I come to Peking for this? . . . I expected to reach to China's mysterious capital, and I find myself landed in a Parisian hotel." [2:4]

(2:3) L.C. Arlington and William Lewisohn *In Search of Old Peking* (Peking, Henry Vetch, 1935; reprinted by Oxford University Press, 1987) p. 10.
(2:4) Henri Borel *The New China: A Traveller's Impressions*, p. 32.

The hotel's clientele, "high, low and middle-class . . . mixed into a social hotch-potch" soon got on his nerves:

"I found it impossible to collect my thoughts in the clamor and rushing to and fro of all these noisy, showy wanderers. Behind the assumed airs of luxury and distinction I

The former Japanese Legation on Zhengyi Road

perceived too much of the snobbishness and vulgarity of Monte Carlo and such places. And I moved into a small, second-rate hotel outside the walls of the Legation Quarter, in the Tartar City, opposite the Italian Glacis on the Viale d'Italia, the Hotel de Pekin." (2.5)

This was the central section of the quadripartite Beijing Hotel on East Chang'an Boulevard, where most famously Chairman Mao entertained Nikita Kruschev, and where all the rooms on a particular floor, possibly the 12th, were bugged. In the old days, however, it served as a catalyst for Borel's enlightenment, despite the fact that it:

. . . was furnished as poorly as possible with ramshackle beds, worn-out mattresses, sheets full of holes, and ordinary iron garden chairs. On entering such a room one feels a sensation of being down on his luck, of having seen better days. . . . The rooms are comfortless, decay stares at one from broken tables and dilapidated ash-trays that seem to be advertisements for whisky. . . . Yet . . . from this miserable little hotel I learned to understand Peking. [2.6]

The last of Legation Street, the steps down to Tiananmen Square

(2.5) Henri Borel *The New China: A Traveller's Impressions*, p. 79.
(2.6) Henri Borel *The New China: A Traveller's Impressions*, p. 83.

Returning to the walk, the pleasant park in the middle of
Zhengyi Road [正义路] was created in 1925 when the canal that
conveyed water from Zhongnanhai, and served as a common
receptacle for rubbish from the neighborhood, was filled in. The
wide east-west road to the south, Qianmen Dong Da Jie, was the
location of the southern wall of the **Tartar City** until that wall was
demolished in the 1960s. Immediately to the south of this wall lay
the **Chinese City**, and the street immediately inside the wall to the
north was called Wall Street. Where the canal passed through the

On the southern wall of the Tartar City, 1873

wall there was a sluice gate, through which the British Indian
troops made their way into the **Legation Quarter** to relieve the
foreign and Chinese prisoners during the Boxer siege in 1900: it
was known as the Water Gate.

In the middle of the next block the former site of the Russian
legation on the north is now occupied by the immense new
building housing China's Supreme Court. The carved marble arch

that stands in isolation near one of the entrances is the original portal to the former Russian site.

On the south side of the street the tall building with no markings was formerly the Banque de l'Indochine et de Suez. Moving on, the squat building with grey Roman columns that started life as the Russia Asiatic Bank, later became the National City Bank of New York—you can see the letters NCB in the shield a the top of the building. Today this building houses the modern Beijing Police Museum, with excellent, if not amusing, displays of historical and present-day law enforcement paraphernalia, including lots of pistols and rifles, as well as an electronic shooting gallery. Across the street again, the single window and mail drop is the High Court's only point of access for Chinese citizens petitioning the court for redress of grievances.

After passing several lawyers' offices on the north side of the street, the building on the corner was the site of the office of the Chinese Eastern Railway, and somewhat beyond this, in the quiet alley running north, there was once an old sign embedded in its wall that read U.S.S.R. Embassy Compound Lane. The Russian barracks once stood to the east of this wall. A bit further back on the south side of Legation Street, the bricked-up gate on the south side used to be the entrance to the Dutch Legation, which remarkably managed to please the usually bilious Dutchman Borel, who described it as possessing:

> . . . something of aristocratic simplicity. It has the stately distinction of the finest old mansions and castles of the Netherlands. It is solid yet characteristic, sumptuous yet sober, and has a genuine Dutch stamp.[2:7]

The next two buildings on the south side of the street are the former American barracks and legation, rebuilt in 1901 after the Boxer catastrophe, and now belonging to the People's Court. The colorful building on the north side of the street, a bit further down, was the French Hospital. This brings us to the end of Legation Street.

(2:7) Henri Borel *The New China: A Traveller's Impressions*, p. 43.

Here you will find a staircase that descends to **Tiananmen Square** [天安门广场] which is open most of the time, 24 hours a day. However it is closed to visitors for major events, whenever high-level ceremonies are taking place at the Great Hall of the People and during the annual National People's Congress in March.

Tiananmen Square is arguably the world's largest public plaza, measuring 880 meters north to south, and 500 meters east to west, but that's stretching it to the very edges (Red Square in Moscow is only 400 meters by 150 meters in size).

Begin by making your way to the prominent **Monument to the People's Heroes** [人民英雄纪念碑], erected in 1958 in the center of **Tiananmen Square**. Six years of planning went into this monolithic political statement, and more than 10,000 people throughout China, including peasants, soldiers and factory workers, were consulted to ensure that the edificatory carved panels on the base of the monument, commemorating a series of revolutions, uprisings and wars of liberation that culminated in the Communist victory in 1949, would be comprehensible to all. The monument was finally unveiled as part of the ceremonies held to celebrate the tenth anniversary of the People's Republic in

Above: *The Chairman Mao Mausoleum as seen from The Gate Facing the Sun*
Left: *The Monument to the People's Heroes*

1959. Along with the Chairman Mao Mausoleum to the south, the monument stands on the once sacred north-south axis that runs through the Forbidden and Imperial cities.

First, a bit of background, beginning with recent history. Here on the night of April 4, 1976, during the Qingming Festival, when Chinese people perform maintenance on the graves of their deceased relatives, Beijing police peremptorily removed wreathes commemorating the recently deceased Premier Zhou Enlai that had been placed at the base of the monument. The response to this act of official desecration of popular sentiment came the next day in the form of a huge protest in Tiananmen Square that led

to mass arrests and the death of hundreds at the hands of armed troops over the next few days. In the aftermath, Deng Xiaoping was dismissed from his posts in the Chinese Communist Party and government by the Gang of Four, a leftist junta headed by Mao's wife Jiang Qing, who blamed Deng for the breakdown of public order. In 1978, following the fall of the Gang of Four, the government's original verdict that the Tiananmen Incident of April Fifth was "counter-revolutionary" in nature was reversed. From then on it was officially declared "a completely revolutionary event." The incident, along with the death of Chairman Mao on September 9, 1976, set off a chain of events that included Deng Xiaoping's rehabilitation in 1977, and the legitimization of the April Fifth Movement, which prepared the ground for unprecedented openness in China. Deng Xiaoping died on February 19, 1997, just months before the former British colony of Hong Kong reverted to China on July 1.

The Square and the area it now occupies has regularly played a dramatic role in modern Chinese history. On May 4, 1919, patriotic university students and intellectuals gathered in front of Tiananmen, the large edifice at the north end of the square, to protest the Versailles Treaty (which ended World War I) and the Japanese occupation of Shandong peninsula, which had been a colony of Germany from 1897 to 1914. The May Fourth Movement that commemorated this event, with its slogan "Democracy and Science," paved the way for the acceptance of Marxism in China and the birth of the Chinese Communist Party in 1921. Anti-imperialist and other public demonstrations of a patriotic and or political nature were also held in here in 1925, 1926, 1938, 1947, 1976 and again thirteen unlucky years later.

From your vantage near the Monument to the People's Heroes a color portrait of Mao Zedong faces you from the north. On October 1, 1949, Mao stood above the spot where his picture now hangs on the rostrum of Tiananmen, the principal entrance to the Forbidden City, and the key element in China's national emblem, and made the famous public declaration "The Chinese

A Manchu officer and ordinary soldiers beneath one of the gate towers of the Pekin city wall, from the Illustrated London News, 1894

The Great Hall of the People

people have stood up." From this same spot in 1912, the warlord Yuan Shikai made a public appearance after being inaugurated the first president of the Republic of China. In 1984, early in his reign, the highly popular Deng Xiaoping presided over a military parade and other self-celebratory events marking the 35th anniversary of the founding of the People's Republic on October 1, after having been driven past the reviewing stands standing up in a large "Red Flag" limousine like a toy soldier. And in 1999, Deng's successor, a jolly Jiang Zemin (president, etc. 1995–2005), mounted the rostrum at the 50th anniversary of the regime. Today, for a modest fee, anyone can mount the gate, inspect the lounge where the leadership took their leisure, gaze down on the square and enjoy a Mao's eye view.

Tiananmen Square is reputed to be the largest urban plaza in the world, with a stated capacity of 600,000 people, each to his own checkerboard square. Geometrically, the square is large enough to accommodate 1,687 tennis courts.

(2:8) For a detailed account of the remaking of Beijing, see Anne-Marie Broudehoux, *The Making and Selling of Post-Mao Beijing* (New York and London: Routledge, 2004)
(2:9) C P Fitzgerald *Flood Tide in China* (London, Cresset Press, 1958) pp. 8–9.
(2:10) The other eight are: the Beijing Train Station (at Chongwenmen), National Art Gallery (Wusi Da Jie), Agricultural Museum, Cultural Palace of the Nationalities, Hotel of the Nationalities, The Military Museum of the Chinese People's Revolution, State Guest House (Diaoyutai), and the Overseas Chinese Hotel, now the Prime Hotel.

The creation of Tiananmen Square was, evidently, part of a greater strategic urban plan. In 1958, the historian C. P. Fitzgerald had observed in his *Flood Tide in China*:

> *The purpose of an imperial city was to enshrine the palace, which indeed occupied a very large part of the whole walled enclosure. . . . Wide straight streets ran from north to south and east to west, streets far wider than the traffic of the age required, a fact which has fortunately saved Peking from the sad necessity of demolishing many ancient buildings to accommodate the traffic of modern times. The purpose of this design was probably not so much a geomantic requirement as a measure of military precaution.*(2:8) (2:9)

As it turns out, the "wide straight streets" are hardly wide enough today to accommodate all the traffic that creeps and flows through this longtime bottleneck of Beijing.

The two top-heavy buildings flanking the square, the **Great Hall of the People** [人民大会堂] to the west (left), and the **National Museum of China** [国家博物馆], formerly the **Museum of Chinese History** and the **Museum of the Chinese Revolution** to the east (right), were completed in 1959 as two of ten major construction projects planned to commemorate the tenth anniversary of the People's Republic of China(2:10); this was

The National Museum of China

during the final years of China's ideological tryst with Russia, and the pile exudes all the gruff charm of Stalinesque neo-classicism. The **Chairman Mao Mausoleum** [毛主席纪念堂] to the south was completed and opened to the public in 1977, one year after Mao died in September 1976. Architecturally it represents an attempt to harmonize with the other buildings flanking the square, but it somehow gives an impression of being temporary. To tone down the deification to Mao, a Museum of Revolutionary Heroes devoted to the exploits of Zhou Enlai, Zhu De, Liu Shaoqi and Mao himself has been installed on one of the upper floors. The little museum features such tricks of the trade as air-brushed photos of the communist leadership and the toothbrush and towel Chairman Mao used in the rural communist base of Yan'an in northern Shaanxi province. Worthwhile stuff for revolution buffs, but not regularly open to the public.

The honor of penning the name of the hall which hangs above the entrance went to Hua Guofeng, Mao's erstwhile successor, whose reign as a lesser but almost look-alike chairman was cut short by the fall of the Gang of Four. It is rare in China for a deposed leader's calligraphy to remain in a public place. In this case, perhaps, the extraordinarily prominent position given to Hua's six words are as much a commemoration of, as well as a writing off, of Mao and Hua's reputations.

If you wish to view Old Mao's embalmed remains in all their Stalinist glory, note that handbags and cameras are strictly NOT allowed inside the mausoleum; you can store them safely in the booths on the east side of the mausoleum. Mao's body lies sequestered in a discreetly lit crystal coffin that is supposedly lowered into an underground fridge during off-duty hours. One curious rumor has it that Mao's left ear nearly fell off and had to be replaced because of shoddy workmanship by the embalmers. Further gritty details on how the nervous technicians nearly botched the preservation of the corpse by injecting many too many chemicals are recorded memorably by Mao's personal physician, Li Zhishui, in *The Private Life of Chairman Mao*, a book that was severely criticized in China when it was published in 1994, naturally spurring international sales. The mausoleum is open daily at 8:30 am and on several afternoons.

Now back to the monument, the tall (38 meters) megalith behind you and Mao's mausoleum further to the south are all standing smack on the semi-sacred north-south central axis of Old Peking. Before the Monument to the People's Heroes was built and Mao was laid to rest, it was theoretically possible for the emperor seated upon his throne in the **Hall of Supreme Harmony** in the Forbidden City, to have an uninterrupted view of his kingdom as far as the south gate of the city, the **Gate of Eternal Stability** (*Yongding Men*), as all the gates on the axis were arranged in a perfectly straight lane.

When the **National Museum of China** reopens at the end of 2009, it will be the world's largest. Over $300 million will have been spent to create 190,000 square metres in which to house more than 600,000 cultural relics.

The portico facing Tiananmen Square has provided display space for a large rectangular electronic countdown clock that has anticipated a series of major events. Beginning in 1994, the clock announced the return of Hong Kong to China on midnight of June 31–July 1, 1997, over the course of some 80 million seconds. As brilliantly interpreted by art historian Wu Hung in *Remaking Beijing: Tiananmen Square and the Creation of a Political Space,*

> *Although called a zhong or "clock," the Hong Kong Clock resembled a giant document...an official certificate.... But this document is not yet finalized. It is still in the making and its function as a certificate is only implied, not consolidated. [This function...can be achieved only when the Clock's changing number stops at zero. The Clock would then freeze and its message, THE CHINESE GOVERNMENT RESUMES EXERCISE OF SOVEREIGNTY OVER HONG KONG, would become eternal. . . . .] Following its removal on July 1, 1997, Tiananmen Square had regained its original balance to represent once again an unchanging Communist order.[2:11]*

(2:11) Wu Hung, *Remaking Beijing*, pp. 136, 164.

Having swallowed Hong Kong, the clock, 14 meters (45 feet) high and 5.5 meters (18 feet) wide), was reset to consume Macao, which timed out and swooned into the Chinese national embrace on December 20, 1999. Then again on September 21, 2004, a new clock face began clicking in seconds towards the opening of the Beijing Olympics, at 8:00 pm on August 8, 2008.

Tiananmen Gate, at noon on a fine February day. The daily flag raising and lowering ceremony takes place just out-of-frame, to the right of the camera

This time, Omega, Official Timekeeper of the Beijing 2008 Olympic Games, added its name to the face of the clock. According to an Omega press release, "The core component of the clock, providing the countdown function, is a special display board shipped directly from Omega in Switzerland, the specialists in the production of electronic scoreboard and information displays.... Omega was the first-ever company to be appointed as timekeeper of the Los Angeles Olympic Games in 1932 and subsequently went on to be the Official Timekeeper of a total of 21 Olympic Games over the past century."

Chairman Mao's Mausoleum fronted by heroic statuary

On the western side of Tiananmen Square, the **Great Hall of the People** [人民大会堂], the venue for important party pomp and government circumstance and meetings between Chinese and foreign heads of state, is open to the public several days of the week and has a room dedicated to each province and autonomous region, including Taiwan, Tibet, Macao and Hong Kong. It has facilities for serving 5,000 sit-down guests at state banquets and 10,000 standing up at cocktail parties.

Before 1949, Tiananmen Square was a narrow corridor on the central axis of the city, which took the form of a T-square, with its top abutting on Tiananmen Gate and its bottom coinciding with the Zhonghua Gate that was demolished in the early 1950s. During the Qing dynasty, the T-shaped plaza was off limits to all but high-ranking officials, and was a major obstacle to east-west traffic in the city. On the east and west sides of this corridor on the land now given over to the square stood the civil and military ministries or boards, respectively, of the Ming and Qing dynasties. This pattern of east/military, west/civil segregation is repeated in the palace gates: only the emperor could use the central entranceway; military officials the west entrance and civil officials the east. Now everyone entering the Forbidden City from the south passes through the central gate of Tiananmen.

There is a little known network of underground tunnels and shelters beneath Tiananmen Square (and many other parts of the city) that date from the late 1950s and 1960s, when Sino-Soviet relations had deteriorated to a point where the Chinese leadership feared Moscow would drop an atomic bomb on Beijing. (Similarly, it is said that Shanghai long remained underdeveloped in terms of basic infrastructure because Mao feared a U.S. naval attack via Taiwan on the once-great port city.) The tunnels were dug by teams of local youth and peasants from the Beijing suburbs who worked for brief stints on small sections of the project in order to prevent anyone from gaining an understanding of the entire system. Some of the resulting fallout shelters have been turned into warehouses, restaurants, shops, hotels and nightclubs.

Rumor has it that there is an automobile tunnel linking the Great Hall of the People with Zhongnanhai, where the top Chinese leaders live, work and play. Another branch of this tunnel supposedly connects Zhongnanhai with the east-west line of the Beijing underground metro, facilitating a quick getaway in a private subway car to the former secret military airport in the western suburbs, just south of the Summer Palace, that was Beijing's main commercial airport before 1949.

On 1 October 1949, Chairman Mao Zedong proclaimed the establishment of the People's Republic of China from the rostrum of the Gate of Heavenly Peace (Tiananmen)

North of the monument stands a flagpole which is the centerpiece of an impressive daily flag raising and lowering ceremony instituted in 1991, following the promulgation that year of the "National Flag Law." The pole and the surrounding plinth occupy a sensitive piece of ground in the square, immediately beneath the gaze of Chairman Mao's image on Tiananmen (see page 68).

The flag raising ceremony, a must-see for Chinese tourists, is rich with hi-tech symbolism. The ritual begins approximately ten minutes before sunrise in Beijing, but at the precise moment the sun breaks over the horizon on the East China Sea.

Peking Railway Station c. 1900

The forrmer Railway Station, 2007

While the background music is a canned version of the Chinese national anthem, "The March of the Volunteers," written in 1935 for a movie, the *subtextual* music is China's nationalist anthem, The East is Red ("The east is red, the sun rises. Mao Zedong has appeared in China..."). On major holidays, 96 soldiers from the People's Liberation Army, each young man standing, or goose-stepping, for 100,000 hectares of (sacred) Chinese territory, parade out of Tiananmen Gate and assemble before the pole. There are 56 balustrades in the marble plinth, each representing one of China's 56 nationalities, or ethnic groups. The actual elevation of the flag is controlled by a computer that ensures the journey up the pole takes two minutes and seven seconds, the precise length of the day's rendition of the national anthem, as well as the time required for the sun to rise. Not a single hair is out of place.

Head south and walk back through the square, crossing the street in the middle on your left side, by the National Museum of China. Continue walking south to the underpass at the end of this long street. Exit the underpass at the broad street where the city wall once stood. This is now Qianmen Dong Da Jie, but, as mentioned earlier, it was formerly the site of Wall Street. The large brick building on the corner is the former **Peking Railway Station**, which served as the terminus of the line from Tianjin. The present main Beijing Railway Station now lies about one mile to the east of here.

Immediately to the west of the wide semi-roundabout here are two large city gates which were at one time part of the south wall of the Tartar City. The southernmost structure is the **Arrow Tower** (*Jianlou*) [箭楼], which burnt down in 1900 and was reconstructed in 1903 following the design of a German architect, who added the slightly odd European-style eyebrows over the windows. The city wall itself extended east and west from the **Gate Facing the Sun** (*Zhengyang Men*) [正阳门], the structure to

The Arrow Tower (left) and the Gate Facing the Sun (right). "Circular Street" from the east

the north, with its single opening. Until around 1915 a semi-circular *enceinte* wall linked the Arrow Tower to the gate, providing shelter for two temples and a number of stalls that conducted their trade inside. Looking at the Gate Facing the Sun from the side, you can get an idea of the impressive height and width of the dearly departed Peking city walls. The Arrow Tower is today closed to individual tourists, catering to overseas Chinese tour groups. The Gate Facing the Sun has three stories, and on the first is an exhibition of photos of the old gates of Peking. On the second floor is an exhibition of Jin dynasty bronze mirrors with dragon patterns, and on the thrd floor is a stall selling souvenirs.

The Gate Facing the Sun houses an excellent museum and has a fine view of Tiananmen

Debates about preserving the old walled city of Peking raged for decades. During the Japanese occupation (1937–45), Japanese planners supported the idea of building a modern New Capital (*Xinjing*, oddly echoing the name of the capital of Manchukuo, now Changchun) in the western suburbs outside the old walled city, and arguments in favor of this plan continued to be raised in the early 1950s, notably by the American-trained architectural historian Liang Sicheng. The Liang camp advocated leaving the old city walls intact and preserving untouched most of what stood inside them. But a directive from Chairman Mao himself sealed the fate of the walls.

As the construction of public housing in Beijing could not keep up with population growth (thanks to Mao's having urged the masses in the 1950s to procreate vigorously as a national defense tactic), a majority of the thousands of traditional courtyard houses (*siheyuan*) in Beijing, essentially composed of four rectangular rooms around a square courtyard, were converted into *dazayuan*, literally "big heterogeneous (mixed-use) courtyards." Thus a courtyard formerly occupied by a single family might have been subdivided and allotted to four, six or as many as eight families depending on the size of the buildings and the number of courtyards. During the Cultural Revolution (1966–76), whatever empty space remained in the courtyards was filled up with jerry-built kitchens, bedrooms, and storage rooms to accommodate the offspring of the post-Liberation baby boom. In the 1950s a few privileged Red-blooded families were assigned spacious traditional courtyard houses (with servants)—the finest of them consisting of three or more contiguous courtyards on a north-south axis— complete with gardens, rockeries and ponds, and of course modern plumbing, hot water, central heating and a garage for the family car. One method the government used to obtain these properties during the first decade of the People's Republic was to accuse the original owners of these homes of being "bourgeois landlords" and then confiscate their "surplus" property, forcing them to live in one corner of their residences. If that didn't do the trick, the government would drive the "feudal landlords" out of their homes by radically raising taxes on the property to the point where the owners could no longer afford to pay them, having already been deprived of their main source of income as landlords.

With the massive building boom that begin in the 1990s and continues breathlessly today, entire traditional, low rise neighborhoods have been demolished to make way for expansive official and commercial (with the line between the two remaining blurred by corruption) real estate projects, new roads, green urban "lungs" and other paraphernalia of modernization, development and Olympics primping.

The Arrow Tower with its so-called European eyebrows

DAZHALAN (DASHALAR) [大栅栏]

With your back to the former railway station continue southwest along the semi-circular street crowded with hawkers and shops, and where **Qianmen Da Jie** [前门大街], undergoing transformation into a huge pedestrian mall, "straightens out" again, cross it and enter the first small north-south alley, **Zhubaoshi Jie** (Jewellery Street) [珠宝市大街].

The area you are now in is locally called **Dashalar**, Pekinese dialect for Dazhalan, literally "big stockades." Stockades of wood or iron were used here in Ming times to close off the streets during the evening curfew. Dashalar and its environs were the most important commercial and entertainment districts during the Ming and Qing dynasties. One reason for this is its location immediately outside of the Imperial City, where certain classes of

establishments were prohibited, notably theaters, shops, restaurants and brothels. Here in the relatively free atmosphere of the Chinese City, Manchu officials would let down their queues, and emperors would come in mufti to taste the pleasures of the common man.

The street life immediately in front of the Front Gate was described by the noted botanist, Robert Fortune, who visited in 1863:

Humble hutongs have additional charm as the demolition teams approach

The noise and bustle about this gate was perfectly deafening. Carts were going to and fro, rumbling along on the rough stone road, and now and then sinking deeply into the broken pavement. Donkeys, horses, and long trains of camels laden with productions of the country, were toiling along; a perfect Babel of noisy tongues was heard in all directions; and the dust was flying in clouds and literally filling the air. Stalls of fruit, hawkers of all kinds of wares, beggars ragged, filthy and in many instances apparently insane, crowded the approaches to the gate.[(2:12)]

Hutong to highrise? Preparing for the future today continues to encroach upon yesterday

Another traveler, writing in 1888, described the same district, which appears to have changed little in the intervening decades:

> *. . . all manner of cheap, useful things, and stores of food are also outspread upon the ground, and became more and more thickly coated with dust [the dust of Peking!] as the ceaseless traffic of the day moves on. The strange market seemed to extend for nearly a mile, and oh! The noise, and oh! The extraordinary variety of smells, all evil, which assailed us as we passed the busy crowd of much-chattering buyers and sellers.*
>
> *On all sides were merchants shouting out descriptions of their wares; blind musicians wandering about in companies, making horrible discords; jugglers exhibiting strange feats to the delight of the crowd; barbers plying their razors on shaven crowns and faces, and carefully plaiting the long black tresses; while quack doctors and mountebanks of all sorts each added their share to the general din. Dentists and chiropodists both shout their invitations to suffering mankind to enter the booths, where, in presence of all who care to gaze, they carry on their work. The chiropodists are said to be exceedingly skilful.*[(2:13)]

(2:12) Robert Fortune Yedo and Peking: *A narrative of a journey to the capitals of Japan and China*, p. 361.

(2:13) C.F. Gordon Cumming *Wanderings in China*, p. 448.

The world's oldest profession has a long history in China, one of the world's oldest continual civilizations, and the Eight Big Hutongs, a district southwest of Dashalar, was where the action was. Like their counterparts in Japan, high-class courtesans were sought out as much for their companionship or for their literary and musical talents, as for their physical charms. Brothels with dreamy names like The Cassia and Lotus Garden, and The Fragrant Clouds, provided a range of services to their male customers. If you were dining out in a restaurant, you could send a boy with a chit to a brothel and your favorite would be delivered to your side by rickshaw in a matter of minutes. Chinese guidebooks to Peking published in the Republican period placed the houses in three classes and listed the girls' "flower names," described the appointments of the rooms (some even had electric fans), quoted prices and outlined brothel protocol. For example, new customers were required to pay in cash, while regulars could sign, and settle their accounts three times a year. Good customers also enjoyed discounts. In the early 1920s there were 78 first-class houses, 85 second-class houses and 57 third-class houses in Peking, in addition to Japanese brothels where Chinese customers might go and brothels for foreigners where Chinese were not welcome. Though morally reprehensible to some, the profession was practiced with the approval of the government, which licensed the brothels and the girls, and carried out regular health inspections. Courtesans and concubines have always had their place in Chinese society, and there were as many dire tragedies as glamorous success stories. Lao She's story, *Crescent Moon* [2:14] chronicles the career of a Peking prostitute in a memorably moving way.

What little is left of the Dazhalan district remains refreshingly seedy today, not all buildings have yet been torn down or modernized, although they have suffered seriously because of a lack of maintenance. Some of the first-class brothels referred to above occupied the solidly built two-storey buildings that may still be spotted.

(2:14) Lao She *Crescent Moon and Other Stories*, pp. 191–231.

Continue south along Zhubaoshi Jie and turn into the second street on your right, **Langfang Ertiao** [廊坊二条], in the old days known in English as Jade Street. For the sake of orientation, on the northwest corner of the street there is a pale green two-storey ornate building. Note the appropriateness of these small *hutongs* for travel by rickshaw and pedicab.

As you stroll down the *hutong*, notice the carved and painted wooden decorative panels on houses **#10, 12** and **14** (there's no house number on **#10**). These were once fairly common on both shops and private homes. The tiny restaurants you will pass by here are privately run.

Make your first left at **Menkuang Hutong** (Door Threshold Lane) [门框胡同] and turn south. Along this street you will see pocket-sized restaurants, hotels, homes, beauty parlors and take out bakeries.

Turn right at the first crossing, and head west once again on **Langfang Santiao** [廊坊三条]. Here the houses appear to jut out and hit you in the face. Before long, you will reach a

Coal-dust briquettes, a major contributor to pollution

large, and probably very new cross street running north/south, **Meishi Jie** (Coal Market Street) [煤市街], once renowned for its restaurants. Today Meishi Jie serves as a conduit for the traffic that once roared down Qianmen Dajie, where the pedestrian mall has been installed.

Cross Meishi Jie, bear right (or north) and enter **Qudeng Hutong** (Matches Alley) [取灯胡同]. Note the old door handles on **#11** and the carved stones at the base of the door. There are two beams in the lintel at **#13**. Beams of this sort appear above the front doors of "better" homes and mansions in Beijing, always in twos and fours depending on the stature of the inhabitants. The double doors at **#17** are peppered with a nailhead design to protect them from being kicked to pieces. No **19**, with its four beams, was the home of a noted Qing-dynasty scholar, who was awarded this property by the emperor. An auspicious couplet is carved on the door of **#21**. Note the decorative stones, functioning as door gods and dismounting stones, at **#23**.

Bear right at the next intersection, go past the shop on the corner, and bear left and enter **Tiaozhou** (broom) *Hutong* [笤帚胡同]. On the first door on the left, note how here again the Chinese character *fu* ,"felicity," on the lintel has been nearly wiped out. During the Cultural Revolution, auspicious inscriptions like *fu* and *shou*, or "longevity," were obliterated as part of the campaign to blot out remnants of the feudal past.

You can inspect a typical big heterogeneous courtyard (*dazayu*an) at **#31**. No need to be shy about walking in to this or any other courtyard where the door is open, as the space inside is shared by multiple families, and thus is not entirely private. The local residents will not resent your presence if you respect the intimacy and privacy of the surroundings.

From there, continue to the end of this *hutong,* turn left and proceed forward for about 50 metres (165 feet). Here you will find yourself in the midst of one of the liveliest hutong markets in the vicinity. This is **Yanshou** (Increasing Longevity) **Street** [延寿街], marked by a sign on the wall above an abandoned millstone. Another minute's walk to the south brings you to the east end of Liulichang, our final destination on this walk.

Please note: the route just taken is a simple one and should not constrain you from exploring further afield. There are traces of Old Peking to be found in every *hutong* in this part of town, and a morning or afternoon spent threading your way on foot or bicycle here will inevitably be rewarding. This is one of the best-preserved *hutong* districts in all of Beijing.

Innumerable images of the Great Helmsman

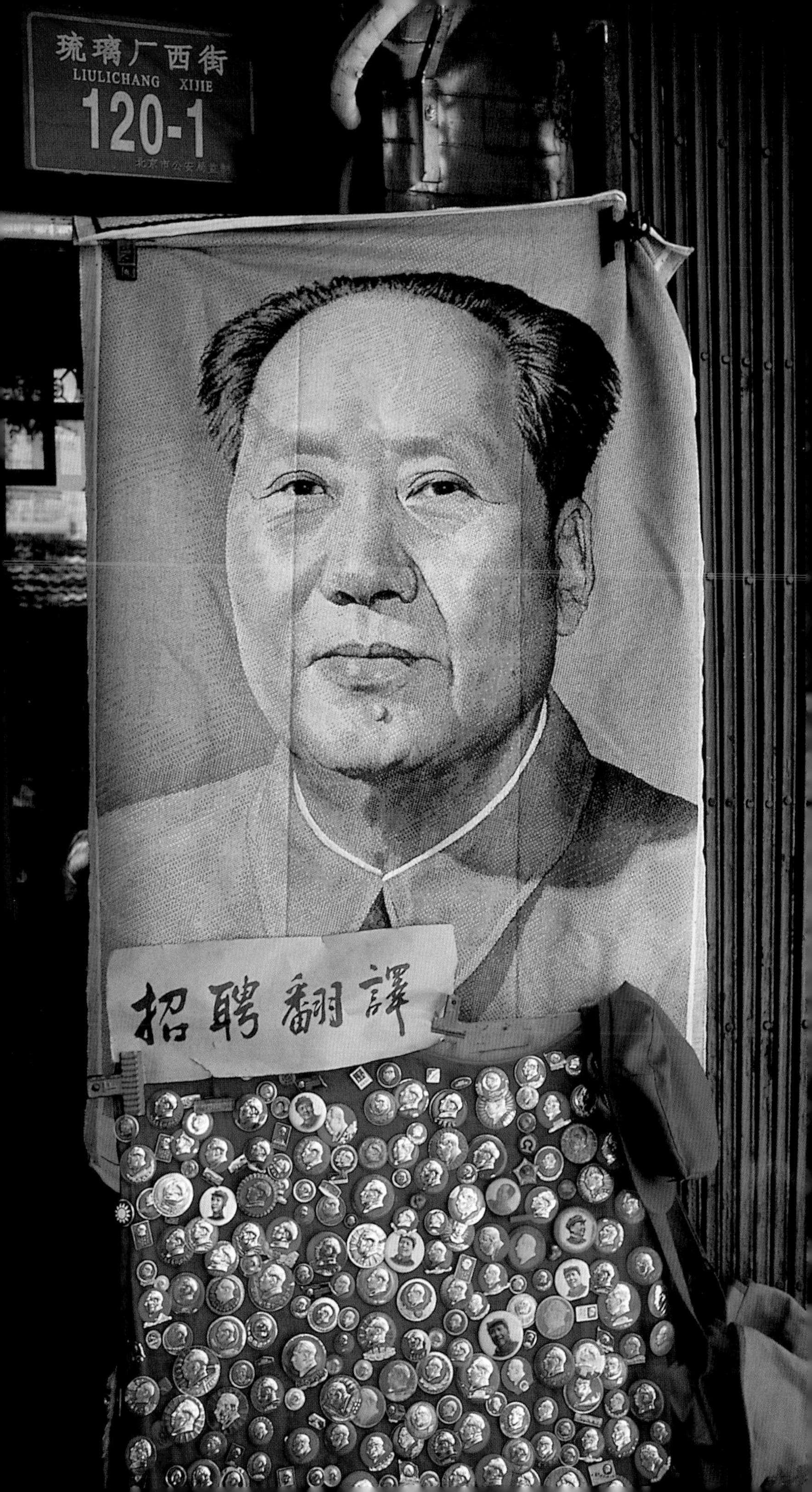
琉璃厂西街
LIULICHANG XIJIE
120-1
招聘翻譯

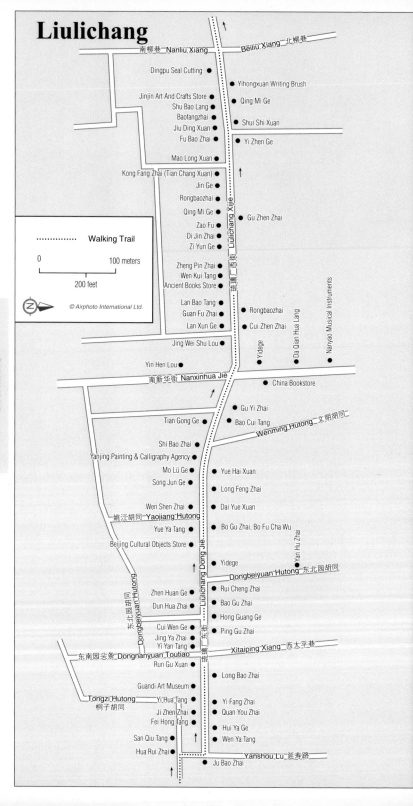

Liulichang

南柳巷 Nanliu Xiang — Beiliu Xiang 北柳巷

Dingpu Seal Cutting ●

● Yihongxuan Writing Brush

Jinjin Art And Crafts Store ●   ● Qing Mi Ge
Shu Bao Lang ●
Baofangzhai ●   ● Shui Shi Xuan
Jiu Ding Xuan ●
Fu Bao Zhai ●   ● Yi Zhen Ge

Mao Long Xuan ●

Kong Fang Zhai (Tian Chang Xuan) ●

Jin Ge ●

Rongbaozhai ●

Qing Mi Ge ●   ● Gu Zhen Zhai
Zao Fu ●
Di Jin Zhai ●
Zi Yun Ge ●

Zheng Pin Zhai ●
Wen Kui Tang ●
Ancient Books Store ●

Lan Bao Tang ●   ● Rongbaozhai
Guan Fu Zhai ●
Lan Xun Ge ●   ● Cui Zhen Zhai

Jing Wei Shu Lou ●

Yin Hen Lou ●

南新华街 Nanxinhua Jie

● China Bookstore

● Gu Yi Zhai
Tian Gong Ge ●   ● Bao Cui Tang

Wenming Hutong 文明胡同

Shi Bao Zhai ●

Yanjing Painting & Calligraphy Agency ●

Mo Lü Ge ●   ● Yue Hai Xuan
Song Jun Ge ●   ● Long Feng Zhai

Wen Shen Zhai ●   ● Dai Yue Xuan

一姚汪胡同 Yaojiang Hutong

Yue Ya Tang ●   ● Bo Gu Zhai, Bo Fu Cha Wu
Beijing Cultural Objects Store ●

● Yidege

Dongbeiyuan Hutong 东北园胡同

Zhen Huan Ge ●   ● Rui Cheng Zhai
Dun Hua Zhai ●   ● Bao Gu Zhai
                    ● Hong Guang Ge
Cui Wen Ge ●   ● Ping Gu Zhai
Jing Ya Zhai ●
Yi Yan Tang ●   Xitaiping Xiang 西太平巷

东南园头条 Dongnanyuan Toutiao

Run Gu Xuan ●

Guandi Art Museum ●   ● Long Bao Zhai

Tongzi Hutong   Yi Hua Tang ●   ● Yi Fang Zhai
桐子胡同   Ji Zhen Zhai ●   ● Quan You Zhai
                 Fei Hong Tang ● ● Hui Ya Ge
San Qiu Tang ●   ● Wen Ya Tang
Hua Rui Zhai ●   Yanshou Lu 延寿路
                 ● Ju Bao Zhai

Liulichang Xijie 琉璃厂西街
Liulichang Dong Jie 琉璃厂东街

Yidege
Da Qian Hua Lang
Nanyao Musical Instruments

Yan Hu Zhai 东北园胡同

东北园胡同 Dongbeiyuan Hutong

琉璃厂东街

········· Walking Trail

0   100 meters

200 feet

N

© Airphoto International Ltd.

LIULICHANG [琉璃厂]

The history of Liulichang, literally "glazed tile factory," as a center of cultural activity in Peking dates back to the first half of the 17th century. During the early Ming, this street was the site of one of the five kilns that produced bricks and glazed tiles especially for the palaces and halls being built in Yongle's new capital. Canals linked the kiln with sources of clay and other raw materials in the western suburbs, and the former presence of bridges spanning these canals is attested to by contemporary street names containing the word "bridge."

During the Qing dynasty, the district gradually became a popular residential neighborhood for Chinese officials serving in the Manchu government who were not permitted to live in the Tartar City. The area was also a popular locale for guesthouses run by provincial and prefectural benevolent associations where native sons from distant parts visiting the capital on business or sitting for the imperial examinations could stay for extended

Intersection of West Liulichang and South Xinhua Street (Nanxinhua Jie)

Liulichang East

Liulichang West

periods. This all-male cadre of officials, merchants and young scholars whiled away their leisure moments in the brothels and restaurants of nearby Dashalar. But they also patronized the many local stalls and shops dealing in scholarly books, brushes, ink, paper, paintings, calligraphy, rubbings, antiques, curios and such scholarly affectations as spectacles and tobacco pipes that had opened here to meet their needs. Another historical factor in the development of Liulichang was Qianlong's late-18th-century project to compile a vast *Encyclopedia of All Knowledge Under Heaven*, for which the court needed to acquire a huge corpus of old and rare books.

After the fall of the Qing dynasty in 1911, Liulichang became an outlet where Manchus recently deprived of their hereditary stipends from the imperial treasury disposed of their private libraries and antiques as a means of survival. Many of the rare Chinese books and works of art that are now in the noted collections of Western and Japanese libraries and museums were acquired at this time.

Regarding the present antiques trade in and around Liulichang, Juliet Bredon's warning written in 1932 still holds true:

Alas, the days of marvelous finds and bargains . . . are over. Do not imagine that if by chance a good piece comes on the market, any stranger will pick it up for a song. . . . Approach all curios, and most dealers, with caution.[2:15]

Writing several years earlier, Gilbert Collins described the curios markets with similar reservations and insight:

There are curio shops all over the city — though most are gathered into such quarters as the Liu Li Chang, in the Chinese City; and the traffic proceeds apace all year round, intensifying a good deal in the open-air markets in certain temple courtyards at times of national festival.

Liulichang East

The whole industry is to a great extent standardized now; even the frauds are standardized. These fall into two main categories: the fraud of fictitious age and prestige, and the fraud of sham material. The first is far the commoner and has the wider range; it reaches from comparatively modern periods well away back toward the dawn of time. . . . At the other end of the scale you have bronze Buddhas of immeasurable antiquity and therefore immense value, which the vendor was lucky enough to dig up out of the earth a week or two ago and is now obliged to offer at a ruinous figure lest the Government should get to hear of his great trove and confiscate. It is a striking, romantic tale, up to a point. That vendor did dig the Buddha up out of the earth a week or two ago, though it was hardly such an accident as he makes out. The man had a pretty shrewd idea where to look, having buried the Buddha there himself, and not so very long ago either. He got it from a foundry in the first place, one of the foundries which are at

"The Lantern Painter" by M Theodore Delamarre

work in China for year's end to year's end turning out nothing but Buddhas of immeasurable antiquity. These articles are interred for two or three months, to give them in tabloid form a two or three thousand years' ration of "patina," and then put on sale as dating from the Zhou Dynasty (1122–255 BCE). Experience has shown that it is practically always a high-frequency type of tourist who secures one of them. As a matter of sober fact, there are Zhou bronzes in existence today, but the place to look for them is not the popular curio-market.[2:16]

For those interested in jade, incidentally, Collins further advises that *"When two pieces of jade are struck together they give out a dull stony clink—nothing more.... [They do not ring] with a prolonged musical tingle. That is the distinctive note belonging to articles made of glass.*[2:17]

There are two types of shops in Liulichang today, government and private. In the state stores prices are fixed, and, particularly on less expensive items, it is futile to attempt to practice the fine art of bargaining. But you would be foolish not to bargain in the privately run shops here, and elsewhere throughout Beijing. Bredon's instructions on how to bargain in

(2:16) Gilbert Collins *Extreme Oriental Mixture*, pp. 101–102.
(2:17) Op cit., p. 104.

the curios markets from 75 years ago remain remarkably apt today. Please heed the following wisdom, and if you are a serious shopper, commit it to memory:

> . . . it is usual for most dealers to ask from a quarter to two-thirds more than they hope to receive — sometimes as much as they dare, or believe the customer can be induced to pay. . . . Offer, as a rule, a little more than half what is asked, then, as the merchant gradually comes down in his price, increase very gradually until neutral ground is reached. Finally, split the difference, and the bargain is yours. If one is in a hurry or shows any enthusiasm for the article in question, it is impossible to make a cheap purchase. Point out the defects in the piece under discussion. . . . A good plan is to leave the shop when the owner, afraid of losing a customer, runs after you with a last offer — the lowest price, or nearly — that he is prepared to accept.(2:18)

As for the shops themselves, Juliet Bredon is an astute judge:

> Some have façades of gilded wood so elaborately carved that we feel they should be put under glass as a protection against the dust, but none have show windows. Indeed, few have windows at all, and the dark, low doorways give little promise of the treasures to be found within. It is fatal to judge, as we would at home, by appearances. . . . The biggest, and the cleanest shops in Peking may not have the best things. Often a merchant hidden away in a blind alley has the rarest treasures. . . .(2:19)

In the mid-1980s, Liulichang was transformed from the ground up into a spick-and-span idealization of its former, more homely seediness. The street is divided into two sections, east and west, by South Nan Xinhua Street. The east section contains dozens of antiques shops; the west, mostly shops selling books and paintings. We enter Liulichang from the east end, and pass a number of privately owned curios shops. Despite the warnings above, these shops are worth pottering around in, if only to train and test your eye. They very occasionally may have museum-

(2:18) Juliet Bredon *Peking*, p. 473.
(2:19) Juliet Bredon *Peking*, p. 444.

Liulichang West

quality pieces for sale, but unless you know your way around antiques, it is unwise to spend large sums here, or anywhere, for that matter.

For many centuries, and as recently as the early 1950s, Liulichang was the site of an outdoor bazaar held every year during the first two weeks of the Chinese New Year, the so-called Spring Festival. This event, known as the Changdian (Tile-factory district) Fair, took place in both East and West Liulichang, in the **Temple to the God of Fire** (*Huoshen Miao*) on East Liulichang Street (now a neighborhood cultural "palace"), and all along Nan Xinhua Street. H.Y. Lowe was a habitué of the fair in its heyday in the 1930s, and gives this colorful, fastidious description of what was on sale in his charming book on Peking, *The Adventures of Wu*:

> . . . *here is a full representation of Peking's own and imported toycraft, from the cheap native jack-in-the-box made of paper and mud to the expensive clock-work toy train or toy airplanes, papier-mâché theater masks complete with*

beards of white or black horse hair, life size wooden replicas of ancient war weapons familiarly seen in the hands of the military heroes of the Chinese stage, little motorboats with oil burners that spin about in a face basin filled with water, and midget movies shaped by the clever hands of the makers from the tinsmith's castaway pieces of tin and from pieces of old films cut into "stills." Paper butterflies operated by a rubber band propeller that actually soar into the sky are sold after demonstration and trial. The toy-balloon sellers bring their chemical laboratories with them, including little pieces of galvanized iron with the indispensable zinc

Fans and seal carving, Liulichang East

coating and bottles of sulphuric acid, with which in a flask hydrogen is "brewed" and balloons filled right under the eyes of the watchful and waiting customers.[(2:20)]

Other handicrafts included pinwheels, paper lanterns (sold especially for the Lantern Festival on the 15th day of the first lunar month), painted kites, diabolos, shuttlecocks rice-flour dough figurines, tiny monkey puppets, birds and butterflies made of dried mud, miniature buildings crafted of colored straw for use in bonsai landscapes, pocket crossbows, and the famous "pupu deng," the gourd-shaped sounding bottle of blown glass in a vicious color of dark red with the bottom end not much thicker than the film on your teeth which are played by alternatingly blowing and inhaling to produce the characteristic sound from which their name is derived.[(2:21)]

So-called Canton goods-dealers sold "old pieces of cut-glass vases and plates from

Mostly reproductions, Liulichang East

(2:20) H.Y. Lowe *The Adventures of Wu: The Life Cycle of a Peking Man*, II, p. 174.
(2:21) H.Y. Lowe *The Adventures of Wu*, II, p. 175.

Hamburg or brass samovars from Tomsk, hardwood boxes and trays with inlay work of mother-of-pearl." (2:22)

In the Temple of the God of Fire one could find the stalls and booths of the jewellery traders, who kept their electric lights burning during the day, quite an extravagance in those times. Here the ladies would haggle generally for precious and semi-precious and not-so-precious stones.

Old books, paintings and calligraphy were displayed along Xinhua Street. The books ranged from rare editions of the Chinese classics to such Western works as "bulky volumes of some old export catalogues of railway locomotives and plumbing or electric fixtures, or even some hoary, old editions of commercial directories of London or Antwerp, older than the booksellers themselves." (2:23)

The book fair has been revived in a way and takes place during the first two weeks of the Spring Festival in the courtyard of the **China Book Store** (*Zhongguo Shu Dian*) [中国书店], the former Ocean King Village (*Haiwang Cun*). The name derives from a merchant in the Liao dynasty (c. 1000 CE) who monopolized the local grain barge business when this was a district of canals. Elsewhere in Beijing, a number of temple fairs are held during the Spring Festival, with traditional *pupu deng* among the goods being offered.

No fair could be complete without its food stalls, and Changdian had its own specialties: sour bean juice (an acquired taste that is said to test the mettle of those who are not true residents of Old Peking); sweet black peas cooked into porridge; spherical dumplings of glutinous rice filled with sweetened walnuts, sesame seed, preserved fruit or date butter; cotton candy; and candied crab apples on a stick.

A number of specialty shops that operate in Liulichang today have venerable histories. Short descriptions will follow the street number, beginning from the east [琉璃厂东街]. None of the antiques stores will be mentioned here, as they have mostly lost

(2:22) H.Y. Lowe *The Adventures of Wu*, II, p. 176.
(2:23) H.Y. Lowe *The Adventures of Wu*, II, p. 178.

their character. But they too are worth a visit as a way of observing the official approach to antique dealing.

#67–**Yidege** [一得阁] has been manufacturing Chinese India ink since 1865. Before the middle of the 19th century, all ink used by calligraphers and painters in China came in the form of dry sticks that had to be rubbed with water on an inkstone. This long, tedious process might have offered leisured poets and scholars an opportunity to meditate on the act of creation while they exercised their elbows, but candidates sitting for the imperial examinations had little time or patience for such practices, so a clever scholar named Xie–who had failed in the examinations himself–came up with the idea of making ink in liquid form and selling it to the examinees before they were sealed up in their cubicles. His venture was an immediate success.

At first Xie used a rather primitive method to make his ink. He combined lamp black scraped off metal plates suspended over oil lamps, tar from burnt rosin collected in chimneys, bone glue and water. Today modern machinery is used and the ingredients are a bit simpler: Sichuan carbon black scented with musk, camphor and borneol. The factory produces over ten million bottles of ink per year.

#73–**Daiyuexuan** [戴月轩] has been selling brushes for Chinese painting and calligraphy since 1916. Great precision is required in selecting, sorting and trimming the animal hairs that make up the tip and securing it in the bamboo handle. The brushes are classified into four types, according to the sort of hair used: goat, fox, rabbit and various combinations of the three.

Crossing Xinhua Street and continuing on West Liulichang Street [琉璃厂西街], walk about four minutes until you come to, on the right:

#19–**Rongbaozhai Studio** [荣宝斋] is the largest and most famous shop in Liulichang. It deals in the "Four Treasures of the Studio"–ink, brushes, paper and inkstones; Chinese scroll

The photographer ate well at this restaurant on South Xinhua Street

paintings and calligraphy; and most notably colored woodblock reproductions of paintings. Rongbaozhai was founded in the 17th century, but not until 1894 did it adopt its present name, a shortened form of the adage "an honorable name is a priceless jewel."

The basic techniques used in woodblock printing date back over 1,000 years to the Tang dynasty, but the Rongbaozhai workshop has devised ways to produce such fine reproductions of brush paintings that noted painters like the late Qi Baishi have mistaken them for their own originals!

Tibetan costumier, Liulichang East

Scholarly books, new and used, in Chinese and Western languages, are sold in the China Book Store on the north side of the parking lot east of South Xinhua Street, and in several shops on the south side of West Liulichang Street. The China Book Store also has a large selection of used books in Japanese and Western languages, as well as rare books published in China. Some of the stock is drawn from pre-1949 libraries, embassies, churches and private collections. This is a fascinating hodgepodge for bibliophiles, with many surprises. Prices range from reasonable to high. A much smaller collection of this type can be found on West Liulichang Street at **#34**, the **Guji (Classic) Bookstore** [古籍书店]. Many of the better art books have English abstracts.

There are several buildings in the immediate vicinity of the crossing of Liulichang and Xinhua Streets where scores of dealers are concentrated in small spaces. As of this writing, none of these places is properly signposted in English. Please see the map on page 140 for the locations.

Advertising in China in the 1920s; it is rare to find original posters, but you might get lucky

From Liulichang you may walk back to Dashalar via a different route through the hutongs, or end the day with a Peking duck meal at the nearby Quanjude Roast Duck Restaurant [全聚德] at Hepingmen [和平门]. You get there by walking north on Xinhua Street [新华街] for about five minutes. The restaurant is the huge multi-storey building to the right (southeast corner) at the major intersection.

Book shop in Liulichang East

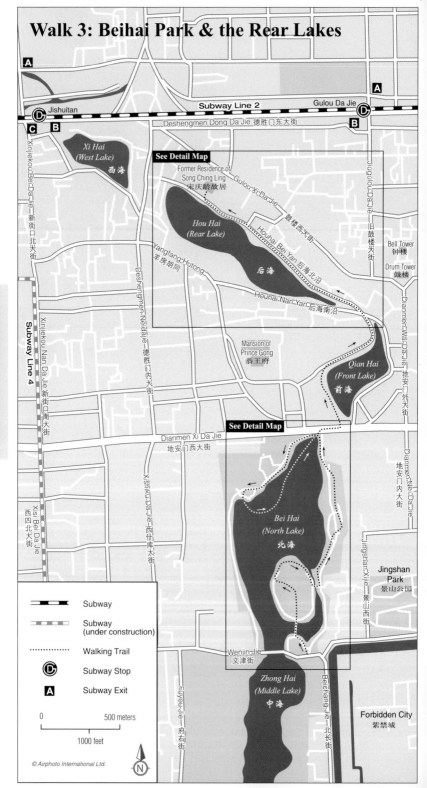

Walk 3: Beihai Park & the Rear Lakes

A

A

D Jishuitan

Subway Line 2

Gulou Da Jie **D**

C

B

Deshengmen Dong Da Jie 德胜门东大街

B

Xi Hai
(West Lake)
西海

See Detail Map

Former Residence of
Song Ching Ling
宋庆龄故居

Gulou Xi Da Jie

鼓楼西大街

Hou Hai
(Rear Lake)
后海

Houhai Bei Yan 后海北沿

Yangfang Hutong
羊房胡同

Houhai Nan Yan 后海南沿

Xinjiekou Bei Da Jie 新街口北大街

Deshengmen Neidajie 德胜门内大街

Subway Line 4

Xinjiekou Nan Da Jie 新街口南大街

Jiuguoluo Da Jie 旧鼓楼大街

Bell Tower
钟楼
Drum Tower
鼓楼

Dianmen Wai Da Jie 地安门外大街

Mansion of
Prince Gong
恭王府

Qian Hai
(Front Lake)
前海

Dianmen Nei Da Jie 地安门内大街

See Detail Map

Dianmen Xi Da Jie
地安门西大街

Xishiku Da Jie 西什库大街

Bei Hai
(North Lake)
北海

Jingshan
Park
景山公园

Jingshan Xi Jie 景山西街

Xisi Bei Da Jie 西四北大街

Wenjin Jie
文津街

Zhong Hai
(Middle Lake)
中海

Beichang Jie 北长街

Fuyou Jie 府右街

Forbidden City
紫禁城

	Subway
	Subway (under construction)
....	Walking Trail
D	Subway Stop
A	Subway Exit

0   500 meters

1000 feet

© Airphoto International Ltd.

N

WALK · 3

BEIHAI PARK AND THE THREE REAR LAKES—SHICHAHAI

DURATION
Approximately five hours.

DESCRIPTION

Visit imperial parks that fit 13th century descriptions written by Marco Polo. Stroll along the shores of man-made lakes once reserved for the imperial family. **Beihai Park** is open from 6:30 am to 8:30 pm in the winter and from 6:00 am to 9:00 pm in the summer. The **Rear Lakes**, known popularly as **Shichahai** ("Sea of Ten Buddhist Temples"), or **Houhai,** have no opening and closing times. It is suggested that you begin in Beihai Park in mid-morning, eat lunch in **Lotus Lane** (Hehua Shichang) on the western shore of the **Front Lake** (Qianhai) and watch the sun set through the willows on the shores of the **Rear Lake** (Houhai) in the early evening. Or return to the Rear Lake area in the late afternoon for a drink, dinner and the noisy nightlife scene that has developed here over the past decade.

STARTING POINT
The Rainbow Bridge that divides Beihai from Zhonghai.

HOW TO GET THERE
Buses 5, 13, 42, 101, 103, 105, 107, 111, 118 stop at Beihai.
Taxi: Beihai Nongyuan Nan Men

HOW TO GET AWAY
From the **Drum Tower** (Gulou) take buses 5, 8, 18, 107, 204, 305 or the Beijing underground (metro) at Gulou Da Jie, about a ten-minute walk north from the tower. From the rear gate of Beihai (Beihai Hou Men) take buses 13, 42, 107, 111, 118, 204.

A string of six contiguous lakes runs north-south through the center of Beijing, fed by a stream that has its source in the northwest suburbs. Practically speaking the six lakes are divided into three areas: the three lakes of **Shichahai** (Ten temples "sea") in the north; **Beihai** (North "sea") in the middle; and **Zhongnanhai** (Central and South "seas") in the south, which are part of the walled compound of the same name, now the headquarters of the Central Committee of the Communist Party of China, a sanctum sanctorum where China's top leaders live, work and presumably play.

Sanskrit inscription within the niche on the south face of the White Dagoba

The history of imperial lakes in China goes back more than 2,000 years. In the third century BCE, so goes the legend, the megalomaniac First emperor of the Qin dynasty (who resided at Xianyang, near present-day Xi'an in central China) dispatched one of his officials and a boat full of children on a crusade in search of an elixir of immortality. They sailed eastward from the China coast in search of the fabled Isles of the Blessed, where the emperor had ordered the official to trade the children for the youth-giving drug. Needless to say, they never returned.

The White Dagoba, Beihai Park

One century later, the Han martial emperor Wu Di (reigned 140–86 BCE), taking a hint from his less than illustrious predecessor, had a pond dug on his palace grounds in Chang'an (now Xi'an) and piled up the sludge in the lake to form three islands, thus creating his own backyard Isles of the Blessed. He called this body of water the **Pool of Great Secretion** (Taiye Chi), also rendered variously as the Pool of Great Fertilizing Spume, or the Great Saliva Pool; the esoteric liquid referred to here is the result of the metaphysical confluence of yin and yang and does not refer to the stuff spittoons are filled with.

Every dynasty that has made Peking its capital has built an imperial pleasure park, complete with pond and islands, in the vicinity of present-day Beihai Park. The nomenclature is rather complex. As early as the Tang dynasty (618–906), there was a park of this nature in Youzhou, the regional capital of that dynasty. When the Liao dynasty (907–1125) made Youzhou its southern capital, they rehabilitated the gardens here. The emperors of the Jin dynasty (1115–1234) constructed an artificial hill in the middle of the lake that they had expanded, and transported Lake Taihu stones from the Song dynasty palace at Bianliang (now Kaifeng) in the south to decorate it. The present name of the island in Beihai Park, **Hortensia Isle** (Qionghua Dao) [琼华岛], dates from this period.

In the 13th century after the founding of the Yuan dynasty, this part of the city became the site of an imperial garden in the Mongol palace, and in the early 15th century emperor Yongle of the Ming dynasty created Nanhai, the southernmost of the six lakes. Throughout the Ming and Qing dynasties, the three southern lakes (Beihai, Zhonghai and Nanhai) formed part of the private gardens of the emperors. Zhonghai and Nanhai were the liquid centerpieces of the Western Garden (Xiyuan), so named because of its location west of the Forbidden City.

After the fall of the Qing dynasty in 1911, the new Republican government established its presidential palace on the shores of Nanhai, but only made use of it until 1925. After the founding of the People's Republic in 1949, Mao Zedong followed suit and chose Zhongnanhai to be the epicenter of communist state power. Many of the Qing-dynasty structures in the compound were removed to other places, torn down or fortified, as one Chinese source puts it laconically, "for practical reasons." Office buildings for the State Council, military barracks, a helicopter pad, subterranean residences, strategic command centers and escape tunnels were installed as part of the apparatus of a modern state.

At present, heads of state and invited guests, such as thoracic surgeons, are the only foreigners who enter Zhongnanhai with impunity. They are usually photographed with the current Chinese leadership in the Ziguang Ge, the **Palace of Purple Effulgence** (also known as the **Hall of Mongol Princes**), the illustrious front parlor of the three governments that have ruled China since 1644. At other times, selected Chinese citizens (such as relatives of the soldier-martyrs who lost their lives in June 1989 during the Tiananmen Incident), groups of school children and a quota of Chinese tourists are allowed to visit a limited section of the grounds and take a peek at Chairman Mao's Spartan study and bedroom.

The most famous description of a Chinese garden is probably found in Marco Polo's 13th century travelogue. Remarkably, however, no Chinese source from the time mentions Marco Polo or anyone vaguely resembling him, and there is increasing doubt among scholars that he ever set foot in China. Regardless of its source, the following passage seems like a reasonable account of the imperial palace garden in the Yuan capital of Khanbaligh ("city of the Khan"), and tallies with contemporary Chinese reports.

Moreover on the north side of the Palace, about a bow-shot off, there is a hill which has been made by art; it is a good hundred paces in height and a mile in compass. This hill is entirely covered with trees that never lose their leaves, but remain ever green. And I assure you that wherever a beautiful tree may exist, and the Emperor gets news of it, he sends for it and has it transported bodily with all its roots and the earth attached to them, and planted on that hill of his. . . . And he has also caused the whole hill to be covered with the ore of azure, which is very green. And thus not only are the trees all green, but the hill itself is all green likewise; and there is nothing to be seen on it that is not green. . . .

The Round City, the starting point of this walk

On the top of the hill again there is a fine big palace which is all green inside and out; and thus the hill, and the trees, and the palace together form a startling spectacle; and it is marvelous to see their uniformity of color! Everyone who sees them is delighted. And the Great Khan [Kublai] had caused this beautiful prospect to be formed for the comfort and solace and delectation of his heart.[3:1]

Ser Marco was likely describing the man-made protuberance that is now Hortensia Isle (Qionghua Dao), where palace buildings stood during the Yuan. He may also have been referring to the **Round City** (or **Round Castle**, Tuancheng), the starting

(3:1) Sir Henry Yule *The Book of Ser Marco Polo*, 3 vols. (London, John Murray, 1921), pp. 365-6.

point of this walk, which at the time was an island in the lake linked by wooden suspension bridges to Hortensia Isle to the north, and to the shores of the lake on the east and west. One section of one of these bridges stood on piles set in two boats, which could be moved out of the way to allow grain transport ships to pass through.

In the early 15th century, a strip of water to the east of the Round City was reclaimed in order to facilitate the transport of bricks, tiles, rocks and timber being used in the construction of the new Ming walls and palaces of Peking. The present brick wall that surrounds the Round City dates from 1745.

The Manchus' first major construction project in these parts, after the founding of the Qing dynasty in 1644, was the huge Tibetan-style White Dagoba that crowns Hortensia Isle (1651). For a full three decades (1741–71) during the Qianlong reign, work continued on the park; the exquisite garden within a garden on the north shore of the lake (see below), the **Studio of the Mirror of Clarity** (Jingqing Zhai), after 1913 known as the **Studio of Quieting the Mind** (Jingxin Zhai), and the **Studio of the Painted Boat** (Huafang Zhai) on the eastern shore of the lake, both date from the reign of Qianlong. For the most part the present layout of Beihai Park follows Qianlong's design.

The Empress Dowager Cixi, a garden fancier whose lavish late 19th century architectural embellishments set the tone for all subsequent restoration work, diverted funds originally designated for the Chinese navy and carried out major restoration work at Beihai Park and the Summer Palace from 1885 to 1888. One interesting 1888 addition to Beihai was a miniature railway line (with an engine built by the French company, Decauville) that ran for about one mile from Zhongnanhai to a small terminus in front of the Studio of the Mirror of Clarity. Though this was not the first railway in China (Englishmen had built a 500-meter demonstration line in 1865), the Zhonghai-Beihai Express was instrumental in convincing Cixi that it was necessary to build railways on a large scale in China. One unsubstantiated legend

One of a pair of majestic marble lions guarding the pailou in front of the Hall of Heavenly Kings

The Hall of Eternal Mercy lies north-west of the Hall of Heavenly Kings in Beihai Park's north-west

tells that after the Decauville engine exploded (the line was maintained by eunuchs), the Empress Dowager ordered that the train be hauled along the tracks by her eunuchs with a golden rope. But she soon tired of this imported toy and had the tracks removed.

In the summer of 1900, following the famous siege of the legations by the Boxers, troops belonging to the Eight Allied Armies occupied a number of buildings in Beihai Park and plundered many of the relics. Traces of their visit remain in the form of bullet holes in some of the older buildings.

Immediately after the fall of the Qing dynasty in 1911, sections of the park were occupied by the troops of Chinese warlords, although officially the grounds remained the property of the deposed last emperor, Puyi. Beihai Park opened to the public in 1925, shortly after Puyi was forced to vacate the Forbidden City and relinquish his other imperial privileges.

During the Cultural Revolution, Mao's spouse, Jiang Qing (a latter-day Cixi in politics but who, in matters of taste, was decidedly inferior to the Manchu dowager), lived for a time in the Studio of the Painted Boat on the east shore of the lake.

Note: On this walk running shoes or hiking boots are recommended, as the distances are long and you will possibly be climbing about some ancient rocks.

The Walk

This walk takes you from the Round City to Hortensia Isle, along the east shore of the lake to the north section of the park, out the rear gate, and along the shores of **Shichahai.**

Begin at the **Rainbow Bridge** that divides **Zhonghai** (Middle Sea) from **Beihai** (North Sea). This elegant Ming-dynasty marble bridge was widened and reinforced in the 1950s to accommodate modern traffic, and the two *pailous* that stood at each end, inscribed "Golden Turtle" and "Jade Butterfly" respectively, were removed at this time. To the south of the bridge lies **Zhongnanhai**, home and offices of China's ruling elite.

Buy your ticket in the kiosk near the parking lot, enter the park, bear left and climb up into the mini-fortress known as the **Round City** (Tuancheng) [团城], which opens at 6.30am.

In the Yuan dynasty, the Round City was the site of palace buildings and the barracks of the palace guard. The main structure in this round enclosure, shaped like an elaborate Maltese cross, is the **Hall of Received Brilliance** (Chengguang Dian) [承光殿], where the Qing emperors occasionally changed their clothing and drank tea while they stopped here for a rest on their journeys from the Forbidden City to the suburban gardens. The present building dates from the Qianlong period, though literary evidence suggests that an earlier building on this spot was round. The hall now houses a large and somewhat chunky **Jade Buddha** that bears a strong resemblance to the image in the Jade Buddha Temple in Shanghai. There are two explanations of its origins. The first is that it was a tribute gift to the Chinese emperor from Tibet. The second, compiled from several sources, is more intriguing.

In 1893, a Peking-based Buddhist monk traveling in Burma made the false claim that he was on a religious mission on behalf of the Empress Dowager Cixi. Suitably impressed, Burmese monks presented him with one large and two small jade Buddhas to take back to China. When he arrived in Peking, he put the

The Beihai Park

to Real Lake

Di'anmen Xi Da Jie 地安门西大街

Rear Gate

Studio of
Quieting the Mind
静心斋

Altar of Silkworms
先蚕坛

Hall of the
Heavenly Kings
天王殿

Nine
Dragon Screen
九龙壁

Beijing Economic Plants
Botanical Garden
植物园

Hall of Pleasant Snow
快雪堂

Studio of the
Painted Boat
画舫斋

Iron Spirit Screen
铁影壁

Little Western
Heaven
小西天

Five Dragon
Pavilions
五龙亭

Boat House

Between the
Hao and the Pu
濠濮间

Bei Hai (North Lake)

北　海

漪澜堂 Hall of Ripples

Fangshan
Restaurant
仿膳

分凉阁 Pavilion of Shared Coolness

Plate for
Gathering Dew
承露盘

阅古楼 Tower for Reading the Classics

White
Dagoba
白塔

East Gate
东门

Temple for Cultivating
Good Deeds
善因寺

Nirvana
Pailou

Hall of
Joyful Hearts
悦心殿

Hall of True
Enlightenment
正觉殿

Hortensia Isle
琼华岛

Pailou

Pailou

Hall of Received
Brilliance
承光殿

Round City
团城
Jade Wine Pot

Ticket Kiosk

Front Gate

·········· Walking Trail

0   100 meters

200 feet

Rainbow Bridge

Wenjin Jie 文津街

**Forbidden
City**

© Airphoto International Ltd.

N

BEHAI PARK

images on display in his temple. But their extraordinary quality drew so much attention to the temple and the monk that an investigation was carried out by the court, resulting in the exposure of the monk's ruse. The monk had little choice but to present the large jade Buddha to Cixi, who instead of punishing him for his presumptuousness, rewarded him generously. Incidentally, before setting out on his trip to Burma, this venerable bonze had sold the contents of his temple to Li Lianying, the fabulously wealthy eunuch who was the Empress Dowager's favorite. The left arm of the serene figure (in *Peking*, Juliet Bredon states that the figure is made of Italian alabaster, and was a gift to Qianlong from the king of Cambodia) bears a scratch that has been attributed to an inconsiderate act by a foreign soldier in 1900.

Another important jade relic in the Round City is the **Jade Wine Pot**, resting in a purpose-built pavilion that stands in front of the **Hall of Received Brilliance** [承光殿]. This huge vessel is

believed to date from the Yuan dynasty, when Kublai Khan used it as a decoration in his Broad Cold Palace on nearby Hortensia Isle. The palace collapsed in 1579, during the Ming dynasty, and the pot was removed to a Taoist temple. When it was rediscovered and identified in the early Qing dynasty, the Taoist priests in the temple were using it as a vat to make pickled cabbage. Qianlong paid a hefty ransom to purchase it from the monks in 1745, and had it installed in its present pavilion after inscribing a wine-drinking song on its interior wall. If this tale is true, then the pot is the oldest cultural relic in Beihai Park.

The priceless Jade Wine Pot was for a while used to pickle cabbage

The Yongan Bridge leads from the Round City to Hortensia Island

In 1915, Yuan Shikai, the soldier-president of the Republic of China, held a series of preparatory meetings in the Hall of Received Brilliance before crowning himself emperor of China, a dream-state that lasted only 83 days before death removed him from the throne he had built for himself. In 1924, the president of the Republic, Cao Kun, was incarcerated in the Round City for two years by the warlord Feng Yuxiang. He was subsequently released by Zhang Zuolin, another influential warlord.

Three trees still flourishing in the Round City so impressed the Qianlong emperor in the 18th century that he conferred imperial titles upon them. The tall Chinese pine, some 800 years old, that covers the Round City like an umbrella, was dubbed the Duke of Shade; the other vintage trees to its north and south were named The Marquis of the Sea Exploration and the White-robed General respectively.

Return to Beihai Park through the north gate of the Round City. Continuing north across the fine marble bridge flanked at each end by pailous (bearing the names "Accumulated Jasper" and

"Heaped Clouds"), you come to **Hortensia Isle** (Qionghua Dao) [琼华岛]. For many decades a number of large earthenware vats were placed at the base of the mountain to the west of the bridge, which contained a collection of marvelous goldfish genetically engineered for grotesqueness. We cannot resist quoting at length Peter Quennell's precise paean to these creatures written after his visit to Peking in the early 1930s:

> *As large very often as a clenched hand, gross and torpid, softly colored and slow swimming, each of them was an Elagabalus [an eccentric Roman emperor] of the fish world, a puffy boneless sybaritic freak, accompanied when it moved by its own draperies, a tail and fins considerably longer than itself, which eddied, rippled and drooped like a gauzy train.*

> *Imagine a group of opulent French bourgeoisies, inconsolable yet voluptuous in widow's weeds. They suggested the catafalque or the crime passionel, the husband slayer sobbing in the dock or the Niobe-like relict of a great man oozing between the arms of her supporters. . . . Many centuries of cultivation lay behind them, the Bourbons and Hapsburgs of their breed, a queer comment on nature's elasticity and the Chinese passion for stretching it to the full and squeezing a strange beauty from horror and ugliness.*[3:2]

Osbert Sitwell, the British writer and world traveler, was similarly taken by these creatures of the shallow depths:

> *...and all of them have eyes that are yet more fantastic than their bodies; protruding, bulbous eyes, eyes at angles, swivel eyes, eyes at the top of their heads, eyes like those of dragons, eyes like those of German Princes in the eighteenth century. . . . So they float, goggling at time itself, flickering and turning, clad in their draperies of sable and gold, engaged, some of them, after the manner of Salome, in an eternal Dance of the Seven Veils. . . . Nevertheless, here these creatures are what—to paraphrase Walter Pater—in the ways of a thousand years, men have come to desire.*[3:3]

(3:2) Peter Quennell *A Superficial Journey through Tokyo and Peking*, (London, Faber, 1932; reprinted by Oxford University Press, 1986), pp. 178–9.
(3:3) Osbert Sitwell *Escape with Me! An Oriental Sketch-book* (New York, Harrison-Hilton Books Inc., 1940), p. 280.

You have now arrived at Hortensia Isle, named after a plant reputed to have immortality-conferring properties. The island, needless to say, was built up from mud dredged out of the lake in the same manner used to create Prospect Hill, which stands to the north of the Forbidden City, and Longevity Mountain in the Summer Palace.

As you begin your ascent of the hill directly in front of the bridge, the first building you will encounter is the **Temple of Eternal Peace** (Yongan Si) [永安寺], the descendant of a Lamaist temple erected here by Shunzhi, the first emperor of the Qing dynasty, in the mid-17th century. The stone lions guarding this temple are resting with their heads facing the temple, rather than facing away from it, the orientation adopted by all the other stone and bronze lions in China. Actually, these lions belonged to another no longer extant temple that stood with its façade directly opposite the Temple of Eternal Peace, where they had been performing their guard duties properly. Inside the courtyard there are typical drum and bell towers.

The next structure on the axis is the **Hall of the Wheel of the Law** (Falun Dian) [法轮殿]. To its north is a courtyard planted with a thorny bamboo grove and two stone steles, each in its own pavilion. The inscriptions on the steles record the history of **White Dagoba Mountain** (Baita Shan) [白塔山], as the man-made hill is called.

Climbing up the stairs to the pailou, inscribed "the purple effulgence of the dragon light," you come to a mid-level plateau which is supposedly strewn with some of the actual Lake Taihu stones that were transported here from the Song capital of Bianliang by order of a Jin dynasty emperor in the 12th century. This lovely park-within-a-park, with its fine south-facing view, is part-wilderness, part manicured garden, and attracts practitioners of taiji and martial arts exercises in the early morning.

To continue your ascent to the **Hall of Universal Peace** (Puan Dian) [普安殿] and the **Hall of True Enlightenment** (Zhengjue Dian) [正觉殿], a sort of duplex temple, you can choose either of

Tsong Khapa, founder of the Yellow Hat sect of Buddhism, in the Hall of Universal Peace

the two interior staircases that begin in the easternmost and westernmost of the six man-made caves. You will emerge into the light again at the base of an observation tower.

On this level, to the west, is the **Hall of Joyful Hearts** (Yuexin Dian) [悦心殿] where the emperors during the latter part of the Qing dynasty held meetings with their high officials. In the courtyard attached to the hall are two special rooms, one formerly used for making tea and the other for making pastries for the imperial breakfast buffet.

The **White Dagoba** (Bai Ta) [白塔], which stands atop a flight of giddily steep stairs, a Tibetan reliquary (in Tibetan, chorten, a tomb for the remains of a Lama Buddhist monk or layman) was in Republican days known irreverently as the "peppermint bottle" by foreigners. The first emperor of the Qing dynasty had this dagoba built on the ruins of a Ming palace in 1651 to commemorate the visit of the first Dalai Lama to the capital. It is made of brick, stone and wood. The dagoba was damaged twice in earthquakes during the 17th and 18th centuries, and large cracks appeared in it during the Tangshan earthquake in 1976, after which it was restored completely. During the restoration, archeologists discovered a repository in the base of the dagoba containing altar tables, Tibetan Buddhist sutras, niches for Buddha images, miniature boat hulls worn around the waist in folk dances, and other sundry ritual paraphernalia. In the interior of the dagoba a column approximately 30 meters (100 feet) tall supports the entire structure. Beneath the decorative hardware at the top of this column, the conservationists discovered a golden Buddhist reliquary containing two sacred bone fragments, most likely belonging to eminent monks.

A lovely park-within-a-park that is part wilderness, part manicured garden–the Hall of Universal Peace

The small sealed-up temple decorated with glazed tile Buddhas on the south side of the dagoba is the **Temple for Cultivating Good Deeds** (Shanyin Si) [善因寺], which once held a gilded bronze image of Yamantaka, a Lamaist deity with a terrifying aspect: 36 arms, 36 eyes, 7 heads and 16 feet. Yamantaka was "slain" during the Cultural Revolution. There is an apt, but chauvinist, Chinese saying that goes: "Only a horrible-looking god like Yamantaka can pacify such wild people as the Mongols (who believe in Lamaism)."

The Qing emperors held shamanistic rituals on this peak, and its elevated strategic location in the city made it an ideal signal tower: flags in five different colors were hoisted to convey military messages by day, and colored lanterns were lit at night. On clear days the peak offers an excellent view of the city.

To climb down, we will take a circuitous, but rewarding, route. If you follow the instructions below to the letter, you should have no problem reaching our desired destination on the shores of the lake. If you get lost, simply do as water does, and seek the lowest level.

1. Go through the round moon gate in the wall behind (north) of the dagoba.

2. Weave in and out of the cave.

3. Walk through a rectangular pavilion, which offers you a view of a rock garden wall.

4. Go down through the gate, turn left through a bottle-shaped opening in the wall.

5. Bear right at the fork and follow the path down the hill, backtracking slightly while hugging the undulating wall. In a matter of minutes you will be on the shore of the lake.

(**WARNING**: don't be tempted to enter the red gate in the wall unless you wish to risk some precarious climbing)

Find your bearings by locating the **Tower for Reading the Classics** (Yuegu Lou) [阅古楼], with its crescent-shaped walls, about 50 meters (165 feet) ahead on the path. The tower contains a collection of stone tablets, dating back to the sixth or seventh centuries, inscribed with calligraphy by some of China's greatest masters. These steles are not meant to be admired in this form, but rather to be used as printing blocks for taking rubbings of their inscriptions.

Heading north you will soon find yourself beneath the eaves of the two-storey veranda that begins at the tower called the **Pavilion of Shared Coolness** (Fenliang Ge) [分凉阁]and snakes along the north shore of the island. Qianlong had this long corridor built in imitation of a similar lakeside structure in a temple in the southern town of Jinshan.

A short way up the north face of the hill, but hard to see up close unless you climb back up among the twisting paths and Lake Taihu stones, is a terrace with a tall column supporting a cast bronze figure of a man holding a brass container over his head. This is the **Plate for Gathering Dew** (Chenglu Pan) [承露盘], the origin of which can be traced back to a Han-dynasty emperor who ordered his underlings to stand outside at night with containers to catch the dew. The emperor believed that drinking condensed liquid from the sky and consuming powdered jade in one gulp could confer immortality upon himself. Qianlong contributed this bronze gewgaw to the garden, as he wrote in an essay, purely for the sake of decoration, and not because he believed in the medicinal properties of jade and dew.

The buildings that lie within the crescent embrace of the two-storey veranda along the north shore of the island are the dining rooms of **Fangshan Restaurant** [仿膳饭庄], a rather staid Beijing institution that is much imitated throughout the city but never equaled due to its surroundings. When Fangshan, literally "imitating, or emulating, imperial cuisine," opened in 1926 on the north shore of the lake where the modest Beihai Restaurant now stands, it was staffed by chefs who had worked in the imperial palace kitchens up to 1924, when Puyi and company were booted out of the Forbidden City. Fangshan opened in its present location in 1959.

Top photo: *The Temple for Cultivating Good Deeds, small but perfectly formed, lies slightly lower than the White Dagoba*

Right: *The Qing emperors held shamanistic rituals on the platform that surrounds the Dagoba*

Opposite page: *The Temple for Cultivating Good Deeds*

In addition to imperial cuisine and the 108-dish Manchu-Chinese feast that is consumed over the course of three days, Fangshan is noted for serving a number of delicate pastries associated through legends with the Empress Dowager Cixi:

1. Baked wheat biscuits stuffed with spiced ground pork, which Cixi supposedly dreamed about one night and was miraculously served for breakfast the next morning;

2. Sweetened pea starch pudding cut into cubes the size of dice;

3. Rolled up kidney-bean cake, which Cixi first sampled when she invited a common street vendor, whom she heard hawking his wares, into the palace; and

4. Thimble-sized cones of sweetened cornmeal. While fleeing Peking in 1900, Cixi got so hungry that she deigned to try the heavy, steamed corn bread (*wowotou*). Shaped like a cone the size of a fist, it's a popular staple food among peasants in north China. When she asked for *wowotou* upon her return to the capital, her pastry chef reproduced them in miniature form, adding sugar to the recipe.

The entrance to Fangshan is located at the northernmost point of Hortensia Isle, where you may board a dragon boat for the five-minute ride to the Five Dragon pavilions on the north bank of the lake. Fangshan itself occupies a group of structures with an elegant name, the **Hall of Jade Ripples** (Yilan Tang) [倚蓝堂]. In warm weather, the Qing emperors and their retinues boarded their pleasure boats here (they were stored in the boathouse that still stands on the eastern shore of the lake) and in the winter observed ice skating displays performed for their edification and entertainment by specially trained soldiers. As many as 1,600 ice troops would participate in these demonstrations on the frozen lake. Rather than go by water or ice, we walk to the Five Dragon Pavilions by a less direct route along the eastern shore of the lake.

From Fangshan, continue east around the northern shore of the island and through the gate tower at the end of the veranda, dubbed the **Tower that Leans Towards the Light** (Yiqing Lou)

[倚晴楼]. On the right beyond the veranda you will pass by a large commemorative stele inscribed by the Qianlong emperor that details some of the wondrous things to be seen in Beihai Park. In particular, he commends a Song dynasty official who brought the gnarled Lake Taihu rocks from southern China and arranged them here in such a way that they resemble the scales of a dragon. Further on is the **Nirvana pailou** in its fine setting, the fancy archway that directly faces the bridge. Crossing the bridge brings you to the east entrance of the park, and by not exiting (though this is an option) turning left, or north, and walking along the path approximately 400 meters (1,312 feet) you come to the first group of buildings on the right, the oddly named **Between the Hao and the Pu** (Haopu Jian) [濠濮间].

Look for the white stele with three Chinese characters on it, and take that path. Bear right to the bridge and pavilion, and go under the pailou.

This architectural complex, dating from 1757, is one of several gardens-within-a-garden in Beihai Park. Qianlong borrowed the name of this garden from a Liang dynasty emperor who around 550 CE had named a garden after two rivers mentioned in the works of the early Taoist philosopher Zhuangzi, the master of touché whose fish tale is told in the chapter on the Summer Palace. The Hao was the name of the stream in which Zhuangzi observed those happy fish swimming, while the Pu River was the scene of another famous incident:

Zhuangzi was fishing in the Pu River one day when the King of Chu sent two ministers to see him: "We have come to entrust you with the affairs of state," they said.

Zhuangzi, continuing to pay attention to hook, line and sinker without turning his head to look at them, proclaimed: "I have heard that in Chu there is a mystical tortoise which died 3,000 years ago, and that your good king keeps it wrapped up in a box in his palace. Tell me, sirs, would the tortoise prefer to be dead and to have its remains revered as something rare and precious by the king, or would it rather be alive, wagging its tail in the mud?'

The ministers said, "Naturally it would rather be alive, wagging its tail in the mud."

"If you will be so kind as to excuse me, gentlemen," Zhuangzi retorted, "I too prefer to wag my tail in the mud."

This elegant little bridge lies on the approach to the Little Western Heaven

Elaborate roofed corridors climb up and down the rockeries here, but the highlight of the complex is the small pond with its lovely pavilion and seven-segment bridge. The water that fills the pond is not drawn from Beihai Lake but rather from a stream that is fed by the **Front Lake** (Qianhai) north of Beihai Park and flows along the eastern wall of the park. After the Summer Palaces were sacked in 1860, this is the place Cixi would come, presumably for consolation, to listen to performances of ballads.

Retrace your steps back to the main path along the east side of the shore of the lake.

Heading north from the Between the Hao and the Pu the large barns built over the water are boathouses, which in their original incarnation date back to the Ming dynasty. The height of the present boathouses, dating from the late Qing, suggests the impressive dimensions of the pleasure craft used by the imperial family.

Qianlong built the **Studio of the Painted Boat** (Huafang Zhai) [画舫斋], the next structure on your right, opposite the tea house, at the same time that the Between the Hao and the Pu was being constructed. Here, outside the main entrance, the emperor would

Nirvana Pailou, Hortensia Island, this faces Doushan Bridge; cross here to reach the path on the eastern shore of Bei Lake

observe annual archery contests held by the Manchu princes, court officials and imperial retainers. The distinguishing feature of the studio is its large square stone-lined pool surrounded by narrow corridors. Cixi is said to have smoked opium in the rooms in the northwest corner of the complex, and in 1900 the French army made its headquarters here. During the Cultural Revolution, Jiang Qing stayed in the secluded northeast courtyard on several occasions, the very place where Cixi had held the Guangxu emperor under house arrest. In 1979, the studio was the venue for the first exhibition of dissident art held in post-1949 China, organized by the group called the Stars.

Further to the north is the now invisible **Altar of Silkworms** (Xiancan Tan) [先蚕坛], which was converted into a teahouse during the Republican period once the ancient rituals ceased being performed. Since the 1950s, however, a nursery school for the offspring of high officials (off limits to the curious) has operated here. The altar was formerly the site of a quaint ceremony (testifying to an early division of labor in China) carried out by the empress in honor of the mythological Goddess of Silkworms, the originator of sericulture, wife of the mythical Yellow Emperor. As Juliet Bredon described the ritual:

> A picturesque note was added by certain details, such as the Empress and her attendants plucking a few leaves from the sacred mulberry-grove near the altar with little sickles, the handing of these leaves to ladies in charge of the precious insects, the inspection at later periods (mostly through delegates) of their growth, of the washing of the cocoons in the sacred moat existing for this purpose, finally of the making of the silk which was used on occasions of Imperial worship, on the same principle as the grain raised by His Majesty's hand at the Temple of Agriculture.[3:4]

The aforementioned agricultural ritual was performed in the third lunar month (late April–early May) by the emperor with the assistance of his underlings and a brigade of 100 aged peasant farmers selected from the capital region. With these worthies at his

(3:4) Juliet Bredon and Igor Mitrophanow *The Moon Year*, (Shanghai, Kelly & Walsh, 1927; reprinted by Oxford University Press, 1982), pp. 66–7.

side, the Son of Heaven would guide a golden plough drawn by a pedigree ox with an unblemished coat and till six furrows in a ritual field. Similarly, in the 1980s, China's paramount leader Deng Xiaoping ventured into the fields on a particular day in the third lunar month—now called Arbor Day or Tree-planting Day. With his own high officials (some of whom were also peasants) at his side, Deng personally planted a symbolic tree to launch the annual nationwide greenification campaign.

Continuing north past the Altar of Silkworms, cross the bridge that leads to the rear gate of Beihai Park, and veer left. Our first destination, the **Studio of Quieting the Mind** (Jingxin Zhai) [静心斋] is an exquisite private garden built by Qianlong in 1758 and first named the **Studio of the Mirror of Clarity** (Jingqing Zhai) [镜清斋]. It was later renovated by Cixi, who often lunched here and used it for storing the imperial seals. During the Qing dynasty, the studio served as a schoolroom for Manchu princes. In 1900 it was occupied briefly by the Japanese army, and in 1913 Yuan Shikai made it available to the Foreign Ministry to use for meetings with foreign guests. Later it was taken over by the Institute of History and Philology of the Academia Sinica, and from 1949 to 1981 it was similarly occupied by a literary research organization and the State Council. Puyi, the last emperor of China, wrote his memoirs, *From Emperor to Citizen*, in this intimate setting. In 1982 it was restored, fitted out with a potpourri of antiques and curios, and opened to the public. Fortunately, it is rarely crowded.

Remarkably, each of the halls in the Studio has its own small pond in front of it, with the exception of the **Chamber of Piled Emeralds** (Diecui Lou) [叠翠楼], which stands at the highest point in the studio in its northwest corner. This particular building was the Empress Dowager's 1885 contribution to the complex when she carried out a major building campaign on many of the imperial properties, settling the bill with naval funds. Like the **Hall for Distant Views** that sits up against the north wall of the Summer Palace, the north windows of the lofty Chamber of Piled Emeralds offered the secluded denizens of the imperial palaces a glance at the outside world.

The Studio of Quieting the Mind, an exquisite private garden built by Qianlong in 1758

There is a vast Taihu stone rockery in the second, rear, courtyard, where a concealed waterfall beneath the rectangular pavilion on the water adds a tranquillizing touch to the rather claustrophobic space. The other structures of note are the **Room for Roasting Tea** (Beicha Wu) [焙茶屋], a tiny room in the east corner, originally used by Qianlong for that very purpose; and the **Studio of the Harmonious Lute** (Yunqin Zhai) [韵琴斋], which is not a music room at all; the name describes the sound produced by the trickle of an artificial waterfall in the tiny courtyard.

Water is an indispensable element in all Chinese gardens, and garden builders display remarkable skill in its disposition. One Western theory of Chinese history posits that the stability of the Chinese state depended on the maintenance of countless hydrology projects throughout the empire, from the tall Yellow River dykes to the capillary-like canals that irrigate the vast Yangzi delta and serve as its principle means of transport. In this garden, water conservancy in miniature is put to aesthetic ends. The finest view in the entire studio is obtained from the easternmost point in the large, rear courtyard next to the Room for Roasting Tea.

The circular route indicated on the map takes you to all the main buildings of the studio: the **Studio of the Mirror of Clarity** (Jingqing Zhai) [镜清斋]; the **Library of Embracing Simplicity** (Baosushu Wu) [抱素书屋]; the **Studio of the Harmonious Lute** (Yunqin Zhai) [韵琴斋]; the **Room for Roasting Tea** (Beicha Wu) [焙茶屋]; the **Studio for Preserving Paintings** (Yanhua Xuan) [延画轩], where a painting of peonies in the hand of the Empress Dowager hangs on the wall; the **Chamber of Piled Emeralds** (Diecui Lou) [叠翠楼]; the **Pavilion that Lies upon the Mountains** (Zhenluan Ting) [枕峦亭]; and the **Pavilion of the Bubbling Spring** (Miquan Lang) [泌泉廊]. Put these elegant names together and you almost have a poem.

Exiting the studio, turn right and head southwest along the willow-lined shore (Cixi would have ridden her French train before it blew up) to the next major complex of buildings with a large pailou in front of it, the **Hall of the Heavenly Kings** (Tianwang Dian) [天王殿], which in the Ming served as a workshop for the

The splendid pailou in front of the Hall of Heavenly Kings

translation and printing (with carved woodblocks) of Buddhist scriptures. It was rebuilt by Qianlong in 1759. In 1945, a pair of gilded pagodas in one of the temples here was completely dismantled by some Japanese "imperialists" with the intention of shipping them to Japan. The crates got as far as Tanggu, the port of Tianjin, when Japan surrendered in World War II. The crates were eventually shipped back to Peking, but the pagodas were too badly damaged in transit to be properly restored. The rear courtyards contain a Qianlong-period pagoda and a two-storey glazed tile hall that closely resembles the Temple for Cultivating Good Deeds that is perched immediately south of the dagoba on Hortensia Isle. From here, exit and turn right and follow the path north.

Further to the northeast, behind the Beihai Restaurant, stands one of China's three **Nine Dragon Screens** (Jiulong Bi) [九龙壁]; the others are in the Forbidden City and in the city of Datong. Why nine? The dragon, a mythical beast modeled after the water snake, the gecko, the alligator, or a permutation of the three, had nine sons, but none of them grew up to be a full-fledged dragon since they each were preoccupied with a specific task, listed here:

Son #1	curls up on the tops of bells and gongs.
Son #2	hangs around the pegs of string instruments
Son #3	rests atop stone steles
Son #4	supports stone steles on his back
Son #5	balances on the roofs of temples
Son #6	lives on the beams of bridges
Son #7	rests on the Buddha's throne
Son #8	is attached to sword hilts
Son #9	guards the gates of prisons

The Beihai dragon wall is unique among the three in that it is a free-standing wall, decorated on both sides with six-color glazed tile dragons swimming in ocean waves. Qianlong built this wall as a "spirit screen" to deter the God of Fire from destroying one of the buildings attached to the workshop for translating and printing Lamaist scriptures that the emperor had built in honor of his mother. The wall performed this function faithfully until 1919, when the workshop building tragically went up in flames. It now confers its protection upon the Beihai Gymnasium, which stands on the site of the former workshop. Statistically minded art historians claim that there are altogether 635 dragons on this wall, counting all the tiny ones in the eaves.

The wall impressed the Frenchman Abel Bonnard on his visit in 1920, who wrote:

> ...an unforeseen spectacle reawakened my interest and curiosity. It was a long wall covered with plaques of porcelain, of which the splendor in full sunlight was quite blinding. Nine dragons are writhing there in high relief. There are two pairs of two, in colors which respond to each other, and they are separated by a single yellow dragon, and are all gloating with their goggle-eyes over the little sphere of a flamboyant jewel which seems to be escaping the convulsive clutch of their claws, while they have all the appearance of breathing fire and brimstone upon it. An art emptied of all substance triumphs upon this lustrous wall, which dates from Qianlong. The dragon, the universal monster, whose sinuous coils can stretch, at a pinch, from Heaven to the abyss of Hell, is here nothing more than a Court dancer, who is performing a violent, concerted measure before the emperor. The same frenetic ballet is reproduced on the other side of the wall, but instead of being enhanced to dazzling excitement by the sunshine, it is soothed and lulled to quiet by the shade.[3:5]

Retrace your steps to the main road on the north side of the lake and then turn right.

The **Hall of Pleasant Snow** (Kuaixue Tang) [快雪堂] and the **Hall of Crystal Waters** (Chenguan Tang), which comprise the complex of buildings to the east of Beihai Restaurant (now a mediocre place for a meal, but when the fashionable Fangshan Restaurant was located here in the 1920s and 1930s one of Empress Dowager Cixi's former chefs earned himself an excellent reputation with his dumplings) was an imperial residence in the Qing dynasty where Qianlong once kept a famous collection of inscribed stone tablets. It was rebuilt twice in the 19th century and in 1900 was occupied by the foreign allied armies, who left it in

(3:5) Abel Bonnard *In China 1920–1921*, (New York, EP Dutton & Co. 1927), pp. 11–12.

One of China's three Nine Dragon Screens

Ceramic decorations, part of the spectacular ensemble at the Hall of Heavenly Kings

Yuan-dynasty carving of a mythological scaly beast with a fiery tail

ruins. Cixi did up the place again in 1901, and between 1913 and 1915 it was the home of Cai E (1882–1916; also known as Cai Songpo), a Yunnan-based general who led the movement to prevent Yuan Shikai from realizing his imperial ambitions. After Cai's death in Japan, the building became the Songpo Library and Cai Songpo Shrine.

In front of the Hall of Pleasant Snow near the boat dock stands another interesting relic, the **Iron Spirit Screen** (Tieying Bi) [铁影壁], actually a slab of dark

The Beijing Economic Plants Botanical Garden, formerly the site of the Temple of Happy Meditation

igneous rock that is not made of iron at all. This Yuan dynasty stone was installed here in 1947, when a patriotic Chinese bought it from a foreigner who was about to ship it out of China. Before this time it had stood in front of a Buddhist convent in the northern part of the city that had housed a bell foundry during the Ming dynasty. The legend that the stone acquired its metallic appearance by absorbing the smoke billowing out of the foundry has no basis in fact. The image carved with remarkable vigor on both sides is a mythological scaly beast with a fiery tail.

Proceeding along the shore, the decorative structures jutting into the lake in the shape of a writhing dragon are the **Five Dragon Pavilions** (Wulong Ting) [五龙亭] which were first built here in the Ming dynasty. Their name arises from the resemblance of the stone balustrades that link them together and the peninsula they stand on to a curling dragon. An anecdote calculated to inspire filial piety tells how the Qing emperor Kangxi settled his mother and grandmother in one of the pavilions, hopped into a boat on the lake, paddled up to where they were sitting, and politely served them snacks. Kangxi's grandson, Qianlong, used the pavilions for fishing. He would angle from the central pavilion while his retinue would fish from the pavilions to the side. One doubts his ministers dared to bait their hooks out of fear of pulling in a bigger fish than the emperor's.

The large complex of buildings to the north of the Five Dragon Pavilions is the **Beijing Economic Plants Botanical Garden**, most frequently visited by school pupils on field trips with their teachers.

The garden was formerly the site of the **Temple of Happy Meditation** (Chanfu Si) [阐福寺], first built by the Ming dynasty emperors to provide their empresses and high-ranking concubines with a place to escape the heat of summer. In the 18th century, Qianlong converted this resort into a temple which, like the Altar of Silkworms described above, was used for the ritual worship of silkworms; later he installed a large Buddha with One Thousand Hands and One Thousand Eyes. The Eight Allied Armies plundered the temple in 1900 and absconded with the jewels encrusting the image. Then in 1919, a warlord army occupied the temple, and shortly afterwards it was destroyed by a fire and never rebuilt.

The most worthy object here, sitting in the neglected northwest corner of the Botanical Garden, is an octagonal pagoda containing 16 portraits carved in stone of lohans, or Buddhist immortals. The original artist was a Tang dynasty monk who was also a gifted painter, although these lively images of eccentric holy men are copies carved in the Qing.

The next pleasant surprise on the itinerary is the huge square pagoda, perhaps the largest of its kind in China, called **Little Western Heaven** (Xiao Xi Tian) [小西天], originally built in 1770 as a shrine to Guanyin, the Goddess of Mercy. Surrounded by a moat, four guard towers and four pailous, this huge square building once housed a tall man-made mountain composed of clay and crowned with an image of the Goddess of Mercy and festooned with 800 smaller lohans, or Buddhist worthies, as well as temples and trees. It was modeled after Mt. Putuo, an island sacred to the Goddess of Mercy, located in one corner of the Buddhist paradise, and in real life off the coast of Zhejiang province. The original mountain was restored by Cao Kun, president of the Republic in 1923–1924, as an act of devotion. But in 1953 a committee of scholars and experts decided that Cao had done a tasteless job of it and had the mountain dismantled. This left the building structurally unsound, so it was later taken apart and rebuilt. In the late 1980s, it was dazzlingly restored and repainted. Note especially the splendid ceiling. In winter, when the weather is cold enough, huge carved ice sculptures are displayed in this part of the park, including a cool Buddha or two.

Inside the Little Western Heaven—note the superb coffered ceiling

Looking east over part of what used to be the Tartar City; unlike the courtyard houses in the foreground, the Drum Tower is not scheduled for destruction

THE REAR LAKES

We now leave Beihai Park, the northern wall of which forms the boundary between the former Imperial City and the former Tartar, or Manchu City, to the north. The Rear Lakes have undergone great changes in the last 1,000 years, yet judging from early descriptions, they still retain something of their original rural character. There are records of lakes here, and poems in praise of their beauty, dating from as early as the third century CE. Today, as of yore, the large private homes of the Chinese leadership dot the south shore of the lake. As H.Y. Lowe, a Manchu who never left China, wrote wryly in the late 1930s:

> *With few exceptions all the [Manchu] princes had their mansions in that neighborhood, a quiet and picturesque district conveniently near to their "jobs" at the Forbidden City—like Beverly Hills is to the movie studios of Hollywood.*[3:6]

(3:6) H.Y. Lowe *The Adventures of Wu: The Life Cycle of a Peking Man*, (Peking, The Peking Chronicle Press, 1941; reprinted by Princeton University Press, 1983), Vol. I, p. 162.

191

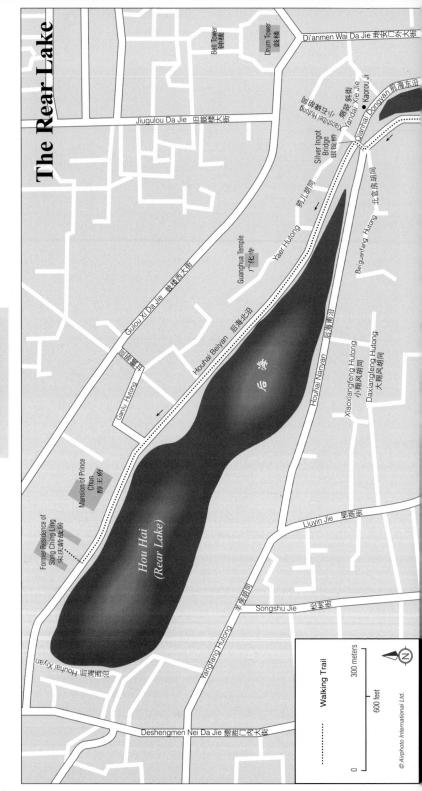

The Rear Lake

Bell Tower 钟楼

Drum Tower 鼓楼

Di'anmen Wai Da Jie 地安门外大街

Jiugulou Da Jie 旧鼓楼大街

Kaorou Ji

Xiaoshibei Hutong 小石碑胡同

Yandai Xie Jie 烟袋斜街

Qianhai Dongyan 前海东沿

Gulou Xi Da Jie 鼓楼西大街

Guanghua Temple 广化寺

Yaer Hutong 鸦儿胡同

Silver Ingot Bridge 银锭桥

Houhai Beiyan 后海北沿

Beiguanfang Hutong 北官房胡同

Ganlu Hutong

Houhai Nanyan 后海南沿

后海

Houhai Nanyan 后海南沿

Xiaoxiangfeng Hutong 小翔凤胡同

Daxiangfeng Hutong 大翔凤胡同

Mansion of Prince Chun 醇王府

Former Residence of Song Ching Ling 宋庆龄故居

Liuyin Jie 柳荫街

Hou Hai (Rear Lake)

Songshu Jie 松树街

Yangfang Hutong 羊房胡同

Houhai Xiyan 后海西沿

Deshengmen Nei Da Jie 德胜门内大街

Walking Trail

300 meters

600 feet

0

© Airphoto International Ltd.

The historical nomenclature of the lakes is complex and at the end of the day it may all seem quite irrelevant. However, there are three lakes (literally "seas") in this district today, **Front** (Qianhai), **Rear** (Houhai), and **West** (Xihai, also called Jishuitan.)

As early as the Wei dynasty (c. 250 CE) conservancy projects carried out in the western suburbs of the city provided a steady flow of water to this area, where a lake was formed. Nearly one millennium later, the 12th century Jin rulers built their pleasure palaces on its shores. When the Mongols established their capital, Khanbaligh (in Chinese, Dadu) upon the ruins of the Jin capital Zhongdu, the lake was incorporated into the new walled city. Later an east-west road was built that bisected the lake; the southern part of the lake was incorporated into the palace grounds and became the **Pool of Great Secretion**, the forerunner of Beihai Lake, while the northern part remained outside the city limits. By channeling additional water from the springs in the western hills, the lakes were enlarged and deepened. The Mongols called them *haizi*, which in Chinese means "small seas;" in Mongolian the meaning of the word swells to encompass the notion of "garden" or "park."

Following the dredging of the Tonghui Canal, which linked the city of Khanbaligh to nearby Tongxian (today Tongzhou, east of Beijing), once the northern terminus of the Grand Canal, these lakes became the major inland receiving port for rice shipments from south China. Early texts describe how during the summer months, the splendid lotus blossoms that filled the lake drew crowds of viewers here, establishing a Peking custom that is still popular today. In Yuan times, the lakes were considerably larger and deeper than the decorative ponds are today, and could accommodate the hefty grain barges that had been hauled 1,000 kilometers (650 miles) to supply the imperial family with their favorite carbohydrate.

When the Chinese Ming conquered the Mongol Yuan and shifted the north wall of the capital approximately three kilometers (two miles) south, the Pool of Great Secretion was

This strip of restaurants, bars and shops is popular with both locals and expatriates

again sliced in two, leaving a good portion of it outside the city limits. The enlargement of the moat around the city walls drained off much of the water that had supplied the lake, and consequently its role as a grain port declined. The construction of another north-south road resulted in the lake being further split into Jishuitan (Reservoir Pond) to the west, and the articulated **Shichahai** (Sea of Ten Buddhist Temples) to the east. At the time (the 15th century), there were numerous temples on the shores of the lake. During the Ming dynasty, the horses in the imperial stables were washed here in an annual ritual that took place on the 12th day of the sixth moon. Horses that had been ridden by the emperor were draped with imperial yellow silk blankets embroidered with dragons, and were led into the water before all the others. Sledding on the ice in winter and boating amidst the lotuses were other popular pastimes in the Ming dynasty.

Another form of "recreation" took place here during the seventh lunar month. Monks and lay Buddhists gathered along the shores of the West Lake (the northernmost of the three Rear Lakes), burned paper boats, floated lanterns on the water and recited scriptures to exorcise the ghosts of those unfortunate souls who had committed suicide by having jumped into the lake.

To supply himself with souvenirs of the temperate climate of the land of his youth, Nanjing, the Ming Yongle emperor, a southerner by birth, imported rice farmers to work the paddies on the shores of Shichahai and stock the imperial pantry with locally produced rice. Buddhist temples, convents and private gardens sprung up around the lake at this time, and in several places fine bridges spanned the lake.

In the 17th century, the Qing court designated the lake as an imperial garden and forbade all commoners from drawing its water. As a result, the convents, monasteries and private gardens that had relied on water from the lake for ornamental purposes were forced to fill in their ponds and streams with soil. During this period, some of these structures were converted into Manchu princes' mansions, a few of which can be visited today.

The Qing dynasty emperors came to the lakes once a year in winter to review the Manchu army skating battalions performing war games on the ice, as they did in Beihai and in the Summer Palace. An observation pavilion in one of the lakes built especially for this purpose was demolished by the foreign allied armies who marched to Peking in 1900 to suppress the Boxer Rebellion.

In the Republican period (1911–1949), a combination of official neglect and increased rice cultivation caused the lake to shrink and eventually it turned stagnant. After 1949, the lake beds were dredged, four large swimming pools were installed, roads were built over some of the old streams, and buildings erected over areas of the lakes that had been filled in with rubble. With the destruction of the city walls near Deshengmen, the narrow body of water outside the gate was turned into a concrete-lined open conduit.

Interior of one of the many bars and restaurants lining the shores of Front Lake

Around the year 2000, a new commercial nightlight district sprouted almost overnight on the western shore of front Lake. Today this blatantly commercial strip of restaurants, bars and shops is popular with locals and expatriates in the evenings in warm and hot weather, and if you fix your gaze upon the lake (or a book or your friends' faces) and avoid the chintzy architecture, it makes for a wonderful setting for an evening out.

In winter, when Front Lake freezes over, the scene is something out of a painting by Brueghel: two-year-olds strutting about in four layers of clothing, women hauling old bamboo baby carriages, youngsters pulling each other in circles on tiny sleds, couples sharing a single pair of ice skates. The sunlight in Beijing at this time of year, filtered by coal smoke and dust, somehow takes on a waxen Flemish quality.

Along with Tianqiao in the former Chinese city, Shichahai was one of the most popular recreation spots for people of modest means in Old Peking. The busting summer scene at Shichahai some 75 years ago is described wonderfully in *The Adventures of Wu*:

> *Enterprising businessmen stake out plots along the wide walk, which serves also as a separating dyke, and erect mat-shed teashops of a deluxe type with elevated floors for better views of everything around. Little variety shows and stalls where popular if rustic kinds of foods are sold, side by side with fruit stalls and those of a number of unexpected businesses which seem to be there more for the fun than for the profits.*
>
> *For here is another world, a little Peitaho [Beidai He] Beach, a Bermuda, nay, a Coney Island in the Chinese standard of judgement. Peking people in every walk of life make excursions here, a few make it their summer resort ....* [3:7]

While watching the magicians, comedians, jugglers and ballad singers, you can enjoy such famous traditional local snacks as sour bean juice (favored by the Manchus), buckwheat cakes, cold starch-jelly, fried sausage, sour plum juice with essence of cassia/osmanthus, corn on the cob, fresh water caltrops, lotus seeds, almonds, walnuts, and lotus seed porridge, to mention a few.

(3:7) H.Y. Lowe *The Adventures of Wu: The Life Cycle of a Peking Man*, (Peking, The Peking Chronicle Press, 1941; reprinted by Princeton University Press, 1983), Vol. I, p. 162.

The Walk

It is a simple one, and mainly atmospheric. From the **Little Western Heaven** (Xiao Xi Tian) [小西天] on the north shore of the lake in Beihai Park, retrace your steps eastward until you come to the rear gate of Beihai Park. Cross **West Di'anmen Street** (Di'an Men Xi Da Jie) [地安门西大街] via one of the underground passageways, and make your way to the entrance of **Lotus Lane** also called **Lotus Flower Market** (Hehua Shichang) [荷花市场] which is now one of the most popular nightspots in Beijing.

Continue the walk by following along the shore of the lake until the string of restaurants and bars ends. When you leave the rear entrance of the market, turn right onto the narrow road that skirts the lake. The two-storey building in front of you, on the left, is the former **Hall of Assembled Worthies** (Huixian Tang) [会贤堂], once a restaurant and meeting place that was popular during the Republican period. When wedding banquets were held here, it was common to invite famous opera singers to perform a number or two. Mei Lanfang, who lived in a courtyard house nearby, was one of those great male divas who came here to sing—until the 1950s, men played the leading female roles in Chinese opera, and were lionized for their hyper-femininity.

Somewhat further on, the well-kept façade to the left of a hole-in-the-wall sweet shop is a large traditional multi-courtyard house once occupied by a former chief of one of the Chinese ministries.

A few minutes' more strolling brings us to the **Silver Ingot Bridge** (Yinding Qiao) [银锭桥] that divides **Front Lake** (Qianhai) from **Rear Lake** (Houhai). Along with the lotus blossoms in the lakes, the view from this bridge of the Western Hills is one of eight cherished Peking look-sees canonized by the Qianlong emperor in the 18th century. Tradition has it that the bridge is at its best at sunrise, sunset, after rain or when it is snowing. The present incarnation of the bridge, which takes its name from its resemblance to a Chinese "shoe" ingot of silver or gold, an ancient

Between the two lakes, pedicabs and policemen

form of currency, was carved out of white marble by stone masons from Hebei province in 1984.

Across the bridge and to the right is the restaurant called **Kaorou Ji** (Ji's Roast Mutton) [烤肉季], where Mr. Ji and his descendants have been serving roast mutton and other fine Muslim (Hui, not Uighur) cuisine for more than 140 years. The grandsons of the founder built the restaurant here in 1927, before which they had been selling from a stall on the lake. The mutton, sliced from the leg according to the desired degree of leanness or fattiness, is barbecued over wood after being marinated in a mixture of shrimp sauce, soy sauce, rice wine, vinegar, sesame oil, chili oil, leeks, coriander, ginger and sugar. Sliced cucumbers, sliced tomatoes, sweet pickled garlic cloves and raw leeks harmonize well with the somewhat gamey meat. Like mutton hotpot, the barbecued mutton here is particularly satisfying and thus most popular in winter.

You can end the walk on this poetic note or continue on past the bridge along the north shore of the Rear Lake.

You will soon pass the former Dazanglonghua Temple on your right. This was previously the ancestral temple of Prince Chun, but is now a nursery school. In a few minutes you will come to the impressive front gate of Prince Chun's mansion, the residential portion of which has been occupied by the Ministry of Health for decades. This was the birthplace of the last emperor, Xuantong, better known as Puyi, and his younger brother Pujie. The tall gate a bit further on belongs to the **Former Residence of Soong Ching Ling**, a European-style home built in the extensive garden of the prince's mansion. Madame Soong (whose status as Honorary Chairman of the People's Republic of China permits her to spell her name in this idiosyncratic manner), the Soong sister who was Mrs. Sun Yat-sen, outlived her husband, the Father of the Chinese Republic, by about half a century. After 1949, Soong Ching Ling pursued a career as an often frustrated figurehead in the Chinese government. She died in Beijing in 1981. Her magnificent solid and spacious home, with its many bedrooms and double windows that filter out the noise and dust, offers a striking contrast to the average Beijing apartment, and candidly suggests the lavishness of the private residences of the Chinese leadership. It can be visited for a modest fee and is highly recommended.

From here you might make a turn around and visit the restored **Mansion of Prince Gong** (Gong Wang Fu) [恭王府] that had served as the living quarters of the officials and families of the Ministry of Public Security before its latest reincarnation; you can also visit the former campus of **Fu Jen University**, one of the finest private universities in Peking, formerly run by the Catholic Church. The garden is finely restored and features a Chinese opera theater where performances are given regularly to tourists. The garden is associated with Cao Xueqin, the 18th century author of the most famous Chinese novel of manners, known in English translation as *The Story of the Stone* (the finest translation, by David Hawkes and John Minford, is published by Penguin Classics, 1974), aka *A Dream of Red Mansions* or *The Dream of the Red Chamber*, Attached to the garden is the classic, consistently decent **Sichuan Restaurant**. The **Former Residence of Guo Moruo** [郭沫若故居] a writer who faithfully served Chairman Mao, is also in this neighborhood.

To get to the Drum Tower, return to the **Silver Ingot Bridge** [银锭桥] and head northwest in the narrow *hutong*.

In spite of large-scale demolition in the area some regional specialty restaurants seem to be thriving; long may they do so

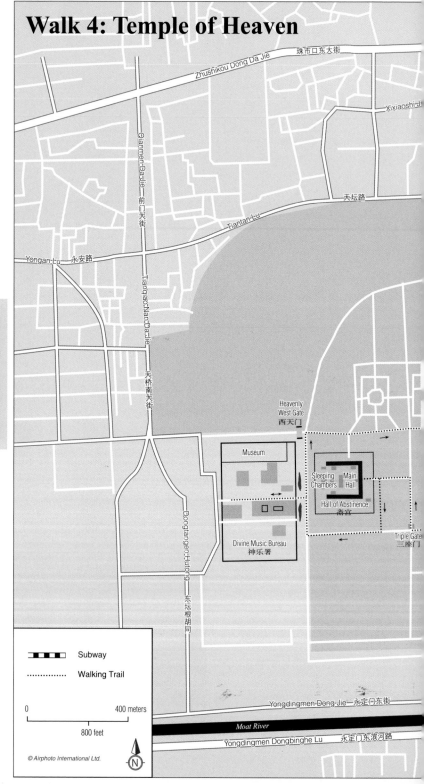

Walk 4: Temple of Heaven

珠市口东大街
Zhushikou Dong Da Jie

Xixiaoshi-J

天坛路

Qianmen-Da-Jie
前门大街

天坛路
Tiantan-Lu

Yongan-Lu — 永安路

Tianqiao-Nan-Da-Jie

天桥南大街

Heavenly
West Gate
西天门

Museum

Sleeping
Chambers

Main
Hall

Hall of Abstinence
斋宫

Triple Gate
三座门

Dongtangenhutong

东坛根胡同

Divine Music Bureau
神乐署

▬▬▬▬ Subway

.... Walking Trail

0   400 meters

800 feet

© Airphoto International Ltd.

N

Yongdingmen-Dong-Jie — 永定门东街

Moat River

Yongdingmen Dongbinghe Lu   永定门东滨河路

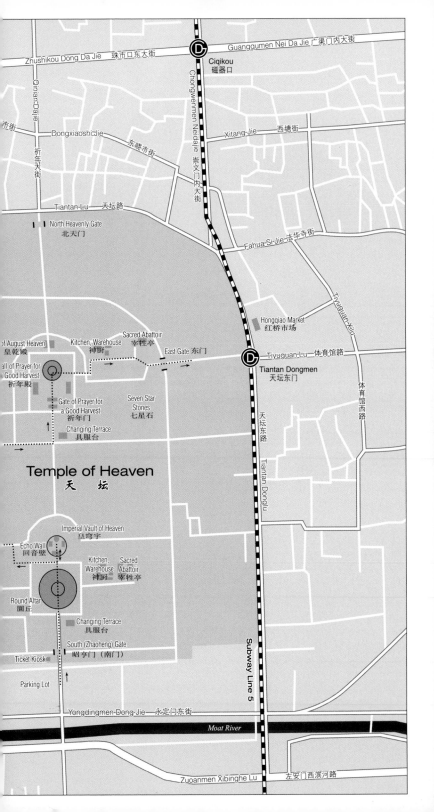

WALK · 4

THE TEMPLE OF HEAVEN, TEMPLE OF SKY

DURATION

Approximately three hours.

E xplore the ritual altars and round blue-roofed buildings where the emperors of China communicated through sacrifice with Shangdi, the Pearly Emperor, Supreme Ruler in the Heaven. This is the least physically demanding walk in this book: total walking distance is less than a mile, although there are a number of staircases to be climbed. The designation **Temple of Heaven** (Tian Tan) does not apply to any particular building here, but is rather the name of the entire complex, which is now called **Tian Tan Park**. In other words, there is no "Temple of Heaven" per se. The imperial rituals were carried out here at three main sites that lie on a north-south axis. Together, they only occupy a small portion of the vast grounds of the park. At

The exquisite Round Altar

the northernmost end of the axis stands the triple-roofed **Hall of Prayer for a Good Harvest** (the building often mistakenly referred to as the "Temple of Heaven"); in the middle, the smaller **Imperial Vault of Heaven**; and further south, the starkly exquisite **Round Altar**. The walk also includes stops at the **Hall of Abstinence** and the **Divine Music Bureau,** which was restored as a fine museum in 2004. The park is open from 7:00 am to 7:30 pm in the winter and from 5:00 am to 9:30 pm in the summer, but the historical buildings keep more conventional office hours: 8:00 am to 6:00 pm.

A toddler watches the sun set on the Imperial Vault of Heaven

"The Emperor comes to this altar in the spring to sacrifice and pray for a good harvest". The Illustrated London News, *February 1873*

Marble bridges cross the moat surrounding the Hall of Abstinence

The best time to take this walk is the early morning. The light of the rising sun casts an ethereal glow on the halls and altar and the park is filled with mostly elderly retirees practicing a dozen forms of early-morning exercise, from *qigong* breath energy posturing (the air, or *qi*, is freshest at this time of day) and martial-arts inspired sword dancing, to opera singing, geriatric disco, card games and polkas. Visitors are always welcome to join in or photograph the scene.

Starting Point

The south entrance of **Tiantan Park** (Tiantan nan en) on **Yongding Men Dong Da Jie.**

How to Get There

Take a taxi to the south entrance, Tiantan Nan Men, or take buses 120, 122, 208, or 814.

How to Get Away

Buses 43, 116, and 208 stop at the east entrance of **Tiantan Park** (Tiantan Dong Men).

> *The Temple of Heaven is stunning in its simplicity, rife with symbols and implications. For more than 500 years the emperors of China came here to carry out rituals to ensure the survival of Chinese civilization—the entire world as they knew it. As one British art historian wrote: "I know of nothing in European architecture capable of producing the same impression of abstract beauty, of a peculiarly concentrated, almost nervous, tension."* [4:1]

The worship of Heaven, (perhaps the word 'Sky' may avoid associations with Western theology, but for convenience, this publication will continue to use 'heaven' as the preferred term, in line with common practice) began as early as the Zhou dynasty, some 3,000 years ago. Heaven was at that time conceived of as a deity that was responsible for maintaining the regularity of the cycle of the seasons and the social order, both of which were perceived as natural phenomena. The Chinese emperor was regarded as the Son of Heaven, and thus the ritual worship of

(4:1) William Willets *Chinese Art*, 2 vols., (Harmondsworth, Penguin Books, 1958), p. 677.

Heaven was for him the fulfillment of filial obligations to his progenitor, who by extension was the ultimate ancestor of the Chinese people. The tripartite universe, consisting of Heaven, mankind and earth, and symbolized in the triple roofs and multiplicands of the number three in the architectural details of the altar made the emperor the ultimate, and most exalted, representative of the human race. The cult of ancestor worship performed in its most sublime form here in Peking was practiced on a smaller scale in the provinces by provincial-level officials, and in further down the pecking order in homes by individual families, who formed the lowest rung of a hierarchical system that was a perfect metaphor of social unity.

As the prime agent of Heaven on earth, the emperor reported regularly to his superior and also submitted appeals for good weather, obedient rivers and plentiful harvests, basic requirements for a peaceful agricultural state. Confucius' pragmatic statement, "To the people, food is heaven," is simply a truncated version of the heaven-earth-man reality sandwich.

Early Western writers about China discovered in the imperial worship of Heaven an expression of the universal original religion. One 19th century cleric cited:

> The probability is that [the rituals performed at the Temple of Heaven] are all survivals of the religious ceremonies observed by the common ancestors of the races before the dispersion of mankind from the Tower of Babel.

In her wonderful guidebook, *Peking*, Juliet Bredon echoed this statement about the Temple of Heaven:

> It is one of the few remaining relics of the original Chinese monotheistic faith—the old, old belief that God is everywhere, invisible and all-seeing, dwelling in a house not made with hand—held in Asia before the gods were personified and their images enshrined in temples. [4:2]

(4:2) Juliet Bredon *Peking*, (Shanghai, Kelly & Walsh, 1931; reprinted by Oxford University Press, 1982), p. 157.

S he described the emperor's participation in the ritual as a worship which,

> ". . . recognizing as sole-divinity the spirit of the great blue dome overhead, discarded, for the occasion, all the idolatrous and superstitious practices of an essentially pantheistic race." [4:3]

Another missionary writer was impressed by the pomp and panoply of the imperial rituals:

> "In position, in attitude, in attitudinizing, enrobing, incensing, and the rest, the Chinese have nothing to learn from the West." [4:4]

And the Dutchman Henri Borel, who had a predilection for religious experiences in all the major tourist sites in Peking, saw the oft-repeated pattern of three found in roofs, platforms, gates and the stones paving the floors of the halls and altar, as an obvious manifestation of the Christian trinity.[4:5] Finally, an anecdote recorded by the American missionary W.A.P. Martin in 1897; "Dr. Legge [1815–97, British translator of the Chinese classics and professor of Chinese at the University of Hong Kong], the eminent missionary, before climbing the steps of this [round] altar heard a still, small voice, saying: 'Put off thy shoes; for the place whereon thou standest is holy ground.'" [4:6] It is recorded elsewhere that Dr. Legge walked barefoot when he was first admitted to the Round Altar.

The **Temple of Heaven** is one of several worship sites in the capital where the emperors offered sacrifices. Its location in the southern part of the city derives from the notion that *yang*, the male vital principle, is located in the south; and as Heaven is *yang*, it should be worshipped in the southern suburbs of the capital. Peking also had altars (*tan*) to the Earth (Ditan, north of the city), Sun (Ritan, east), Moon (Yuetan, west), Silkworms (Xiancantan in Beihai Park), Agriculture (Xiannongtan, to the west of the Temple

(4:3) Juliet Bredon *Peking*, (Shanghai, Kelly & Walsh, 1931; reprinted by Oxford University Press, 1982), p. 161.
(4:4) John Ross *The Original Religion of China*, (New York, Eaton and Mains, no date), p. 312.
(4:5) Henri Borel *The New China: A Traveller's Impression*, (London, T Fisher Unwin, 1912), pp. 245–60.
(4:6) W.A.P. Martin *A Cycle of Cathay, or China, South and North*, (New York, Fleming H. Revell, 1987), p. 243

of Heaven), and the Gods of the Soil and Harvest (Shejitan, in the center of the city in what is now Zhongshan Park). Nearly all of these former places of worship were turned into public parks in the early years of the Republic, having ceased functioning in their original capacity, and most remain parks today. Curiously enough, the Altar of Silkworms in Beihai Park is located off-limits inside the walls of a nursery school traditionally reserved for the pupae of bigwigs in the party and government.

In the 1950s the grounds of the **Temple of Heaven Park** (*Tiantan Gongyuan*) were reduced to approximately two-thirds of their dimensions during the Qing dynasty, when the surrounding wall was 5.6 kilometers (3.5 miles) long. The now-missing slice of land, on the west flank, is occupied by the Museum of Natural History, Tiantan Dental Hospital, Tiantan Hospital, a hotel and housing blocks. Observed from the south on a map or from the air, Tiantan Park takes the form of a squat rectangle topped by a semi-circle: an apple sitting low in a box. Everything here is charged with symbolism. In traditional Chinese thought, Heaven is round, Earth is square. The rounded north section functions like the semi-circular spirit wall around a traditional Chinese grave, diverting the evil influences originating in the north from the temple complex.

Though, in principle, access to the grounds of the ritual temple was as "forbidden" to the common man as the Forbidden City itself, during the latter part of the Qing dynasty,

The Hall of Prayer for a Good Harvest, the main attraction for most visitors to the Temple of Heaven

entrance could be gained by anyone willing to offer the gatekeeper a small tip. A 1904 guidebook to Peking remarked:

> As a rule visitors have now to pay a small trifle for admission. On quitting each of these temples [in the Temple of Heaven] a little civility over and above this to the guardians of the Temples will generally elicit civility in return and greatly enhance the pleasure of the visit. Chinese value courtesy highly.[(4:7)]

In fact, the sacrificial altars of Tiantan Park were never in use more than six or eight days in the year. After the Boxer Uprising in 1900, the park became the headquarters for the Bengal Cavalry under the British General Gaselee, whose troops staged theatricals on the altars in their leisure hours. There are also reports from around this time of impious foreigners dancing on the Round Altar under the moonlight. The **Hall of Abstinence**, the only formal residence on the premises, became the British officers' mess for a short time. Imperial cattle bred especially for the sacrifices that had become infected with the plague, were once burnt on the Round Altar by the British. In the decades before the Temple of Heaven was opened as a public park, the grounds surrounding the ritual precincts were used as a polo ground, and after 1911, the government gave a plot of land and the buildings formerly occupied by the Music Bureau to the Forestry Bureau which converted them into an experimental farm. At the same time a radio station was set up in the

(4:7) Mrs. Archibald Little *Guide to Peking*, (Tientsin, Tientsin Press, 1904), p. 22.

"Yesterday we went to see the Temple of Heaven...We went a long way past what seemed miles of enormous walls, gates, and pagodas; then walked along a wall, so as to approach the gate of the Temple unperceived, and then burst through. They saw that they were too late to stop us, so the gatekeepers and all laughed. One keeper we took as a guide, and gave him a little money afterwards. The quantity of the stone used for these buildings is enormous. There are many fine flights of steps, marble terraces and balustrades, fine old yew-trees, and oak groves, with bronze

tripods, and ovens to burn sacrificial silk in. One stone platform is curiously meted out, mathematcially. There is one large round stone in the centre, for his Imperial Majesty to stand upon, when the bullocks and sheep are sacrificed on the great day; there are nine other stones, surrounding it; eighteen more, outside these; and twenty-seven again, placed round those, forming radii of nine stones in length from the centre." Mr. Michie F. A. Fraser, of the British Legation at Pekin, as reported in *The Illustrated London News, February 1873*

southwest corner of the grounds. In 1917, the troops of the warlord Zhang Xun camped in the Temple of Heaven, and a small battle broke out between them and the Republican army when Zhang Xun attempted to re-establish the monarchy by restoring Puyi to the throne.

The construction of the oldest building on the Temple of Heaven ritual grounds was completed around 1421, just as the Ming emperor Yongle was putting the finishing touches on the rest of his new capital. At first, the worship of Heaven and Earth was conducted simultaneously here and at a corresponding temple in Nanjing. In 1530 the Ming dynasty reverted to the older practice of worshipping Heaven and Earth at separate altars, and constructed the Round Altar for the worship of Heaven at its present site, while a **Temple of Earth** (*Ditan*) was built in the north of the city. The splendid round **Hall of Prayer for a Good Harvest** was first built in 1545, replacing an earlier square hall. During the Ming and early Qing, the tiles on the triple-tiered roof of this building were in three colors: the uppermost roof was blue, symbolizing heaven; the middle roof was yellow, representing the emperor; and the lower roof was green, representing the common people.

For about a century, from the early Qing until the time of Qianlong (reigned 1736–96), the rituals continued to be carried out in the old manner. But the growing prosperity and self-confidence the empire was enjoying in the mid-18th century, and a series of successful military campaigns in the northwest, made Qianlong eager to build. The Round Altar was enlarged to nearly double its original size, and the triple roof of the Hall of Prayer for a Good Harvest was tiled in a uniform cobalt blue. Annual ritual worship continued uninterrupted until the first decade of the 20th century; however it stopped for a few years around the turn of the century when the Empress Dowager Cixi placed the Guangxu emperor under house arrest.

A fire started by lightning destroyed the Hall of Prayer for a Good Harvest in 1889. Legend has it that the fire began when a centipede climbed to the golden knob at the summit of the roof

This golden knob is in fact the summit of the Imperial Vault of Heaven

and was struck by lightning as punishment for its boldness. In any case, 30 officials accused of being "responsible" for the insectivorous accident were executed. It took seven years to rebuild the hall due to a scarcity of timber as well as a lack of blueprints. The four giant columns that bear most of the weight of the roof are hewn of Oregon fir and were imported to China in the 1890s by the American lumber dealer and shipping magnate, Robert Dollar, whose Dollar Shipping Lines, with a Shanghai headquarters on the Bund, evolved into American President Lines. As a contemporary guidebook describes:

> *"[The Hall of Prayer for a Good Harvest] was struck by lightning in 1889 but the Chinese sent to America for immense timbers and spent a considerable sum on its reconstruction."* (4:8)

This is further attested to by Frank Dorn, an American army officer and language student in Peking from 1934 to 1938, who wrote:

> *"... it was struck by lightning and burned down. The rebuilding began at once when the American shipping*

(4:8) Madrolle's Guide Books *Northern China, The Valley of the Blue River, Korea,* (London, Hachette & Co., 1912), p. 37.

A venerable (500 years old) pagoda tree shades the Divine Music Bureau

magnate *Robert Dollar provided the main pillars for its circular colonnade with a shipment of great logs of Oregon fir."* (4:9)

And as the long-time China resident, businessman and author Carl Crow wrote in his self-published *Handbook for China* in 1921:

"When rebuilt every care was taken to reproduce the older building in all details but it was impossible to find native timbers strong and long enough to support the massive roof. Oregon pine was turned to and the pillars used were secured and transported from Portland [Oregon] to Peking at great expense."

(4:9) Frank Dorn *The Forbidden City: The biography of a palace*, (New York, Scribner, 1970), p. 62.

The ritual at the Round Altar was performed by a member of the imperial clan for the last time in 1910, when Prince Chun stood in for the Xuantong emperor (Puyi), who was then only four years old. On October 10, 1912, the first anniversary of the founding of the Republic of China, the Temple of Heaven was opened to the public for the day. To celebrate the occasion, the age-old sacrifice was carried out, with significant modifications of a republican nature, by a civil official acting on behalf of the president of China at the time, the warlord general Yuan Shikai. On December 23, 1914, Yuan himself donned imperial-style robes and performed the winter solstice ritual for the very last time in Chinese history. The ceremony was filmed for posterity, and stills of it remind one of a Cecil B. de Mille spectacular. In 1918, the Temple of Heaven was formally opened as a park.

In 1948 some of the old cypress trees on the grounds were felled in preparation for the construction of an airfield that was never completed. Before this, the air force had made do with an emergency airstrip closer to the city center, in present-day Dongdan Park. The American scholar Derk Bodde, who was studying in Peking in 1948 as one of the first American Fulbright fellows, reported on the scene on the Temple of Heaven grounds in the fall of that year:

> . . . all the buildings are filled with hundreds of young men. . . . They are wartime student refugees from Shansi, some of whom seem hardly older than 12 or 13. Most of the stone terraces outside, as well as the floors of the temple itself, are covered with their sleeping pads and meager possessions. . . . The marble balustrades of the Altar of Heaven [the Round Altar] are festooned with bedding drying in the sun. The columns of the great temple and adjoining buildings, much faded from their former brilliant red, are covered with ugly written notices, and dust and debris lie everywhere on the once gleaming marble . . . the mental condition of these boys is far worse than that of the poorest coolies. . . . Portions of the courtyard, and even of the lower tiers of the Altar of Heaven itself, are littered with their half-dried excrement.[4:10]

(4:10) Derk Bodde *Peking Diary: 1948-1949, A Year of Revolution*, (New York, Abelard-Schuman, 1950; reprinted by Fawcett World Library, 1967), pp. 31–2.

The Walk

Beginning at the south entrance of **Tiantan Park**, visit the triple-tiered **Round Altar** and the exquisitely roofed **Imperial Vault of Heaven** on the main axis, then detour for a look at the **Hall of Abstinence** and the **Music Bureau**, returning to the axis and exploring the domineering **Hall of Prayer for a Good Harvest**, before exiting the park's east entrance.

To make the walk efficient, and to eliminate backtracking, we will not follow precisely in the emperor's footsteps, although we will go everywhere he went.

Although this was not required of the emperor, purchase your ticket at the ticket kiosk at the **south gate of the Temple of Heaven Park** (*Tiantan Nan Men*) [天坛南门], pass through the broad gate and begin by walking north.

The Hall of Abstinence, one of many marble waterspouts surrounding the Beamless Hall

After about 200 meters, just before the Round Altar,, you will come to the **Changing Terrace** [具服台] on the right (east), a rectangular platform whereupon a yellow tent was erected in which the emperor changed out of his imperial yellow robe and donned a more humble blue robe worn especially when conducting ritual sacrifices.

The emperor would have come here before sunrise, after spending the night in the **Hall of Abstinence** (which we will visit shortly). Three days previously to that, the Son of Heaven would have begun a pre-ritual fast in the Forbidden City. This was no starvation diet, but rather entailed refraining from meat, wine, pungent vegetables such as onions, garlic or scallions (though he was permitted tea, snacks and blander vegetarian dishes, to stave off hunger), and avoiding pleasurable liaisons with his empress or concubines. Nor was he allowed to discuss criminal cases, visit the infirm, listen to music or visit the tombs of his ancestors during this period of self-purification. Finally, on the eve of the sacrifice, the emperor took a ritual bath.

Returning to the ritual, pass through the triple *pailou* archways of white marble that resemble both the *torana* gateways at the mound-like Buddhist temple at Sanchi in India and the elegant *torii* gates that stand before major shrines and temples in Japan, to the **Round Altar** (*Yuan Qiu*) [圜丘], the uncovered temple where the emperor would communicate directly with Heaven. Two major rituals took place here each year: at the winter solstice, the shortest day of the year, the emperor would report to Heaven the key events of the year in the ceremony called "communicating with heaven;" and in the fourth lunar month, usually around May, the emperor would appeal to Heaven for rain and a good harvest.

The Round Altar is encircled by two sets of walls, an outer square wall, symbolizing the earth and an inner round wall in the shape of Heaven. The green-tiled structure south of the altar is the oven used for the sacrificial incineration of an unblemished ox. A number of iron censers, now here in replica, were used for burning

Altar for burning the sacrificial bullock, Temple of Heaven, Pekin,
The Illustrated London News, February 1873

the other objects used in the ritual, a way of delivering them
through the medium of smoke to Heaven.

The design of the altar itself follows a strict numerological-
symbolic pattern, based on the old *yang* (male, bright as opposed
to dark, vigorous) numbers three, five, seven and nine. To begin
with, the altar is composed of three platforms. The top platform is
nine *zhang* (a measure equal to about three meters or ten feet) in
diameter, the middle platform is 15 *zhang* (3 x 5) in diameter, and
the lower platform 21 *zhang* (3 x 7) in diameter, which adds up to
a total of 45 (5 x 9). In the *Yi Jing (I Ching), The Book of Changes*,
an early treatise of divination and philosophy based on
numerology, the combination 5:9 stands for the relationship
between a man and his superior, which in turn is analogous to the
relationship between the emperor and Heaven. The number of
panels in the three balustrades, all multiples of the auspicious
number nine, is also significant. On the first platform, there are 36
(9 x 4); on the second 72 (9 x 8); and on the third, 108 (9 x 12)
which make a total of 216, or 9 x 24.

Similar formulas are repeated in the stones paving the surface of the platforms. The round stone in the center of the uppermost platform—perhaps the most sacred bit of turf in the Chinese empire—is surrounded by nine stones. Moving outward, each ring increases by nine; thus the second ring consists of 18, the third of 27, and the outermost ring, 81 (9 x 9), a highly auspicious number. On the second platform the innermost ring has 90 stones and the outermost ring, 162 (2 x 81); on the third platform the numbers run from 171 to 243 (3 x 81).

The foods offered to Heaven during the ceremonies range quite literally from soup to nuts. The following menu is taken from an illustrated ritual text of the Qing dynasty, which specifies the placement of some 30 containers:

Grains	Fruits and Vegetables	Meats
rice	plums	fish
sorghum	dates	venison
millet	hazelnuts	hare
white cakes	salted chives	spleen
black cakes	salted bamboo	suckling pig
roast grain	salted celery	pickled venison
rice flour	salted shallots	pickled pork
chestnuts		veal

One of the two Sacred Kitchens that connected to the Hall of Prayer for a Good Harvest complex via the Long Corridor

Add to this soup, rice gruel and wine served up in bronze ceremonial vessels, along with candles, lamps, incense and baskets of jade and silks, which were eventually consigned to the flames as a burnt offering. These dishes were prepared in a Sacred Kitchen and abattoir located to the east of the altar.

The Round Altar cries out for reverent silence, but it is usually mobbed with people standing in the center trying out the remarkable echo effect here by clapping or shouting at the top of their voices. Its plainness, when visible, was much appreciated by the French author Abel Bonnard, who visited in 1920:

> Like the neighboring temple, it is all of white marble, in three circular terraces, retreating one from the other, with staircases turned to the four cardinal points, and open balustrades. It is not lofty. It only exacts your respect by its appeal to the mind and makes not the slightest effort to astonish the eye.[4:11]

Round Altar Ritual: What follows is the script of the major sacrifice conducted here at the winter solstice during the later part of the Qing dynasty. Though tedious and involved, the entire procedure takes no more than two hours.

First, imagine the shortest, darkest day in the year in the cold, dry climate of North China, when the *yang*, or male, principle is at its nadir and begins to stir afresh. Two hours before noon on the day before the solstice, the Director of the Sacrificial Court goes to the Gate of Heavenly Purity (*Qianqing Men*), the entrance to the palace residential quarters in the Forbidden City, to escort the emperor from the palace on the journey to the Hall of Abstinence in the Temple of Heaven. Wearing a blue double-dragon robe designed exclusively for this ceremony, the Son of Heaven mounts his sedan chair and escorted by 12 high officials proceeds to the Gate of Supreme Harmony (*Taihe Men*), where he reviews the text of the prayer that he will deliver the next day. At the gate he changes from his palace palanquin into a larger sedan chair. While in the palace he is accompanied by 20 men of

(4:11) Abel Bonnard *In China 1920–21*, (New York, E.P. Dutton and Co., 1927), p. 8.

The Round Altar and one of its monumental pailou

the "leopard-tail" guards armed with rifles and swords, and 20 others with bows and arrows. As the procession moves south through the Meridian Gate (*Wu Men*) [during the Ming, the emperor traveled by Burmese elephant, and one Ming emperor obsessed with the notion of appearing humble, managed to make the journey on foot, considerably irritating his advisors], the bell in the gate tower sounds, and all the princes, dukes, civil and military officials who will not accompany the emperor, assemble and kneel to see off those who will. Here the procession is joined by additional uniformed men holding colorful ensigns and standards.

As the imperial procession, now 2,000 strong, moves south, "the city seems to hold its breath." The deep ruts in the streets formed by cart traffic have been filled in with golden sand to smooth the imperial passage, and auspicious couplets written on red paper strips have been posted on all the shops and police stations along the way. It was forbidden, upon penalty of death, for commoners to gaze upon the emperor as he passed, but this

was unlikely anyway as he was cozily concealed in his sedan chair. In the late 19th century all rail traffic in the south part of the city was ordered to a halt during the procession. As the entourage enters the Temple of Heaven complex through the west gate, the bell in the Hall of Abstinence is rung in a continuous peal.

The emperor's first destination in the Temple of Heaven complex is the Zhaoheng Gate (south of the Round Altar), where he alights from his sedan chair. Escorted by the Director of

Stone pavillion for a missing bronze statue, the Hall of Abstinence

Sacrifices and the Sacrificial Prompter, he proceeds to the Imperial Vault of Heaven, where he burns incense before the spirit tablets of Shangdi, his ultimate ancestor, and the deceased Qing emperors, and performs for the first time the ceremony of three genuflections and nine kowtows.

The emperor then goes to the Round Altar to inspect the lavish silken tents and shrines that have been placed there to hold the spirit tablets, the sacrificial vessels and the edible offerings. The shrine of Shangdi is placed inside one of the round tents of blue silk that stands slightly to the north of the center of the altar; the shrines of the former emperors are placed in square tents to both sides. The emperor then climbs back into his Jade Chariot and returns to the Hall of Abstinence. The members of the imperial clan and the officials who take part in the sacrifice wait outside the gate of the hall as he passes and only retire after the emperor enters. They will camp out for the night in tents put up nearby.

The next morning, precisely one and three-quarters hours before sunrise, as determined by court astronomers, the Director of Sacrifices goes to the Hall of Abstinence and announces the time to the emperor. The emperor dresses in his sacrificial robes, and mounts the sedan chair which conveys him to the gate of the Hall of Abstinence, where he changes for the Jade Palanquin to the accompaniment of a sounding bell. Bearers haul the Jade Palanquin to the Zhaoheng Gate, where the emperor alights, walks through the gate, and proceeds along the Sacred Way to the yellow silk tent set up on the Changing Platform. The emperor now washes his face and hands carefully and changes into another set of sacrificial robes.

The emperor then proceeds through the *pailou* gates set in the square and circular walls around the altar and takes up his position on the middle step of the second tier of the Round Altar. (Try it for size. Oddly enough no tourists have carved their name on it.) The Director of Sacrifices then escorts the princes, *beile* and *beizi* (high-ranking members of the imperial clan), to their

The Imperial Vault of Heaven seen from the south aspect

respective places on the lower tier. The entire ritual contingent of about 230 people, including musicians and dancers in colorful garb, also take their places on and around the altar. All face north.

At the same time, the president of the Board of Rites leads a small group of officials to the nearby Imperial Vault of Heaven to supervise the transfer of the spirit tablets, in miniature sedan chairs, to the Round Altar, and sees to it that they are placed properly in their respective altars. Then the Director of Sacrifices invites the emperor to perform the three genuflections and nine kowtows again.

The ceremony that follows is divided into nine parts. Naturally it was forbidden for any of the participants to shed tears, spit or cough during the ceremony. Those who erred in the execution of the ritual, such as by allowing a candle to go out, were severely punished.

1. The officials in charge of incense approach the emperor with their incense containers. A drum is struck three times and the musicians begin to play the tune "First Peace" accompanied by a chorus. The prompter escorts the emperor to the uppermost tier of the altar and brings him before the spirit tablet of Shangdi. The emperor kneels down on a yellow silk cushion and makes an offering of incense sticks to Shangdi, and then repeats this offering before the tablets of the deceased emperors of the dynasty. He then returns to his place on the second tier, where he again performs "the three and the nine."

At this point a wooden percussion instrument in the shape of a tiger (an example of this can be seen in the building to the east of the Hall of Prayer to a Good Harvest) is sounded three times, indicating for the music to stop. The princes and other members of the imperial clan follow the emperor's example and offer incense before the shrines.

2. To the tune "A Smooth Prospect" the emperor now repeats the ritual described above in front of all the spirit tablets, only this time the offering consists of jade and silks in baskets instead of incense. When this is over, the emperor returns to his place.

3. The large container (*cu*) is now brought in, and the musicians commence playing "Complete Harmony." The emperor turns to the west and receives the *cu* which has just been filled with the fresh blood and fur of a sacrificial ox. The emperor brings this reverently before the spirit tablets of Shangdi and the emperors, kneels down, and raises it over his head. The *cu* is then wiped clean three times while the emperor returns to his place. The music "Complete Harmony" is performed again.

4. Martial dancers perform an interlude to the tune "Eternal Peace" holding a flute in one hand and a baton with a feather attached in the other. The emperor ascends to the uppermost tier of the altar and offers a vessel of wine to Shangdi. He then stands nearby while the prompter picks up the tablet inscribed with the prayer they had rehearsed the previous day in the Hall of Supreme Harmony. The music and

Four marble staircases, rich in detail, lead up to the Vault of Heaven

dancing cease, and the emperor kneels down and reads the prayer, an appeal to Heaven to treat its subjects kindly and to provide the proper natural conditions to ensure a good year. The prompter then places the written prayer on a table in front of the spirit tablet of Shangdi.

5. An official leads the subordinate officials onto the platform. They stand before the spirit tablets of the sun, moon, and stars, and offer up incense, silk and wine. Once this is completed, they return to their original positions.

6. The martial dancers are replaced by the civilian dancers. The musicians play "Excellent Peace" while the dancers perform their movements with feather batons and flutes. The emperor ascends to the uppermost tier and presents a second flagon of wine to Shangdi.

7. The emperor makes a third offering of wine in a similar manner accompanied by the music "Eternal Peace."

8. In the next to last offering, meat and wine are placed before the spirit tablet of Shangdi. Once the offerings are properly laid out, the emperor approaches the tablet, drinks the wine and eats the meat in a climactic act of communion with Heaven. The offerings are removed and the emperor kneels down. He then returns to his place on the second tier, where he performs "the three and nine," which is repeated by the entire assembly.

9. The written prayer, jade, silk, food and incense are removed from the table in front of the tablet of Shangdi and taken to the braziers to the south. The emperor again leads the assembled worshippers in "the three and nine," and the music "Pure Peace" is played. All the spirit tablets are now replaced in the Hall of August Heaven.

The emperor descends from the second terrace and stands before the furnace while the music "Great Peace" is played. The offerings are burnt concluding the ceremony. At this time, the tail, fur and blood of the sacrificial ox are buried in the "fur and blood pit" next to the furnace as a symbolic way of providing sustenance to the ancestors.

The emperor then returns to the golden tent to change his robes, mounts his Golden Chariot and is escorted out of the Temple of Heaven to the accompaniment of the music "Protecting Peace." When he arrives at the Meridian Gate of the Forbidden City, the officials who did not accompany him are once again waiting in their ceremonial robes, and kneel before him. The assembled officials enter the palace and escort the emperor as far as the River of Golden Water, where they halt while the emperor disappears into the palace.

Having completed this ritual, continue walking north to the Imperial Vault of Heaven (*Huangqiong Yu*) [皇穹宇], which is surrounded by a circular wall. The building itself resembles a simplified and somewhat shrunken version of the Hall of Prayer for a Good Harvest, which we will see at the end of the walk. Note the elegant white marble platforms on which all three buildings here stand, the single roof, and the bracket systems supporting the roof. The Imperial Vault of Heaven is so named because it is designed in the shape of Heaven—round. Yet despite its fancy title, it was little more than a storage place for the spirit tablets that were used in the rituals held on the Round Altar. No rituals were carried out in the building or courtyard itself. In the Qing dynasty, as today, the spirit tablets of Shangdi and the deceased Qing emperors were stored in the round building, while the tablets of subsidiary spirits occupied the two rectangular side buildings.

The round courtyard offers two entertaining acoustical phenomena:

—Two people standing at any two points along the interior of the Echo Wall (*Huiyin Bi*) [回音壁] (the circular wall enclosing the courtyard) who speak facing the wall in a normal voice with their heads at the same altitude will be able to hear what the other is saying.

—If you stand on the first of the Three Echo Stones [三音石] at the very foot of the inclined carved marble slab—resembling a carpet—that leads up to the hall from the southern approach, and clap your

The Imperial Vault of Heaven's East Annex Hall, storage place for ritual objects

The Imperial Vault of Heaven's circular wall offers intriguing acoustics on a quiet evening in 1978

hands once, you will hear a single echo of your clap; if you clap once standing on the second stone, you will hear two echos; and from the third stone, a single clap will produce three echos.

Unfortunately, the wall and courtyard are usually so crowded with an overwhelming babel of tourists that it is impossible to reproduce these phenomena. These forms of echo can be explained by the fact that the Imperial Vault of Heaven does not sit in the precise center of the round courtyard but rather slightly to the north.

The Hall of Abstinence is surrounded on all sides by a broad moat, here without water

Exiting the circular wall at the same gate you entered, turn right and head west to the **Hall of Abstinence** (*Zhai Gong*) [斋宫] along the main path. When you reach the Triple Gate (*Sanzuo Men*) [三座门] turn right and walk to the entrance of the Hall of Abstinence, which will be on your left side (the sign here refers to the compound as the Fasting Palace). The Hall of Abstinence is a well-defended miniature citadel, surrounded on all sides by a broad moat, with a second U-shaped moat inside. In the covered corridors, which run around the outside of the walled complex, eunuch sentinels would patrol during the emperor's one-night residence here, as he prepared for the early-morning sacrifices. We learn from history books that during the Ming dynasty the eunuchs on duty were, like the emperor, expressly forbidden to eat meat, drink wine or expectorate while their sovereign was in residence.

The Hall of Abstinence differs in two respects from other imperial habitations: first, it is built on an east-west axis, facing east, rather than south as do most imperial buildings and temples; and secondly, the roof tiles are green, a color that stands for the common people, rather than the usual imperial yellow. These features can be interpreted as symbolic gestures of humility in the presence of Heaven.

As very little is known about the original furnishings of the Hall of Abstinence, the display in the Main Hall and the disposition of furniture in the Imperial Sleeping Chambers are educated guesswork on the part of the curators, based on similar quarters in the Forbidden City and Summer Palace.

In the central room of the **Main Hall**, constructed without rafters or beams, the emperor would confer with the officials in charge of the rituals. The side rooms served as waiting rooms for attendants.

The small white marble altar on the south corner of the patio in front of the hall held a series of removable plaques indicating the hour of the day, one way of reminding the emperor that he should practice self-cultivation and meditation in a timely manner. The square-roofed pavilion on the patio held a bronze statue of the semi-legendary Leng Qian, an official of the Music Bureau, and an inscribed ivory plaque. The figure's closed mouth was a hint to the emperor that he should remain silent during his night of abstinence.

There are two bedrooms in the Sleeping Chambers behind the Main Hall. The emperor occupied the south chamber at the summer sacrifices, and the north bedroom on the eve of the sacrifices that took place at the winter solstice and in early spring. The north bedroom is appropriately equipped with a *kang* bed warmed by a system of underground flues. In 1807 a fire broke out in this old-fashioned heating plant and consumed the entire building. It was rebuilt shortly afterwards.

In the early 1980s the Hall of Abstinence fell prey to the vagaries of the Four Modernizations policy and became for a while the *Marco Polo Shop*, featuring Pierre Cardin fashions manufactured in China. The building has since been restored.

Exiting the Hall of Abstinence, turn right and return to the path, where you make another right, and then walk west until you reach the **Divine Music Bureau** (*Shenyue Shu*) [神乐署], exactingly restored and reopened to the public in 2004.

When the Yongle emperor moved the capital of the Ming dynasty from Nanjing to Peking in the early 15th century and constructed the Temple of Heaven complex, he built a Temple of Music (*Shenyue Guan*) on the present site of the Bureau, also known as the Temple of Heaven Taoist Temple (*Tiantan Dao Guan*), as it was operated by monks of the Tianyi sect of Taoism and contained a temple to Guandi, the God of War, and other shrines dedicated to Taoist deities. The buildings were rebuilt on a large scale by the Ming Hongzhi emperor (reigned 1488–1505) and the Qing Kangxi emperor (reigned 1662–1722), who provided wine and tea shops for visitors to the temple. In 1742, the Qianlong emperor issued a decree that banned the wine shops and forbid the imperial musicians from practicing Taoism. He further ordered that the ritual musicians and dancers who performed at the Music Bureau had to belong to the eight Manchu banners, and be members of the imperial clan.

The large freestanding spirit wall in front of the entrance of the bureau was reputed to have the power to exorcise the "five poisons" (referring generally to summertime pests and infestations, but specifically snakes, centipedes, toads, lizards and scorpions) if rubbed by a visitor, and thus local visitors flocked to the temple at the Dragon Boat Festival, which takes place on the fifth day of the fifth moon.

The Bell Tower, note the green roof tiles

The massive bell within the Bellfrey adjacent to the Main Hall, Hall of Abstinence

The small museum with numerous replicas of ancient instruments

The principal courtyard and "concert hall" of the Divine Music Bureau

The principle formal activity of the Divine Music Bureau was to train the musicians and dancers who took part in the imperial rituals at the Temple of Heaven as well as all the other ritual altars in Beijing. At times the bureau was staffed by as many as 3,000 teachers, performers and administrators.

Today the rebuilt quarters of the Divine Music Bureau, probably the only extant such "bureau" from imperial times in China, contains numerous informative exhibits relating to classical Chinese music theory and musical instruments, and displays of the ritual music and dance performed for imperial ceremonies, including costumes and ritual paraphernalia.

Exiting the Music Bureau turn left and walk down to the next path to the West Celestial Gate (*Xitian Men*) [西天门]. Turn right here and walk east through the neat rows of scholar trees to the raised **causeway** (*Danbi Qiao*) [丹陛桥], known in Chinese as "the bridge of cinnabar steps" that connects the **Imperial Vault of Heaven** with the next item on the itinerary. The causeway is 360 meters (1,170 feet long) and is higher at its north end than at its south end. Turn left and head north on the causeway, which functioned as a sort of *camino real* during the rituals, until you get to the gate that leads to the courtyard enclosing the **Hall of Prayer for a Good Harvest** (*Qinian Dian*) [祈年殿]. On the right before the entrance to the hall is another **Changing Platform,** (*Jufu Tai*) [具服台] where the emperor would change his clothing in preparation for the rituals. During the Ming dynasty, the emperors followed the Hindu custom of removing their shoes here before proceeding with the sacrifice in the Hall of Prayer for a Good Harvest. During the sacrifices, the entire length of the causeway was covered with a coir mat to protect the imperial toes and soles.

The Gate of Prayer for a Good Harvest (*Qinian Men*) [祈年门] is the only Ming building in the temple complex (though its roof was replaced during the Qing). North of this gate lies the famous **Hall of Prayer for a Good Harvest** (*Qinian Dian*) [祈年殿], with its three-tiered roof and tall three-tiered terrace of white marble, which is known as the **Altar of Prayer for Grain** (*Qigu Tan*) [祈谷坛], arguably one of the best known buildings in

China—its image appears on dozens of commercial products, from cigarettes to soaps.

The triple roof—symbolizing heaven, earth and man—of the Hall of Prayer for a Good Harvest is as blue as the sky. Its three circular roofs are supported by three sets of columns; the lower two roofs by two sets of 12 columns each, one set representing the 12 months of the year, and the other the 12 two-hour periods of the day, while the uppermost roof rests upon the four Oregon tree trunks (pine or fir, previously mentioned) that represent the four seasons. There are 28 columns altogether, just as there are 28 constellations in the Chinese heavens. The hall is nine *zhang* (a traditional measure equal to about three meters or ten feet) tall; nine is the ultimate *yang* number, virile, creative, and solar. The uppermost roof is 30 *zhang* in circumference; there are 30 days in a lunar month.

The hall offers particularly fine examples of the decorative and functional systems of bracketing that appear in every traditional wooden building in China. The entire weight of the roof is distributed through the brackets and supported by the columns; the walls are merely screens and support none of the weight. The result is a highly stable and attractive structure that is flexible enough to withstand strong earthquakes.

On the floor in the center of the hall is a round stone with a "found" picture of a dragon and phoenix. If you have difficulty distinguishing these two imaginary celestial creatures, it is because the heat of the fire of 1889 supposedly distorted the pattern beyond recognition. The dragon had originally resided in the cupola in the ceiling and descended to join the phoenix who for years had occupied the circular stone all by herself. The interior cupola here with its resident dragon is rivaled in splendor only by a similar installation in the Hall of Supreme Harmony in the Forbidden City. The three marble balustrades on the altar, complete with dragon-head rain spouts, are also of the same genre as those framing the Three Great Harmony Halls. They appear yet again at the Round Altar.

Top: *The Gate of Prayer for a Good Harvest*
Bottom: *Looking east from "The Bridge of Cinnabar Steps"*
Right: *The Hall of Prayer for a Good Harvest*

The rituals practiced in this hall were quite straightforward. On the 15th day of the first lunar month (around February or March) the emperor made a sacrificial offering before the spirit tablets of Heaven and the deceased emperors of the dynasty to obtain their blessing for the year and to ensure the proper natural conditions for a good grain harvest. Replicas of the spirit tablets, inscribed with the names of the deities in Manchu and Chinese characters, stand on high platforms in the hall, and there is a complete set of ritual paraphernalia (again in replica) laid out as if the ritual were about to take place.

To the north of the Hall of Prayer is the **Hall of August Heaven** (*Huangqian dian*) [皇前殿], where the spirit tablet of Shangdi, the Pearly Emperor Supreme Ruler in the Heaven, the emperor's ultimate ancestor, was stored. In recent years this hall has been used for the dissemination of public hygiene information. But it now performs its original function with replicas. There are two other rectangular halls in the courtyard, today used for historical displays. The original purpose of these two halls was to store all the tablets used in the ritual, except the tablet of Shangdi. In the Ming dynasty, these included the spirit tablets of the Ming emperors, the moon, sun, stars, oceans, wind, clouds, thunder, rain, rivers, mountains, early mythological emperors, etc. A vast quantity of these tablets had accumulated by Qianlong's day, so he burned them all leaving only five belonging to the deceased members of his own Aisin-gioro clan, including the founder and first three emperors of the Qing dynasty.

Descending from the triple-tiered platform, head east through the gate and go down the incline to the lengthy covered corridor, consisting of 72 bays, which connects the sacrificial altar with the **Sacred Kitchen** (Shen Chu) [神厨], the **Abattoir**, or Butcher House (Xingsheng Ting) [宰牲亭] and the **Sacred Warehouse** (Shen Ku) [神库], where the sacrificial animals and foodstuffs for the nearby rituals were prepared. When the offering was completed, the remnants of the sacrifices were burned in the tile ovens, iron censers and disposal pit located in the southeast corner of the

courtyard near the Gate of Prayer for a Good Harvest, again
similar to the procedures at the Round Altar. These "sacred"
buildings are no longer used for their original purposes, although
floral displays and other exhibitions are held there. As you walk
east through the corridors, making several 90-degree turns, note
how the live acoustics of the corridors attract amateur opera
singers, gamblers and their respective audiences and kibitzers
throughout the day, a scene of great delight.

To the south of this corridor stand the so-called **Seven Star
Stones**, which are not meteors as has been suggested, although
they do form a pattern that resembles the Big Dipper. Legend has
it that when the Ming emperor Yongle was shopping around for a
location to build his Temple of Heaven, these seven lucky "stars"
fell out of the sky and landed in this auspicious place, hence
inspiring the emperor to break ground nearby. The pitted surface
of the stones is not the result of extraterrestrial physics but rather
the result of superstitious people having chipped away good luck
souvenirs over the past six centuries.

Continuing east when the corridor turns north once again
brings you to the eastern entrance of Tiantan Park. A three
minute walk to the north, and across the street, is the **Hong
Qiao Market** [虹桥街市], a department store popular with
foreign tourists, featuring endless shops selling billions of fresh-
water pearls on the third and fourth floors, and hundreds of
dealers offering shoes, clothes, watches, luggage, antiques and
more on the first, second and third floors.

The Long Corridor, scene of impromptu opera, patriotic songs and jazz, daily calisthenics and gossip

The Hall of Abstinence's Main Hall's central room was constructed without beams or rafters, so the entire weight of the roof is distributed through brackets

Walk 5: Confucian & Lama Temples

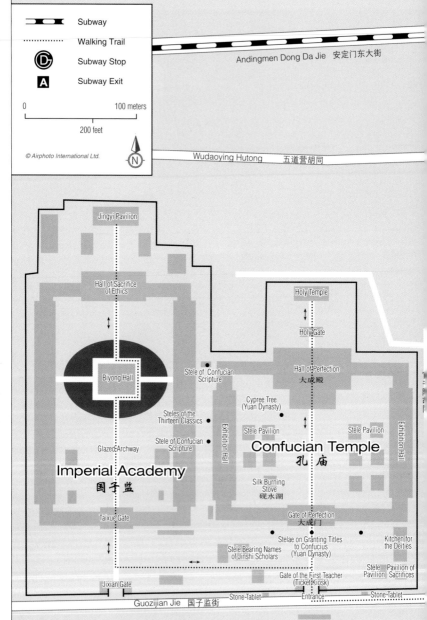

Subway

Walking Trail

Subway Stop

Subway Exit

0   100 meters

200 feet

© Airphoto International Ltd.

N

Andingmen Dong Da Jie 安定门东大街

Wudaoying Hutong 五道营胡同

Jingyi Pavilion

Hall of Sacrifice of Ethics

Holy Temple

Holy Gate

Biyong Hall

Stele of Confucian Scripture

Hall of Perfection 大成殿

Cypree Tree (Yuan Dynasty)

Steles of the Thirteen Classics

Stele Pavilion

Stele Pavilion

Exhibition Hall

Exhibition Hall

Stele of Confucian Scripture

Confucian Temple 孔庙

Glazed Archway

Silk Burning Stove 砚水湖

Imperial Academy 国子监

Taixue Gate

Gate of Perfection 大成门

Stelae on Granting Titles to Confucius (Yuan Dynasty)

Kitchen for the Deities

Stele Bearing Names of Jinshi Scholars

Stele Pavilion

Pavilion of Sacrifices

Jixian Gate

Gate of the First Teacher (Ticket Kiosk)

Entrance

Stone-Tablet

Stone-Tablet

Guozijian Jie 国子监街

Screenwall

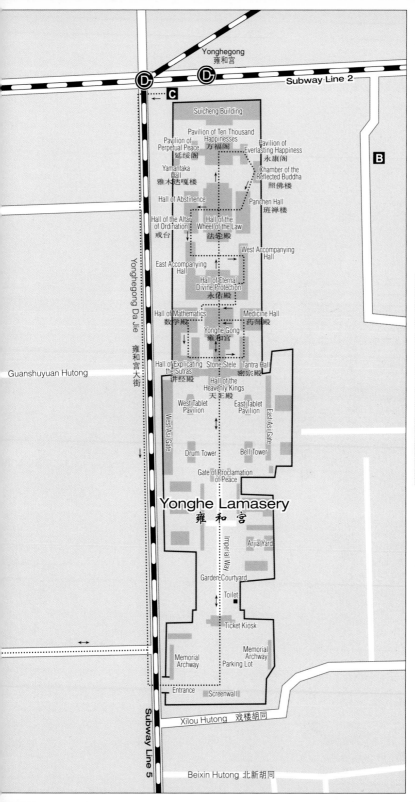

Yonghegong
雍和宫

Subway Line 2

C

B

Yonghegong Da Jie
雍和宫大街

Guanshuyuan Hutong

Suicheng Building

Pavilion of Ten Thousand
Happinesses
Pavilion of
Perpetual Peace
延绥阁
万福阁
Pavilion of
Everlasting Happiness
永康阁

Yamantaka
Hall
雅木达嘎楼
Chamber of the
Reflected Buddha
照佛楼

Hall of Abstinence
Panchen Hall
班禅楼

Hall of the Altar
of Ordination
戒台
Hall of the
Wheel of the Law
法轮殿
West Accompanying
Hall

East Accompanying
Hall
Hall of Eternal
Divine Protection
永佑殿

Hall of Mathematics
数学殿
Medicine Hall
药师殿

Yonghe Gong
雍和宫

Hall of Explicating
the Sutras
讲经殿
Stone Stele
Tantra Hall
密宗殿

Hall of the
Heavenly Kings
天王殿

West Tablet
Pavilion
East Tablet
Pavilion

West Asi Gate
East Asi Gate

Drum Tower
Bell Tower

Gate of Proclamation
of Peace

Yonghe Lamasery
雍和宫

Arjia Yard

Imperial Way

Garden Courtyard

Toilet

Ticket Kiosk

Memorial
Archway
Memorial
Archway
Parking Lot

Entrance
Screenwall

Subway Line 5

Xilou Hutong 戏楼胡同

Beixin Hutong 北新胡同

WALK · 5

CONFUCIAN TEMPLE, IMPERIAL ACADEMY, LAMA TEMPLE

DURATION

Approximately three hours.

DESCRIPTION

This walk covers three destinations within a few minutes' walking distance of each other in the northeast section of the city. While the **Lama Temple** (*Yonghe Gong*) is a Lamaist temple both in name and superficially in practice, the **Confucian Temple** (*Kong Miao*) and **Imperial Academy** (*Guozijian*) have had a more checkered history. Until recently, the Confucian Temple housed the **Capital Museum** (*Shoudu Bowuguan*), a collection of artifacts related to the history and culture of Beijing from its neolithic beginnings to the present. In 2005, a new huge modern Capital Museum, costing US$150 million, opened in Fuxingmenwai on the west side of the city. It is very much worth a visit. And until the year 2000, the Imperial Academy was home to the **Capital Library** (*Shoudu Tushuguan*), with rich holdings in the social sciences and Beijing local history. The library's new home is on the Third Ring Road near Beijing Curios City and the Panjiayuan Market.

As the opening and closing times of the three sites on this walk may vary, it is recommended to plan your visit between 9.00am and 4.00pm.

STARTING POINT

The Confucian Temple on Guozijian Jie near Andingmen.

HOW TO GET THERE

Bus 13, 106, 107, or 116 to Yonghegong. Take the Beijing underground train to the Yonghegong station on the circle line.

HOW TO GET AWAY

Take the same bus or train you came on.

The central arch of the splendid pailou within the Imperial Academy, and the Qianlong period biyong *beyond it*

CONFUCIAN TEMPLE [孔庙]

The Confucian Temple in Beijing is one of the largest temples of its kind in China, and second only in importance to that in Confucius' ancestral home in Qufu, Shandong province.

About Confucius (551–479 BCE) the man, few personal details are known except what can be inferred from his principal work, the *Analects (Lun Yu)*, a collection of short statements attributed to the sage and dialogues he held with his disciples. The picture that emerges from this evidence is one of an upright man with the courage to speak out against injustice, yet fastidious in his personal habits. Living in a period of civil war, Confucius, or Kongzi as he is known in Chinese, envisioned a peaceful, ordered world run by a moral elite.

Confucius believed that men were bound together by *ren*, "human heartedness" or "humanity," a quality that manifested itself in five cardinal relationships: ruler and subject, parents and children, older and younger brother (sisters were not considered), husband and wife, friend and friend. Held together with the glue of *ren*, these relationships were ideally conducted according to a code of ritual and etiquette (*li*) that reinforced the status quo.

Confucius had his own mirror version of the Golden Rule. He said: Do not do unto others what you would not have them do unto you. He also attached great importance to practical matters and shied away from the occult and the question of death because, as he stated, he did not, and could not, know enough about them. In this respect Confucianism differs from Buddhism and Taoism (pronounced like "Dow" is in the Dow Jones of stock market fame), philosophy-religions that offer salvation, self-realization through personal cultivation and, eventually, enlightenment. Summing up the differences among the Three Religions of China as practiced by the elite, one could say: the proper Chinese gentleman was a Confucian from Monday to Friday and a Buddhist and Taoist on the weekends.

Thirteen Chinese texts, carved into about 200 slabs of marble for preservation, in the Confucian Temple's Hall of the Classics, The Illustrated London News, March 1873

The worship of Confucius was part of the imperial ritual repertoire since as early as 175 BCE, when a Han-dynasty emperor first offered sacrifices at the Kong family temple in Qufu where Confucius was born. A later Han emperor promoted this worship in schools throughout the empire, and before long Confucianism became a religious cult based on a kind of hero-worship and borrowing from nature-deity and ancestor worship. Confucian thought is also associated with the Chinese civil service examinations, the world's first practical system for staffing a bureaucracy. For 2,000 years, from the Han dynasty to the early 20th century, the Chinese examination system supplied the empire with its mandarins great and small by testing candidates' knowledge of a canon of ancient books that are attributed to the pen of Confucius: anthologies of poetry, history, rituals, the brief Analects of Confucius, the lengthy writings of Mencius and two short essays, *The Doctrine of the Mean (Zhong Yong)* and *The Great Learning (Da Xue)*. Chinese government was exercised

249

through moral suasion by gentlemen of purportedly high ethical cultivation who were also equipped with fantastic memories—it is said that the top candidates memorized texts of 400,000 Chinese characters in length—and the ability to write formulaic essays on didactic subjects; practical knowledge, such as mathematical or scientific ability, was of little consequence.

The Mongol Kublai Khan, the first great foreign ruler of China, established the earliest Confucian temple in Peking during the Yuan dynasty in the late 13th century, while the Confucian Temple on the present site dates from 1306. In a curious symbolic gesture some 450 years later, the Qianlong emperor replaced the green roof tiles on all but one of the major halls in the temple with yellow tiles, thereby elevating them to imperial status; the single exception was a hall used for sacrifices to Confucius' parents and ancestors. In 1906, two years before her death, the Empress Dowager Cixi rebuilt the temple and raised the status of the ritual worship of Confucius even higher, putting it on a par with the worship of Heaven, Earth, the Imperial Ancestors, and Land and Grain.

After the founding of the Republic of China in 1911, the worship of Confucius continued as it had for centuries, but under the aegis of the president of the republic rather than the emperor, while the other major imperial sacrifices to heaven, the sun and the moon were discontinued, with a few exceptions.

In her guide to the city, *Peking*, Juliet Bredon describes a visit to a dress rehearsal of the ceremony here—foreigners and common Chinese were not allowed to witness the actual ritual—in the 1920s. In the ceremony she witnessed a ritual resembling the imperial sacrifice to Heaven in Tiantan (the Temple of Heaven); offerings of animals, silk, jade, grain, fruit and wine were placed before the spirit tablets of Confucius and his key disciples. Music was played, prayers recited and the chant "Confucius, Confucius! How great is Confucius!" repeated by a chorus. Finally the text of the prayer was burnt, just as in the grand finale of the worship of Heaven. Local magistrates performed similar rituals on the same day, but on a smaller scale, at Confucian temples throughout the empire, and the practice was carried out as well in schools.

Few personal details are known about Confucius

The Wall of Beijing viewed from Andingmen, October 21, 1860

The colorful pageant continues to be performed on September 28 every year in the numerous Confucian temples throughout Taiwan, where the day is a public holiday called Teachers' Day.

Confucius and his school of worldly thought did not fare well under communist rule until quite recently. The Confucian temples that were a regular fixture in every country town in China were either demolished, converted into warehouses or factories, or simply abandoned and neglected in political movements that rooted out the influence of "feudal" culture perceived as inimical to the dictatorship of the proletariat. One major cloak-and-dagger campaign of the early 1970s specifically attacked Confucius and Lin Biao, Mao's appointed successor, as "feudal reactionaries," while pointing a finger at Premier Zhou Enlai as a renegade contemporary "sage."

In the 1980s, Confucian studies enjoyed a revival in China, as the country's leaders sought out a native-born ideology to replace Marxism-Leninism-Mao Zedong Thought that would justify both the resurgence of market capitalism Chinese style and the continued practice and consolidation of power in the hands of the party and military.

Beginning in 1989, Confucius' birthday was celebrated annually on the mainland. In 1994, then-president of China, Jiang Zemin, publicly praised Confucius, an about-face that can be viewed as much as a clear repudiation of Mao and communism as an indication of a cultural and ideological identity crisis. More recently, Confucian schools have opened, and Confucian studies are enjoying a new-found popularity on university campuses around the country. State-sponsored Confucian Institutes are now opening in many foreign countries too.

The Walk

Guozijian Jie, the street running in front of the Confucian Temple and Imperial Academy, was once an enclosed area where, according to the message inscribed in six languages on the old stone tablets now stuck in the pavement, "military officials must dismount from their horses, and civil officials must descend from their sedan chairs." Such tablets appear in front of all Confucian temples in China.

Guozijian Jie is one of the only streets in Beijing where the decorative archways called *pailous* are still standing. The three-character inscription on the first *pailou* reads "Perfecting Virtue Street" as Guozijian Jie was known before such concepts became intolerable to the city fathers. The inscription on the second *pailou* more laconically reads "Guozijian." The wall on the south side of Guozijian Jie, indented for a length of about 15 meters (50 feet) in front of the temple entrance, functions as a spirit wall to protect the front entrance of the temple. Like most of the important buildings in Beijing, the temple lies on a north-south axis, with the principal buildings facing south.

A Mandarin's sedan chair with attendants, Beijing: 1870–80
Photographer: T. Child

Purchase your ticket and enter the Confucian Temple through the central **Gate of the First Teacher** (*Xianshi Men*) [先师门] built in the style of the Yuan dynasty, and formerly off limits to all mortals save the emperor; all others would enter by side gates. The first courtyard contains an important collection of 198 stone tablets inscribed with the names and home towns of 51,624 successful candidates in the capital examinations held during the Yuan, Ming and Qing dynasties. The earliest degree holder on record here passed his examination in 1313. During the Ming, however, most of the names of the Yuan graduates (the conquered) were filed off the stones and replaced with the names of Ming scholars (the conquerors); now only three Yuan steles remain. These tablets provide a permanent record of what is probably the most ancient old boy network in the world.

In a very long and narrow north-south corridor to the west of the second courtyard, to the left of the **Hall of Perfection** (*Dacheng Dian*) [大成殿], is another huge set of stone tablets, 189 in all. Carved on both sides by a single hand, these tablets preserve the texts of 13 Confucian classics (in 630,000 Chinese characters) in non-flammable, anti-bookworm and water-proof form; quite literally, a set of hard discs containing the core contents of Chinese civilization. By taking page-size rubbings from the tablets—actually the only way to read clearly and thus truly appreciate their contents—autographic texts can be reproduced and thus preserved in perpetuity. Artisans who specialized in carving calligraphy on hard stone could reproduce all the idiosyncrasies of calligraphic brush strokes, down to the single brush hair, with remarkable fidelity. This set of classics is a rare example of this skill.

Heading north through the first courtyard we come to the **Gate of Perfection** (*Dacheng Men*) [大成门], where you may inspect a set of ten ancient **stone drums** surrounded by scholarly controversy. These "drums," which resemble squat round garden seats, and which were carved at the behest of the Qianlong emperor in the 18th century, are copies of another earlier set of drums that date back over 2,500 years to the eighth century BCE. The inscriptions consist of poems on hunting, a favorite imperial

Round, black stones, inscribed with an ode to one of Emperor Sieun-Wang's hunting trips, are amongst China's oldest documents c. 800 BCE. The Illustrated London News, March 1873

pastime since ancient times (the Qing emperors had several hunting parks in the Peking suburbs). The poem on the first drum reads:

> Our chariots were strong,
> Our steeds alike swift,
> Our chariots were good
> Our steeds tall and sleek.
>
> A numerous array of nobles
> With a waving cloud of banners;
>
> The hinds and stags bounded on,
> The nobles in close pursuit.
> The strings of black bows resounded,
> The bows held ready for use,
> We pursued them over the hills,
> Coming on with audible roll.

"Place for competitive examinations at Pekin". The Illustrated London News, March 8, 1873

In a close packed mass,
The charioteers driving at full speed,
The hinds and stags hurried on,
We drew near upon the wide plain,
We pursued them through the forest,
Coming up one after the other
Shooting at the same time the wild boars.[5:1]

According to one source, the original set of drums was excavated in Shanxi province in the Tang dynasty, brought to Nanjing in the Song dynasty, shipped to Peking during the Jin dynasty and placed in the Confucian Temple here in the Yuan dynasty. In the late 1940s, the Nationalist government removed the original drums to Nanjing for safekeeping, and they are now in the collection of the Palace Museum, much of which is still stored in that Yangzi River port. The stone tablet mounted on the wall to the right (east) of the drums records a testimonial to Qianlong's good works in preserving these relics.

The courtyard beyond this gate, lined with ancient cypress trees, is the main courtyard of the temple. Of interest here are the eleven **tile-roofed chambers** (there are three more in the first courtyard), each housing a giant stone tablet resting on the back of a mythological tortoise, a symbol of stability, longevity and literacy (the patterns on the tortoise shell are said to resemble Chinese characters), literally a "rock of ages." The inscriptions on these tablets chronicle the military exploits of the Ming and Qing emperors at the apex of their power and glory.

Stroll north towards the **Hall of Perfection** (*Dacheng Dian*) [大成殿]; on the left of the paved path is a covered well that Qianlong dubbed the **Pool of Water for Inkstones** [硯水湖]. The idea was that anyone who drank this water would have sage thoughts flowing from his brush, but the well dried up years ago.

One of the gnarled trees here is known as "the cypress that struck the wicked official." In the Ming dynasty, a notoriously

(5:1) Translation by the sinologist S. W. Bushell, quoted in Mrs Archibald Little *Guide to Peking* (Tientsin: Tientsin Press, 1904), pp. 31–2.

A giant stone tablet (stele) rests on the back of a mythological tortoise
while the courtyard beyond this gate is lined with ancient trees

In the Confucian Temple, a few of the 198 steles listing the names of ancient scholars

cruel official named Yan Song was worshipping Confucius on behalf of the emperor one day, when a strong wind blew up and a branch of the tree knocked off his hat.

The Hall of Perfection, the principal building in the Confucian Temple, was the venue for the annual sacrifice to Confucius. In the centre of the hall is the altar where the spirit tablets of Confucius were placed during the rituals; the spirit tablets of his disciples were arranged to the side. In the early Ming dynasty, a statue of the sage stood here as the principal object of worship, but later in the dynasty it was replaced by a portrait and a spirit tablet. When the statue was later restored, it was decked out in imperial robes. Legend has it that when the Eight Allied Armies plundered Peking in 1900, the portrait of Confucius was stolen by German troops and eventually fell into the hands of a foreign sinophile, who humbly returned it to the temple. During the Cultural Revolution, the temple buildings were occupied by a printing school and a drama academy. Today copies of the ritual implements and musical instruments used in the ceremony are on display, including stone chimes and bronze hanging bells.

Signage concerning steles of Jinshi scholars

Another tale tells how the offering table used to hold the ritual vessels and sacrificial food presented to Confucius was at first quite low, as a way of emphasizing the elevated status of the sage. Then a Ming official pointed out that such a low table forced Confucius, or his spirit, to bend down uncomfortably when he was partaking of the sacrificial meal, and suggested that the table be made higher. Other improvements followed, such as replacing live animal sacrifices with offerings of cooked meat, and serving them up in porcelain bowls instead of wooden trenchers. At one point the floor of the hall was covered with coir matting, suggesting that the emperor may have performed the ritual barefooted, as in the Temple of Heaven during the Ming.

Behind the Hall of Great Perfection is the last courtyard of this complex, with its temple dedicated to Confucius' parents.

Make your way to the west side of the temple and look for the gate that leads to the next stop on our journey, the **Imperial Academy** [国子监]. The ticket for the Confucian Temple includes entrance to the Imperial Academy.

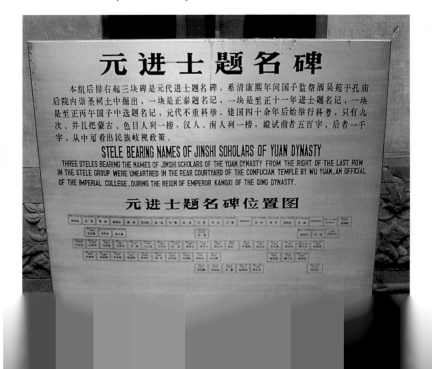

IMPERIAL ACADEMY [国子监]

In 1306, the Yuan dynasty court founded the *Guozi Xue* ("school for the sons of the state"), an institution where Mongol boys (the Yuan rulers were Mongols) studied the Chinese language and Chinese boys learned the Mongol language and martial arts. Built in the same year as the Confucian Temple next door, its location was determined by a traditional formula, "left temple, right academy," which does make sense if you are facing south. In 1313 an important library was installed here, an act repeated in the 20th century. Later that century, following the fall of the Yuan and the rise of the Ming dynasty, the school was upgraded to an institution of higher learning, with dormitories (located to the south of the main entrance) and a vegetable garden to supply the school kitchen. In 1462, the academy had more than 13,000 students. During the Yuan, Ming and Qing dynasties—from the

Plain grey roof tiles have replaced the former yellow tiles

Qing dynasty sun-dial

13th to the early 20th century—a total of more than 48,900 *jinshi* (the highest degree in the examination system, as well as the title accorded its holders) attended the school. Beginning in the Ming dynasty the academy enrolled students from the tributary states of Siam, Korea and Annam, as well as a number of Russians. In the Qing dynasty, one Manchu and one Chinese supervisor were especially assigned to take care of the Russian students.

A word about the roof tiles here and at the Confucian Temple. When the Ming Wanli emperor restored the buildings in 1600, he provided them all with green glazed roof tiles. The Qing Qianlong emperor raised the status of the buildings in 1737 when, as mentioned above, he replaced the green, standard-issue palace tiles with the imperial yellow. Later, however, the yellow tiles were replaced with plain grey. But in 1783, when Qianlong built the present version of the main structures, which was completed in 1784, he ordered yellow tiles once again.

The Walk

Enter and walk through the second courtyard with its **drum and bell towers** into the second large courtyard, where there is a massive **glazed-tile *pailou*** bearing an inscription from the Confucian *Analects*, "All under heaven benefit from the teachings." This particular *pailou* deeply impressed Henri Borel in 1909:

> *Suddenly a vivid melody resounds from this dead old transient mass; a glorious p'ai-lou of marble and porcelain with three arches, red, white, and yellow, lifts its song to the sky, filling the soul with joy, as if the immortality of life were revealed to it.*
>
> *This p'ai-lou is certainly the greatest wonder of all the stately arches of honor in Peking. In the midst of all the old decrepit ornamentation of the antique palace, behind these churchyard trees, wrinkled by the centuries, from the dull stillness of somber hues, this miraculous p'ai-lou shouts its joy into the blue sky, a gleam of eternal youth, of stainless beauty unassailable through the ages.*[5:2]

Beyond the *pailou* stands the Qianlong period **biyong** (1784), an elegant hall where the emperor would deliver an annual spring lecture based on a subject drawn from the Confucian classics. The rest of the year the building served as a venue for a

(5:2) Henri Borel *The New China: A Traveller's Impressions*
(London, T Fisher Unwin, 1912), p. 202.

"A glorious p'ai-lou of marble and porcelain with three arches, red, white, and yellow"

sort of graduate seminar for candidates preparing for the capital examination (*jinshi*), whose names, if they passed the test, would be recorded on the stone tablets in the Confucian Temple next door.

The term *biyong* dates back to the Western Zhou dynasty (11th century BCE–771 BCE) when the early kings convened discussions in a school of this name in the suburbs of the capital. The *biyong* of yore, like that in the Guozijian, sat in the middle of a round pool known as the **River of Crescents**, so named because four marble bridges divide the pool into four arcs. The water in the pool is supplied by two wells and a culvert, and flows into the pool through four dragon-head spigots of carved

The biyong *in the River of Crescents*

marble. The white marble balustrades encircling the building and the pool add a delicate touch to the bulkiness of the building.

The hall to the north of the *biyong* sheltered the throne on which the emperor would rest before presenting his lecture. Beyond it are a number of buildings formerly occupied by the officials in charge of the school.

Exit the Guozijian through the south gate, turn left, and walk east towards the north-south street in front of you (Yonghegong Da Jie). Cross the street and turn right and walk south for a few yards to the entrance to the Lama Temple, located on the east, or left, side of Yonghegong Da Jie.

LAMA TEMPLE [雍和宮]

Our third and final destination on this walk is the **Lama Temple**, or **Yonghe Gong**, one of the best preserved and maintained temples of any faith in China today. Before entering, however, rest assured that security here is much better now than it was in the 1920s when a famous guidebook gave the following warning:

> Visitors are advised not to venture alone into the maze of buildings with any of the lamas. In former days the Yung Ho Kung [Yonghe Gong] had a very bad reputation indeed for assaults on foreigners and sometimes the complete disappearance of solitary sightseers. . . . As recently as 1927 one of the authors was enticed into one of the buildings on the pretence of being shown some rare ornaments and nearly had the door closed on him. When he pulled out his revolver which from experience he had taken along, the lama at once let go of the door explaining that he had only closed it because he did not want the Head Lama to see him showing visitors around.[5:3]

I n 1694, the Kangxi emperor built a mansion on this site for his fourth son—and eventual successor—Prince Yong, the Yongzheng emperor-to-be. When the prince ascended the throne and moved into the Forbidden City in 1723, a number of buildings in the mansion were converted into a Lama temple, while the rest became a "detached palace," or *pied à terre*, for the emperor. Fire destroyed these quarters shortly afterwards. When Yongzheng rebuilt them he named the place Yonghe Gong (palace of peace and harmony; "yong" is the same "yong" in his reign title) and installed his notorious secret intelligence agency and hit squad here. Yongzheng died suddenly in Yuanmingyuan in 1735, and was replaced on the throne by his son Qianlong, who had been born in the mansion in 1711. Qianlong had his father's remains moved into the Yonghe Gong and ordered that the green roof tiles on all the major buildings be changed to imperial yellow within 15 days, thereby elevating their status to that of the buildings in the Imperial Palace. In 1744, at his mother's bidding, Qianlong formally consecrated the Yonghe

(5:3) L.C. Arlington and William Lewisohn *In Search of Old Peking* (Peking: Henri Vetch, 1935; reprinted by Oxford University Press, 1987), p. 195.

The Lama Temple, or Yonghe Gong, one of the best preserved and maintained temples in China today

Gong as a lamasery, enlarged the southern section, and invited 500 lamas from Mongolia to staff it. Several factors have been suggested as an explanation for this:

—Qianlong's mother wanted to atone for the deaths of all those murdered by her husband Yongzheng's secret agents;

—Qianlong wished to show his respect for his father's belief in the Lamaist religion;

—As a boy Qianlong had studied the Chinese, Manchu and Mongolian languages for 11 years in the company of a "Living Buddha" his age, who became his friend. When Qianlong became emperor, he wanted to provide this friend with a respectable place to practice his religion;

—Qianlong sought to conciliate the politically powerful Mongols and Tibetans by displaying a deep interest in their religion; and

—According to imperial usage, the birthplace of an emperor cannot be inhabited by his descendants or relatives.

The late 18th century was the golden age of the Lama Temple. Lamas of Tibetan, Mongolian and Manchu origin numbering in the thousands studied here alongside Chinese eunuch monks who served in the palace and at the imperial tombs. In the 19th and early 20th centuries, the monastic population diminished rapidly. The majority of monks who remained were Mongol, as they are today. Curiously, the chief lama of the temple was required to have had smallpox, because the sixth Panchen Lama died of this disease in Peking during the Qianlong reign.

After Qianlong's death, the five subsequent Qing emperors personally performed rituals in the Yonghe Gong three times a year: on Qianlong's birthday, on the anniversary of his death and immediately after carrying out the sacrifice at the Temple of Earth (*Ditan*).

During the Qing dynasty, the Lama Temple was closed to the public except for the annual performances of the "devil dances" (see page 271). In 1900 the Eight Allied Armies occupied the temple briefly, and during the early Republican era it came under the auspices of the Bureau of Mongolian and Tibetan Affairs. Poor management and corruption among the monks during the ensuing decades resulted in the loss of many precious relics.

Few foreign writers had favorable comments about the inhabitants of the Lama Temple. The following, written in 1888, is typical:

Lama Temple, October 6, 1860. No trace of this impressive structure is visible today

> These monks are Mongol Tartars of a very bad type, dirty and greedy of gain; and, moreover, are known to be grossly immoral. They are generally offensively insolent to all foreigners, many of whom have vainly endeavored to obtain access to the monastery—even the silver key, which is usually so powerful in China, often failing to unlock the inhospitable gates.[5:4]

Ten years later, according to another English visitor, the situation had hardly improved:

> Here twelve hundred lazy monks, filthy and vicious, are housed in the palace of a prince, who, on coming to the throne, gave them his dwelling and ordered them to be fed at his expense. So greedy are these recluses, whose first law is self-abnegation, and so indelicate is their mode of picking pockets, that a visitor always departed with the conviction that instead of visiting a house of prayer he had fallen into a den of thieves.[5:5]

(5:4) C.F. Gordon Cumming *Wanderings in China*
(Edinburgh and London, William Blackwood & Sons, 1888), p. 392.
(5:5) W.A.P. Martin *A Cycle of Cathay, or China,
South and North* (New York: Fleming H. Revell, 1897), p. 144.

Closeup of a prayer wheel

Lamaism, the principal religion of Tibet, Mongolia, Sikkim and Bhutan, has never been widely practiced or generally understood in China proper. Unlike Mahayana Buddhism, which underwent sinicization from the Han through the Tang dynasties, and became the dominant school of Chinese Buddhism, theologically speaking Lamaism is relatively free of Chinese content, although the Lama Temple itself has some of the features commonly found in Chinese Buddhist temples. And while a vast corpus of Mahayana scriptures has been translated into Chinese, the Lamaist canon (written in Tibetan) has not been, and there were few Han Chinese followers of the faith. On the other hand, Indian and Tibetan influence is evident in Chinese sculpture and architecture in Peking beginning in the Yuan dynasty; the Western Yellow Temple (*Xihuang Si*) and the Five Pagoda Temple (*Wuta Si*) are two such examples.

Before Buddhism entered Tibet from Nepal and China in the seventh century, Tibetans practiced an ancient shamanistic cult known as Bon. The advent of the faith supposedly took place when the first historical king of Tibet, Songtsen Gampo (608–650 CE), took two Buddhist princesses to be his wives, one from China and the other from Nepal, who converted him to their beliefs. Lamaism, which replaced and to some extent absorbed elements of Bon, consists of three strands of Indian Buddhism: Hinayana, the monastic teachings of the Buddha, Sakyamuni (fl. c. 500 BCE); Mahayana, a later popular elaboration of Hinayana; and Vajrayana, esoteric practices that make use of sounds, visual symbols and meditation.

Believers in Buddhism use a variety of means in their search for *nirvana*, an indescribable state in which the individual transcends pleasure and pain, life and death, by stepping beyond the cycle of death and rebirth.

The word "lama," from which the religion derives both its vernacular English and Chinese names, means 'guru' or teacher in Tibetan. But a lama is not necessarily a monk, and most monks are not lamas.

Several other curious customs were practiced here besides the well known devil dances. Once a year in winter, the monks in the Lama Temple cooked up huge cauldrons full of a sweet porridge of rice, fruit and nuts called *labazhou. La* refers to the twelfth month of the lunar calendar; *ba* means the eighth day of that month, and *zhou* means "gruel" or "porridge." Buddhists celebrate this day because it marks the Buddha's attainment of enlightenment, but there is another story behind it.

For six years before he attained nirvana, the Buddha lived a life of austerity. He had grown gaunt and his clothing was in tatters. One day he was sitting on a riverbank, begging for something to eat, when a girl cowherd brought him a bowl of fresh milk. After drinking it, the Buddha recovered his strength rapidly. Buddhists in ancient India celebrated this event by distributing food to the poor. In China Buddhists, and especially the monks in lamaseries, commemorated the day by preparing a pot of this delicious mush.

uring the Qing dynasty, all the ingredients, pots and serving bowls used to prepare the super stew in the Lama Temple were supplied by the imperial palace department of domestic affairs, which would also dispatch a supervisor and numerous underlings to help in the kitchen, a hall to the east of the **Hall of the Heavenly Kings** (*Tianwang Dian*) [天王殿]. One of the huge bronze pots used to cook the brew still stands in the courtyard before this hall today.

In the early Qing dynasty, the monks annually prepared a total of six vats of gruel with different ingredients. Three of the vats were made with huge dollops of yak butter combined with dried fruit. Of these, the contents of one were presented as offerings before all the supposedly-hungry Buddha images in the temple; the second went to the emperor and his ladies in the palace; and the third was decocted to Mongolian VIPs and high-ranking lamas. Bowl number four was made with butter but without the dry fruit, and went to some lucky civil and military officials, while the fifth vat, made of rice and red dates without butter, went to the hundreds (and sometimes thousands) of monks who lived in the Yonghe Gong. A smaller sixth pot of gruel had bits of mutton added to it. The custom as practiced in the Lama Temple ceased in 1937 at the start of the Japanese occupation of Peking, but local residents continue to make *labazhou* before the Spring Festival (Chinese New Year) for their friends and family.

Another noted delicacy of the Lama Temple was Dragon Whiskers Noodles, a form of superfine pasta made of wheat flour. At the summer solstice, the emperor sacrificed at the Temple of Earth (*Ditan*), just as he would do at the Temple of Heaven at the winter solstice. After completing the sacrifice, the emperor proceeded to the Yonghe Gong, where he placed stalks of freshly picked wheat before all of the Buddha images as a way of thanking them for having produced the harvest. Then he would remove his sacrificial robe, don a more mundane costume, and eat a bowl of cold Dragon Whiskers Noodles seasoned with sesame sauce before returning to the palace.

The Walk

The **Lama Temple** stands on a long north-south axis. The itinerary takes you through the main ceremonial buildings on the central axis and then back through the auxiliary halls, all of which contain interesting displays of Tibetan art, including many bronze images and *tanka* scroll paintings.

Purchase your ticket in the kiosk on the north side of the parking lot, a square flanked by three *pailous* and a spirit wall. The columns supporting these *pailous* were originally made of *nanmu*, a precious hardwood, but during the Japanese occupation (1937–45), troops removed them and shipped them to Japan. Since then they have been replaced with columns of concrete.

Head north through the long garden courtyard. To the east of here once stood the beehive-like complex of residences for the hundreds, and sometimes thousands, of monks who lived in the temple. Pass through the first gate into the first courtyard, which contains the standard Chinese-style drum and bell towers that are found in the front courtyards of Buddhist temples, Taoist monasteries and even the Forbidden City, two tall pavilions holding carved stone tablets, and a pair of bronze lions. The inscriptions on the stone tablets (in Chinese and Manchu on the left, Mongol and Tibetan on the right) are the text of Qianlong's essay "On Lamaism."

Following the pattern of most Chinese Buddhist temples, the first building in the complex is the **Hall of the Heavenly Kings** (*Tianwang Dian*) [天王殿], where an image of the Buddha of the future, Maitreya, in his manifestation as the Laughing Buddha, is guarded by four giant heavenly kings. Note how this quartet of subcontinental ruffians, responsible for keeping the peace in the four directions and throughout the four seasons, are engaged literally in stamping their feet to the north, in the direction of incarnations of evil. Guarding the rear entrance of this hall is a statue of Weida holding a scepter and facing north in the direction of the next courtyard. Weida's job is to protect the image of Sakyamuni located in the next hall.

The Gate of Proclamation of Peace on the Lama Temple's north-south axis, running parallel to Yonghegong Da Jie

The second courtyard contains a **square stone stele** inscribed on four sides, again in four different languages, with an essay by the Qianlong emperor. Here the sovereign outlines the origins of Lamaism, candidly explains how his own belief in the religion stems from a practical need to assuage the Mongols, and acknowledges the importance of the Lamaist practice of selecting "Living Buddhas" to act as spiritual leaders. The elaborate bronze incense burner to the north of the stele, manufactured in 1747 by the imperial foundry in the Forbidden City, is regarded as one of the finest works of art in the temple. It was designed to represent Mt. Sumeru (*Xumi Shan* in Chinese), a microcosm of the world. Its rare "eel green" color was achieved by adding several ancient bronzes from the imperial collection to the molten bronze when the piece was being cast.

This particular courtyard was the scene of pandemonium as witnessed by Osbert Sitwell, who along with a vast crowd visited the temple one winter day to see the "Devil-Dancers":

One of the handsome bronze lions that guard the Lama Temple

The Gate of Yonge Gong, announced in Manchu, Chinese, Tibetan and Mongol

> *The crowd of pleasure-seekers—for such, rather than devout, their demeanor showed them to be—behaved as though it were a Rugby-football scrum; . . . . Pent up for a while, just as we entered, it broke like a flood through the heavily guarded gates. Police with batons and thronged whips and long poles laid about them, but got as good as they gave.*[5:6]

The next hall, the **Yonghe Gong** (*Palace of Peace and Harmony*) [雍和宫], where Prince Yong held official audiences before he became the Yongzheng emperor, is now the main hall of the temple. The three presiding images here are the Buddha of the Past (left), the savior of the world before the birth of Sakyamuni; the Buddha of the Present (center), Sakyamuni himself; and the Buddha of the Future (right), here making his second appearance in the temple. Sakyamuni is attended by his two loyal disciples, the young Ananda and the older Kasyapa. Up against the walls are 18 statues of *lohan*, or arhats, Sakyamuni's disciples. The paintings on the rear walls depict Sakyamuni in his various manifestations. There is a fascinating clutter of ritual implements and containers crowded onto the tables before the images.

(5:6) Osbert Sitwell *Escape with Me! An Oriental Sketch-book* (New York, Harrison-Hilton Books, Inc., 1940), pp. 192–193.

The odd gold-plated four-head Guanyin (or Avalokitesvara, the Goddess of Mercy), made in Thailand and installed in the next courtyard in 1987, is no longer to be found here.

The next building is the **Hall of Eternal Divine Protection** (*Yongyou Dian*) [永佑殿], originally Prince Yong's residence. When the Yongzheng emperor died in 1735, his sarcophagus was laid to rest here before being buried in the western tombs of the Qing dynasty emperors. The Qing emperors are buried at two mausoleum complexes to the east and west of the capital; Puyi, the last emperor, who died in 1967, the only Qing emperor to be cremated., was moved to the western Qing tombs, in 1995. Later the images of the Amidha Buddha (center), a reincarnation of Tsong Khapa, the 14th century founder of the Yellow Sect of Tibetan Buddhism (right), and the Medicine Buddha (left), were

Note the splendid bronze incense burner

277

placed here. A set of the "eight precious objects" of Buddhism, each symbolic of one aspect of the Buddha's teachings, stands before each image.

The next hall, the most spacious in the Lama Temple, is the **Hall of the Wheel of the Law** (*Falun Dian*) [法论殿]. The elaborate roof is a combination of Tibetan and Chinese architectural elements. Here, five times a day, the resident lamas attended religious and philosophical lectures seated on the cushions set out in long rows. The large central statue is of Tsong Khapa, the founder of the Yellow Hat Sect and the creator of the Ganden Monastery in Tibet. Tsong Khapa was the teacher of the first Dalai and Panchen Lamas, whose successive incarnations have continued to act as the leaders of the sect. The Dalai and Panchen Lamas, like all other Living Buddhas, reveal themselves to the world in their childhood after undergoing a series of religious tests. The throne to the left of Tsong Khapa's image is set aside for the Dalai Lama, that to the right for the Panchen Lama. Both lamas conducted religious services here in 1954.

The main entrance to the Lama Temple

Right: *Falun Dian, Hall of the Wheel of the Law*

The elaborate wall paintings in the Hall of the Wheel of the Law depict events in the life of Sakyamuni, beginning with his birth from his mother's armpit. Here displayed in a plastic box at the north end of the hall is the large carved *nanmu* wood basin in which the infant Qianlong was bathed on his third day; it is often filled with donations by Chinese parents hoping to give birth to a "dragon" son. Another important artifact is the diorama of the **Mountain of Five Hundred Immortals** in a vertical case in the northern part of the hall. Five hundred is a magical number in the lore of India. The mountain itself is carved of hardwood, and the figures on the mountain are crafted of gold, silver, bronze, tin and iron. The walls of this hall are lined with stacks of cloth-covered Tibetan Buddhist scriptures printed from woodblocks on long rectangular sheets that are left unbound.

The hall in the next courtyard, the **Pavilion of Ten Thousand Happinesses** (*Wanfu Ge*) [万福阁], houses an awesome image of Maitreya, here making his third and final appearance in the Yonghe Gong. The statue is 26 meters (85 feet) tall, though one third of its length is below ground to prevent it from toppling over in the event of an earthquake.

The story goes that in 1750, Qianlong sent troops into Tibet to quell an uprising but they arrived long after order had been restored. To express his gratitude, the seventh Dalai Lama offered a gift of Buddhist images and other precious relics to the emperor. At the time, Qianlong had been concerned that the northern section of the Yonghe Gong, then occupied by a temple to the Goddess of Mercy, needed a tall building to prevent evil influences from the north from entering the premises, and he decided to erect a giant image there. Coincidentally, at this time the king of what is today Nepal was shipping a huge cedar trunk 2.7 meters (nine feet) in diameter from India to Tibet (the cedar is native to the Himalayas), and when the Dalai Lama learned of Qianlong's intentions, he traded a quantity of precious jewels for this tree and had it shipped to Peking; it took three years to reach its destination. Qianlong demolished the Goddess of Mercy temple occupying this spot in the northern section of the Yonghe Gong, laid the foundation for the new pavilion, had the huge

Andingmen c. 1861. The Gate of Serene Peace was just north of the Lama Temple

The Guinness Book of Records issued this certificate for the 26-meter (85 feet) tall Maitreya carving

image of Maitreya carved out of the tree trunk by artisans from the Forbidden City and built the pavilion around it only after it had been set on its base. The "10,000 happinesses" refer not only to Maitreya and his good works but to the innumerable Buddha images of clay, wood and stone found on the second and third stories of the pavilion. The huge standing image has earned a place in the Guinness Book of Records.

Pierre Loti, the romantic, sensitive French writer, described the pavilion after his visit in 1900:

> As we expected, this last temple... is only a repetition of the other two, save for an idol in the center, which, instead of being seated and life-sized, is colossal and standing....To see the face one must go close to the altars and look up between the rigid flowers and the incense-burners. It then looks like a Titanic mummy in its case, with a downcast look that makes one nervous. But on looking steadily, it exercises a sort of spell; one is hypnotized and held by that smile so impartially bestowed upon all this entourage of dying splendor, gold, dust, cold, twilight, ruins, and silence.[5:7]

The "flying bridges" that connect the Pavilion of Ten Thousand Happinesses to the two tall towers to the east and west are unique examples of a form of architecture seen only in frescos in the Dunhuang Caves dating back to the Han and Wei (fourth-sixth centuries) periods.

(5:7) Pierre Loti *The Last Days of Pekin*, (Boston, Little, Brown, and Co., 1902), p. 137.

The Pavillion of Ten Thousand Happinesses and the bridge connecting it to the Pavillion of Perpetual Peace on its west flank

The east tower, the **Pavilion of Everlasting Happiness** (*Yongkang Ge* [永康阁]), contains an immense temple-sized prayer wheel set in an octagonal pavilion and suspended on a steel axle that runs through the wheel from the floor to the ceiling. This is a jumbo version of the standing prayer wheels found in other places in the temple, and of the miniature hand-held and wind-driven prayer wheels common in Tibet. The significance of the prayer wheel can be explained in three ways: it symbolizes the "wheel of the law," the ceaseless cycle of death and rebirth; it symbolizes an altar where Sakyamuni is preaching—every time it is spun the Buddha's blessings absolve the spinner of all his sins; and it can confer instant merit on whoever turns it. As the interior of the prayer wheel is filled with Buddhist scriptures, one revolution of the wheel is equivalent to reciting all the scriptures contained inside. The giant prayer wheel was spun when the emperor came to worship Maitreya.

This late 20th-century stele lists the names of temple donors

The west tower, the **Pavilion of Perpetual Peace** (*Yansui Ge*) [延绥阁], houses a huge wooden automaton lotus with petals that open and close around a baby-faced seated image of Sakyamuni. This bit of carnival side-show ingenuity was originally a product of a Qing-dynasty palace workshop. Now restored, it still "performs" on certain holidays.

To the west of this courtyard there was once an interesting complex of buildings that were mostly dismantled after 1949 when the road beside the temple was widened. It contained a small **Hall of the Four Heavenly Kings** and shrines to the Goddess of Mercy and to Guan Di, the god of war and patron saint of the Qing dynasty. Here also were the headquarters of Yongzheng's shock troops, staffed by monks trained in the martial arts and other professional thugs. But Yongzheng cleverly disguised this organization as the office responsible for providing the imperial household with pet animals and insects, including fish, cicadas and dragonflies. It is said that for reasons of security these buildings were connected to Prince Yong's residence by an underground passageway. This area now contains a toilet for visitors.

Finally, to the north of the Pavilion of Ten Thousand Happinesses is a courtyard with three buildings in which were stored the masks, costumes and other paraphernalia used in the famous "devil dances" performed here once a year and revived in the 1980s. They are not open to the general public.

Having seen the giant Maitreya, all other Buddhas may seem anticlimactic, but don't overlook the image in the **Chamber of the Reflected Buddha** (*Zhaofo Lou*) [照佛楼] on the east side of the courtyard in front of the Pavilion of Ten Thousand Happinesses, and just southeast of the Pavilion of Everlasting Happiness. The Chamber was the private chapel of Qianlong's mother.

A legend surrounds the name of this place: when Sakyamuni, the original Buddha, was about to ascend to heaven to deliver a scripture to his mother, his disciples asked him to leave an image of himself in the mundane world. To satisfy their request, Sakyamuni invited an artist to paint his portrait. The painter, however, was unwilling to gaze directly upon the Buddha's countenance, and asked his subject to stand on the shore of a river so that he could paint his image from the reflection in the water. From then on, all images of Sakyamuni were copied from this reflected likeness. The image in this hall is cast of bronze, crafted and painted to resemble wood. The two accompanying figures are the young Ananda and aged Kasyapa. Note the intricate wooden carving decorating the niche, with its 99 golden dragons disporting in the waves—carving 100 dragons, a perfect sum, would have been considered presumptuous.

On the west side of this courtyard is the **Yamantaka Hall** (*Yamudaga Lou*) [雅木达嘎楼], now closed but once home to a grotesque image of a diety who, like Guan Di, was worshipped as a god of war. The Qing emperors kept weapons here that had been captured on military campaigns in the border districts as well as Tibetan weapons received by the court as tribute. These trophies are now on display in the Hall of the Altar of Ordination.

Working your way south you may stop in some of the less important buildings lining the sides of the courtyards that have been converted into museums containing excellent displays of Tibetan art.

To the west of the **Hall of the Wheel of the Law** is the **Hall of the Altar of Ordination** (*Jie Tai*) [戒台], where Qianlong celebrated his 70th birthday in the company of the sixth Panchen Lama. The wooden throne, set on a square three-tiered marble platform that nearly fills the room, was used by Qianlong when he took part in Lamaist rituals. Numerology inspired the unique design of this building: the upper storey is 3 x 3 bays, and the lower storey 5 x 5 bays. Both this and the Panchen Hall (see below) are museums today. The Hall of the Altar of Ordination contains a number of valuable relics associated with Qianlong and the later inhabitants of the temple, including ceramics, bronzes, cloisonné, ritual implements, snuff bottles, skull drums, trumpets, robes and hats worn by the Dalai Lama in each of the four seasons.

Across the courtyard to the east of the Hall of the Wheel of the Law is the **Panchen Hall** [斑阐楼], built to celebrate the sixth Panchen Lama's visit to Beijing in 1780. Identical in design with the Hall of the Altar of Ordination, it contains a throne and platform on which the Panchen Lama, the second most important figure in Tibetan Buddhism, sat when holding formal audiences. This throne had first been used by Qianlong when he sat atop the Altar of Abstinence. When Qianlong moved the throne to the Panchen Hall, he had a copy made for himself.

The buildings flanking the next courtyard to the south contain numerous interesting items. The east hall features a group of Tantric images veiled in yellow and white *hata*, or Tibetan scarves. These are the famous Joyful Buddhas, bronze gods and their consorts welded in sexual embrace. The guard might explain that they are kept under wraps because Chinese people cannot understand their esoteric significance: they are cosmic symbols of the unity of opposites. In the old days, the monks could be persuaded to lift these veils for a penny or two. One guidebook commented, "the figures are very crude indeed and, as a pornographic exhibition, disappointing." The two large stuffed bears on display here are believed to have been shot with bow and arrow by Qianlong in one of the imperial hunting parks in Manchuria.

The hall on the west side of the courtyard contains a number of Buddhas of lesser interest as well as *tankas*, or religious paintings. Unfortunately some of these displays are so poorly lit it is difficult to appreciate them.

The first of the **Four Study Halls** set around the four corners of the Yonghe Gong is, moving counter-clockwise, the **Hall of Mathematics** [数学殿] (northwest), where the monks learned astronomy and geography. There is an image of Tsong Khapa here, and some astronomical instruments. Proceeding counter clockwise we come to the **Hall of Explicating the Scriptures** [讲经殿] (southwest), the **Hall of Tantra** [密宗殿] (southeast), where the precepts of this branch of abstruse learning were studied, and the **Medicine Hall** [药师殿] (northeast) where traditional Tibetan medicine, with its vast pharmacopoeia of plant and animal drugs, was transmitted to the assembled monks. This brings us back to the Hall of the Heavenly Kings.

The Tibetan "devil dances"—a Peking "entertainment" mentioned by nearly all early foreign visitors as an event not to be missed—took place on the last day of the first lunar month and marked the conclusion of the Chinese New Year celebrations. If you happen to be in Beijing at this time of year, consult a lunar calendar as they are mentioned in the press only *after* they have taken place.

There are several interpretations of the significance of the devil dances. Scholars of Buddhism believe that they are an object lesson in vanquishing symbolic "devils," here referring to a particular sextet of human weaknesses: wine, sex, covetousness, anger, recklessness and killing. These evils are attributed to the followers of the Red Hat Sect of Lamaism, and hence the protagonist in the dances is the founder of the opposing Yellow Hat sect, Tsong Khapa.

Another traditional view, held primarily by Manchus in old Peking, is that the hero in the dances is the Kangxi emperor, who twice in his reign sent troops to Tibet in support of the Dalai

Lama. A third view popular among monks is that the devil dances are an ancient Indian form of ritual opera, symbolizing the union of opposites, or the resolution of contradictions, similar to the esoteric message conveyed by the Joyful Buddhas. Chinese scholars set little store on this theory. H.Y. Lowe, in his *Adventures of Wu*, described the dances in the 1930s:

> The front court of the temple would be crowded to capacity with sight-seers from early morning. To prevent mobbing of the inner precincts, where most of the temple's images and various religious and sacrificial attributes are kept . . . these are forbidden to the visitors of the day. By noon the dance party would come out to the front court for their mystic antics, performed in full public view.
>
> To get a vantage point to watch a Devil Dance is not an easy matter . . . in the center of the courtyard the attendant priests with the help of the police manage to make a clearing with the help of long whips and the tossing of handfuls of lime powder, and within the cordon thus thrown are seen the various characters of this colorful paganistic show, all clad in conventional garbs of rich embroideries though shabby from age and wearing big, top-heavy masks of various kinds, some representing the various Lamaist deities and others the devilish members with ugly faces, some with their hats decorated with facsimiles of human skulls and others brandishing short religious weapons and others wearing the heads of cows and deer.
>
> In the center is the figure of buttered dough painted red and carried ceremoniously on a small wooden stand—the embodiment of the devil. Chanting of Tibetan scriptures and playing of religious music, echoing drums and horns, accompany the mimicry subduing process. A few minutes later the entire group form into a procession and make for the gate of the temple where the dough figure is cut into pieces and burned, thus ending the Devil Dance.[5:8]

(5:8) H.Y. Lowe *The Adventures of Wu: The Life Cycle of a Peking Man* (Peking: The Peking Chronicle Press, 1940–41; Princeton University Press, 1983), II, pp. 188–9.

Another visitor, Osbert Sitwell, became more involved with the events:

> Here, surrounded by a mob of excited Chinese spectators,
> the Devil-Dancers, in carved and painted masks and rich,
> fantastic dresses, were whirling round and indulging in
> various significant antics to the sounds of gongs, drums,
> trumpets and stringed instruments.... Some [of the monks]
> were merely watching, or only joining in to the extent of
> uttering short, sharp yells at regular, rhythmic intervals, while
> those actually taking part squatted cross-legged on the floor,
> turning prayer-wheels and howling—so they gave out—for
> Universal Peace.... I hope it was for that purpose, because
> I subscribed a sum toward it. But I nearly withheld my
> pence, for, judging purely from the sound, I had my doubts
> concerning it at the time. And the course of events in the
> subsequent few years seems to have borne them out.[5:9]

Finally, Richard Wilhelm, the German sinologist and translator of the *I Ching* who lived in Peking in the 1920s, compared these devil dances to the gyrations of another sort of devil:

> When, to the accompaniment of a jazz band, the
> foreigners perform on hot summer nights their negro dances
> on the airy roof of the Hotel de Pekin, there is not a very great
> difference from the cult dances in the Yong Ho Kung [Yonghe
> Gong] Temple in the north of the town, according to Chinese
> ideas. There the Mongols dance in the winter and their
> Lamas are wrapped up and are masked, so that almost
> nothing of their original appearance can be seen and the horn
> and skull-drums beat the rhythm to it. Here, in the summer, the
> Europeans dance and their ladies are so décolletés that
> almost nothing of their original figure can be seen, and the
> negro saxophones and wooden rattles beat the rhythm. Of
> course their gods are different....[5:10]

(5:9) Osbert Sitwell *Escape with Me! An Oriental Sketch-book* (New York, Harrison-Hilton Books, Inc., 1940), pp. 192–193.
(5:10) Richard Wilhelm *The Soul of China* (London: Harcourt Brace, 1928), pp. 264–5.

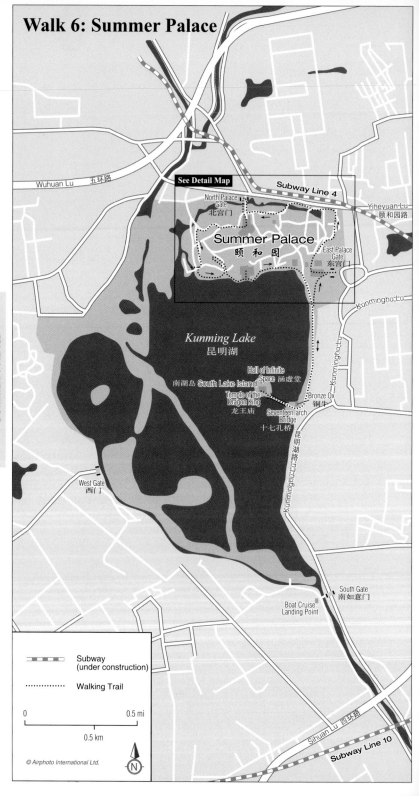

Walk 6: Summer Palace

Wuhuan Lu 五环路

Subway Line 4

See Detail Map

Yiheyuan-Lu 颐和园路

North Palace Gate 北宫门

Summer Palace
颐和园

East Palace Gate 东宫门

Kunminghu-Lu

Kunming Lake
昆明湖

Hall of Infinite Space 涵虚堂

南湖岛 **South Lake Island**

Temple of the Dragon King 龙王庙

Seventeen-arch Bridge 十七孔桥

Bronze Ox 铜牛

Kunminghu-Lu

West Gate 西门

昆明湖路

South Gate 南如意门

Boat Cruise Landing Point

Subway (under construction)

Walking Trail

0   0.5 mi

0.5 km

Sihuan Lu 四环路

Subway Line 10

© Airphoto International Ltd.

N

Walk · 6

Yihe Yuan, The Summer Palace

Duration

Not less than three hours.

Description

This walk holds many pleasant surprises in store. Beginning in the mid afternoon, we visit the **Summer Palace** ceremonial quarters; a garden-within-a-garden; and the relatively wild north side of the man-made mountain *before* exploring a huge abandoned **Lama Temple** and viewing **Kunming Lake** from the highest point in the park. We then view the famous **Marble Boat**, stroll along the **Long Corridor** and visit the other major buildings on the south face of the mountain before rounding the east shore of the lake and crossing the **Seventeen-arch Bridge** as the sun sets over the **Western Hills**. The idea is that as the crowds disperse you will have the Summer Palace almost to yourself—just as the emperors intended it to be.

This is perhaps the most physically demanding walk in this book, and includes a bit of hill climbing. It is suggested that you wear hiking boots or comfortable running or walking shoes. You may also want to bring a picnic lunch, as there is only one large, famous and timeworn restaurant on the premises, the Hall of Listening to the Orioles Sing (*Tingli Guan*), which is often a mob scene at meal times.

Starting Point

The East Palace Gate of the Summer Palace (Donggong Men) [东宫门].

How to Get There

Buses 332, 333, 346, 362, 374, 375. Bus 332 begins at the Beijing

Zoo. By bike it takes a little over an hour to get from Tiananmen Square to the Summer Palace, but traveling in this manner requires heroic courage and infantry lungs. A taxi from the Tiananmen Square to the Summer Palace should take 30–50 minutes, depending on traffic. You can also take the underground/light rail Line 13 (orange on the station maps) to the Wudaokou station, and take a taxi or bus 375 from there to the East Palace Gate. A subway line is now being built that extends to the Summer Palace.

Less traffic but a bumpier ride

How to Get Away

The same way you got here, as the walk begins and ends at the East Palace Gate.

> *"See the Summer Palace," said an old Pekinese, "and you will have seen all that China has to offer in art and architecture," and we found verily that not only in the tout ensemble but in every detail of porcelain roofs, canopied walks, marble caves, arched bridges, lotus ponds and rockeries, there was a plan apparent which showed that a whole empire had been drawn upon to furnish the scheme of this gigantic effort of man to combine the beauties of his craft with those of nature's own art.*[6:1]

Plan to begin your visit to the Summer Palace in the middle of the afternoon on a clear day (may luck be with you) in order to catch the sun setting over the Western Hills at the completion of the walk. By five to seven o'clock, depending on the season, the swarms of visitors begin to stream out of the palace. The Summer

(6:1) Paul Myron *Our Chinese Chances through Europe's War*, p. 87.

Palace is at its best in spring and summer, when the willows cast their shadows on Kunming Lake, and the resident staff and neighborhood folk come out to enjoy the cool breezes in the lakeside pavilions and take part in improvised performances of Peking opera and ballads. But on a clear day at any time of year, the sunset here is one of the most memorable sites in the city. When Kunming Lake freezes over in the winter—nowhere is it deeper than two meters (six feet)—skaters sometimes defy safety warnings and spin circles in the lip-cracking air. Though Beijing has four clearly demarcated seasons, spring and autumn are regretfully fleeting. The Summer Palace is a perfect place to spend these elusive days in *relative* solitude.

During the Qing dynasty there were five imperial gardens in the northwestern suburbs of Peking. The Manchus also built a

Yuanming Yuan, the Old Summer Palace, which was destroyed by European troops in 1860 and again in 1900 has never been reconstructed. Photographed by F. Beato, October 1860

summer getaway at Chengde (Jehol) and a palace in honor of the founding of the dynasty at Shenyang (formerly Mukden). The extant Summer Palace, or *Yihe Yuan* (**Garden of Peace and Harmony in Old Age**), was known in English as the **New Summer Palace** after it was rebuilt in the late 19th century. This was to distinguish it from the even more splendid *Yuanming Yuan*, the Old Summer Palace, which had been destroyed in 1860 and was never reconstructed.

The Chinese names of both of these gardens—*yuan* in fact means "garden," not palace—contain no references to summer; their English names derive from the fact that several of the Qing emperors, and the Empress Dowager Cixi, often spent all but the coldest months of the year living, working and taking their leisure in them. The *Yihe Yuan* was twice destroyed (in 1860 along with the Yuanming Yuan, and again in 1900) and twice rebuilt (1888 and 1902). It was renovated on both occasions in accordance with Cixi's instructions and by dint of her shrewdness in controlling the imperial purse. Its present incarnation still bears the personal stamp of this remarkable and notorious woman, and indeed much of her career as the virtual ruler of China was played out on these grounds. The Swedish art historian Osvald Siren wrote, in 1949:

> Tzu Hsi's [Cixi's] summer palace was the last product of a tradition that can be traced back to the beginning of our era, a last attempt to render in concrete form a phantasmagoria of art and Nature which might serve as a residence for the divine ruler of the Middle Kingdom. It is easy to understand that she loved this place above all others, and accounted the periods she spent here as the best in her life.[6:2]

All that remains of the original Yuanming Yuan, the **Garden of Perfection and Light**, are a few sadly crumbled stone columns and plinths, though local officials allowed the French to rebuild the maze in 1988. The three contiguous gardens designated by this name were built during the reigns of the Kangxi, Yongzheng and Qianlong emperors (grandfather, son and grandson) in the 17th and 18th centuries. One of its best-known sections, the well-

(6:2) Osvald Siren *The Gardens of China*, p. 134.

documented Western Buildings, was designed in Italian baroque style by the Jesuits Castiglione, Benoist (who was placed in charge of the fountains in 1747) and Sichelbarth, who, as some of the earliest foreign consultants in China, served the emperor at the Manchu court ca. 1730–50. The magnificent Yuanming Yuan was sacked and burnt in 1860 by the English and French troops, with unhappy local residents contributing to the plundering of its riches, but it has never been significantly restored or rebuilt. The idea of reconstructing it was proposed several times in recent decades. Conservative opinion holds that *not* rebuilding it provides a more persuasive historical lesson in the depredations of foreign imperialism as opposed to fabricating a shiny-new, or fake-old, park on the theme of imperial extravagance, with foreign cooperation. Now both imperialism and extravagance seem to have won the day.

Another noted garden in the western suburbs, now off limits to visitors, is **Jade Spring Mountain** (*Yuquan Shan*), with its fine porcelain pagoda, which stands about one and a half kilometers (one mile) to the west of **Longevity Hill**, the principal protruberance in the Summer Palace grounds. The Qianlong emperor built himself a cozy summer retreat here, and for centuries the water from its numerous springs was transported daily by donkey cart to the Forbidden City to fill the imperial teapots. Jade Spring water was so highly regarded that the emperors also had large jugs of it transported along with them on their journeys away from the capital. In Republican days Jade Spring Mountain was converted into a spa, and a soft-drink bottling plant was built nearby. Since its occupation after 1949 by the Chinese Air Force, it has served as a watering place for high ranking soldiers. Jade Spring Mountain is clearly visible immediately to the west of the Summer Palace.

According to an unsubstantiated but widely circulated report, it was on the southwest slope of Jade Spring Mountain that Mao's appointed successor, Lin Biao, was "liquidated with rocket launchers" after a failed coup. If this is true, Lin did not die in the officially publicized and carefully documented air crash in Inner

Mongolia when his plane ran out of fuel during his escape flight to the Soviet Union.[6:3] There is a military airstrip about one mile to the southwest of Jade Spring Mountain, one of several Peking airstrips used for civil aviation before 1949. But this airport, visible from some points in the Western Hills (Xiangshan Gongyuan), is curiously eliminated from all publicly available Beijing maps published since 1949, and does not even appear in a reconstructed 1947 map of Peking published in a 1988 historical atlas of the city. A satellite photograph of Beijing shows it in the light of day.

The earliest imperial parks in the western suburbs of Peking date back to the 12th century, when a Jin dynasty emperor built a summer retreat in the Western Hills. Around 1190 he diverted a stream from Jade Spring Mountain to provide water for the urban center to the southeast, and at the same time dredged a lake in the marshy land immediately south of Jug Hill, the molehill that eventually became today's Longevity Hill.

In the 13th century, the hydraulic engineer Guo Shoujing built canals from the Western Hills and nearby Changping Country for the purpose of supplying water to the Yuan dynasty capital, Khanbaligh (*Dadu* in Chinese), thus enabling the urban waterway system to be linked to the Grand Canal. The lake was considerably enlarged at this time.

Though the Ming emperors were not active as suburban garden builders, one of them erected a temple on Jug Hill. Centuries later, in 1750, Qianlong of the Qing dynasty enlarged this temple and the hill it stood on (using mud dredged from the marsh) on the occasion of his mother's 60th birthday. He called it the Temple of Mercy and Longevity; renamed Jug Mountain Longevity Mountain in her honor; and radically remodeled the lake with dykes and bridges based on the model of West Lake in Hangzhou, which he had admired on his half a dozen or so trips to the former capital of the Southern Song dynasty (1127–1279). He dubbed the new body of water Kunming Lake, after a pond of the same name in the Tang-dynasty capital of Chang'an where the

(6:3) Yao Ming-le *The Conspiracy and Murder of Mao's Heir*, pp. 160–3.

imperial navy had conducted war games. Qianlong built a fleet of boats for the same purpose on Kunming Lake, and recruited seamen from the coastal areas to man them. Construction of the new garden lasted 11 years; Qianlong called his creation the Garden of Pure Ripples.

Pagoda bridge at the Summer Palace, Beijing: 1870–80

Qianlong's formulaic birthday greeting to his mother is a model of modesty and hyperbole, scented with filial piety:

> *My Holy Mother, the Empress Dowager, Eminently Fortunate, Manifestly Merciful, Peaceful and Gracious, Sincerely Agreeable, Liberal and Venerable, is naturally kind and benevolent . . . meets all under Heaven with justice wherefore all within our realm honor her . . . .*
>
> *I, who have sometimes failed to be a filial son . . . have built this temple and assembled priests to chant their scriptures . . . hoping to requite my Mother's goodness . . . .*
>
> *Before the temple spreads a lake, sweet as koumiss [fermented mare's milk]. [My mother] is charmed with the scene, she clasps her hands in devotion, and her face beams with joy, a joy which comes partly from what I have done for her.*[6:4]

In 1860 the Garden of Pure Ripples was destroyed by the British and French armies as an afterthought to the looting and burning that took place at the Yuanming Yuan. This violence began as an act of revenge arising from disputes over trade, diplomacy and the question of the rights of foreigners residing in China. The troubled Qing dynasty remained without a suburban summer palace until 1873, when the Tongzhi emperor reached his majority and ascended the throne, whereupon the Empress

[6:4] Carroll Brown Malone *History of the Peking Summer Palaces Under the Ch'ing Dynasty*, pp. 110–111.

Dowager Cixi (Tongzhi's mother) began to carry out repairs to
provide herself with a place for her retirement. When Tongzhi died
in January 1875, the work came to a halt. In 1886, with the young
Guangxu, Cixi's nephew, now on the throne, Cixi procured funds
that had been earmarked for the Chinese navy and started work
again on the garden, which she renamed—one might say self-
indulgently—*Yihe Yuan*, The Garden of Peace and Harmony in
Old Age. The work was completed in 1891. She spent 24 million

The European racecourse in the Western Hills, June 1867

taels of silver on the project, equivalent at the time to
approximately six million British pounds. Cixi concentrated her
building efforts on the south face of Longevity Mountain, leaving
most of the structures on the north face untouched.

In 1900 Russian, British and Italian troops visited
destruction upon the Yihe Yuan in the wake of the Boxer Uprising
and siege of the Peking legations, and occupied the garden for a
year. But in 1902 Cixi returned from her temporary, self-enforced

exile in Xi'an and in the course of the next two years restored the palace, for the most part, as it stands today. As before, Cixi's sense of largesse was cramped by limited funds and she directed most of her attention to the structures on the south face of the mountain. In 1905, Cixi erected the tall walls that surround the palace and

installed a telephone as well as troops to guard her. Cixi died in
1908, and the Qing dynasty fell in 1911. In 1914, the
grounds were opened to the public for the first time,

*"A portion of the Emperor of China's Summer Palace, near
Pekin ". The Illustrated London News, April 27, 1861*

although the high price of admission was beyond the means of the average Peking family. Several years before this, visiting the Summer Palace presented other problems, as a cynical Henri Borel wrote in 1909:

> *The summer palace is no longer open daily to tourists: they damaged, and even robbed it. Visitors are admitted on two Wednesdays of each month [another contemporary source says on the 5th, 15th and 25th of each month], provided they can present an order for admission, applied for by their Legation [embassy]. These Wednesday visitors are solemnly received at the palace entrance by mandarins of the Wai-wu Pu, the Foreign Office, on behalf of the Chinese authorities. They thereby display the diplomatic courtesy that so often is the gilded shell of distrust and contempt. Their Chinese hosts, after conducting the visitors into a reception-room where tea and refreshments are offered, then show them over the palace, ostensibly to be of service to them by giving information, but in reality to watch them so that they may not do more damage or steal.[(6:5)]*

Major rebuilding and dredging of Kunming Lake was carried out in 1959–60, and in 1966, at the start of the Cultural Revolution, the Summer Palace was renamed People's Park. However, this name did not stick for long. Kunming Lake was drained and dredged again in 1991. This time the crews discovered European-style bullets that were conveniently attributed to the visit of the Eight Allied Armies, fragments of Qing dynasty porcelain that had once graced the palace and a large number of wedding rings. It was apparently an old Peking custom for married couples in the process of obtaining divorces to toss their wedding rings into Kunming Lake.

While the grand symmetry of the Forbidden City and the Temple of Heaven can be best appreciated from the air, the Summer Palace is a visual feast for earthbound strollers. As Juliet Bredon observed:

(6:5) Henri Borel *The New China: A Traveller's Impressions*, p. 228.

Unlike the Forbidden City, the Summer Palace is not a collection of remarkable buildings, impersonal, aloof, almost cold, which seem to look down contemptuously on the tiny ant-like humans that hurry between them. But what [Yihe Yuan] loses in magnificence, it gains in sympathy.[(6:6)]

When you are there, try not to forget that this lavish resort was designed for the pleasure of a single imperial person and his (or in Cixi's case, her) retinue, rather than for the millions of tourists who visit it every year.

The Yihe Yuan has several "controlled views"—pavilions, terraces and windows so designed that an observer standing in the proper place is presented with a framed picture of a fine landscape. The best example of this is the pavilion appropriately named **Strolling through Painted Scenery**, described below. Another such view is obtained from the terrace of the **Hall of Infinite Space** (*Hanxu Tang*) on the north shore of South Lake Island.

As in all gardens in China, the whole of the Summer Palace is greater than its parts. Many of the buildings, under close scrutiny, are tiresome Qing kitsch, a judgment that applies to the period furnishings as well as the several post-Mao paint jobs. But Thomas Cook's guide to China noted in 1917: "The [Summer Palace] might be garish in any other part of the world but it is a fairyland in China."

On the other hand, the relatively neglected section of the Summer Palace on the north side of Longevity Hill is especially quiet and very much off the beaten path. Here, where wheat, millet and vegetables were once grown to supply the imperial kitchen, one can feel pleasantly isolated from the hustle and bustle of Beijing.

(6:6) Juliet Bredon *Peking*, p. 297.

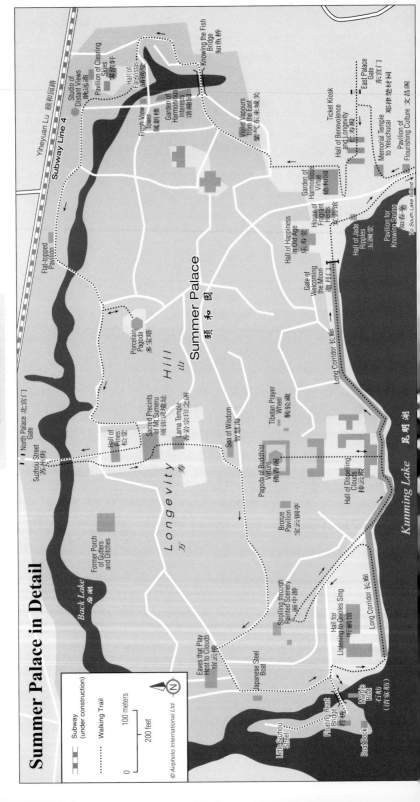

Summer Palace in Detail

SUMMER PALACE

Subway (under construction)

Walking Trail

0   100 meters

0   200 feet

© Airphoto International Ltd.

N

Yiheyuan Lu 颐和园路

Subway Line 4

Studio of Distant Views 眺远斋

Pavilion of Clearing Skies 霁清轩

Hall of Far Vistas 澄爽斋

Knowing the Fish Bridge 知鱼桥

Fresh View Tower 城新楼

Garden of Harmonious Interests 谐趣园

Violet Vapours from the East 紫气东来城关

East Palace Gate 东宫门

Ticket Kiosk

Hall of Benevolence and Longevity 仁寿殿

Garden of Harmonious Virtue 德和园

Memorial Temple to Yeluchucai 耶律楚材祠

Pavilion of Flourishing Culture 文昌阁

Flat-topped Pavilion

North Palace Gate 北宫门

House of Fragrant Herbs 益寿堂

Hall of Happiness in Old Age 乐寿堂

Hall of Jade Ripples 玉澜堂

Pavilion for Knowing Spring 知春亭

To South Lake Island

Porcelain Pagoda 多宝塔

Gate of Welcoming the Moon 邀月门

Summer Palace 颐和园

Longevity Hill 万寿山

Suzhou Street Gate

Hall of Pines 松堂

Sacred Precincts of Mt Sumeru 须弥灵境遗址

Lama Temple 善岩宗印之阁

Sea of Wisdom 智慧海

Tibetan Prayer Wheel 转轮藏

Long Corridor 长廊

Former Porch of Gutters and Ditches

Pagoda of Buddhist Virtue 佛香阁

Bronze Pavilion 宝云铜亭

Hall of Dispelling Clouds 排云殿

Suzhou Street 苏州街

Back Lake 后湖

Eaves that Play Host to Clouds 宿云檐

Strolling through Painted Scenery 画中游

Hall for Listening to Orioles Sing 听鹂馆

Long Corridor 长廊

Kunming Lake 昆明湖

Japanese Steel Boat

Little Suzhou Street

Floating Heart Bridge 荇桥

Marble Boat 石舫 (清晏舫)

BoatDock

The Walk

The Summer Palace contains more palaces, temples, *pailous*, summer houses, tea booths, terraces, pagodas, gazebos, studios, gardens, lakes, islands and bridges than can possibly be described here or visited in a single day. The walk that follows is a selection of highlights rather than a complete inventory.

Buy a ticket in the kiosk near the **East Palace Gate** (*Donggong Men*) [东宫门]. The East Palace Gate was the entrance most frequently used by foreigners after 1902, on the several occasions when they were invited to the Summer Palace to meet the Empress Dowager and the Guangxu Emperor. The slab of carved marble set in the staircase that leads up to the gate was moved here from the Yuanming Yuan, and the two impressive bronze lions that guard the gate date back to the days of Qianlong's Garden of Pure Ripples.

The emperors traveled to the Summer Palace from the city by an interesting water route. Boarding a boat immediately outside the northwest corner of the city walls, they would often make a two-day journey of it, stopping for the night, or for tea, at **Wanshou Si** [万寿寺], a temple to the west of today's **Purple Bamboo Park**, where there was a lock which made it necessary for the imperial entourage to change boats. Wanshou Si, which had been occupied by the People's Liberation Army since the Cultural Revolution, was entirely refurbished in the 1980s and is now home to the Beijing Art Museum, a municipal-level entity with a fine collection of Buddhist art and more. They continued their floating journey northwest on the still-extant canal that runs for 24 kilometers (9.15 miles) to the southernmost corner of Kunming Lake, whence they passed under a lovely camel-back bridge, called the **Bridge of Embroidered Ripples,** or less eloquently the **Hunchback Bridge**. They would then proceed to **South Lake Island** in the center of Kunming Lake, disembark, and offer a prayer of gratitude to the Dragon King for having ensured the safety of their journey by keeping the waters calm along the

Top: *East Palace Gate ticket kiosk*; Middle: *Marble dragon "carpet" salvaged from the Yuanming Yuan*; Bottom: *The Summer Palace museum, the Wenchang galleries*; Left: *One of the huge Lake Taihu stones that grace the Summer Palace*

307

way. Tourists boats now ply the watery route in season, and the Shangri-la Hotel, located near the Wanshou Si, can arrange luxury private sailings with food and entertainment on board.

Upon entering the East Palace Gate, proceed through a tree-shaded courtyard (where there is a map of the grounds) to the first *pailou*-style gate, **The Gate of Benevolence and Longevity** (Renshou Men) [仁寿门], which leads to a courtyard and the **Hall of Benevolence and Longevity** (*Renshou Dian*) [仁寿殿]. In addition to the huge, much-photographed, Lake Taihu stone, taken from the Shaoyuan Garden (presently on the campus of Beijing University), and much-rubbed bronze incense burners now encaged in wire, note the delicate stone carving on the gates and the stands on which the bronzes sit.

The large bronze image of a mythological beast standing in the center of the courtyard is a kylin, or chimera, or as it is popularly known in Chinese, a *si bu xiang*—a quadruple non-resemblance, for it defies biological classification with its deer horns, dragon head, lion tail and bovine hooves. Cast in the Qianlong period, the beast was one of a pair that survived the depredations at the Yuanming Yuan. The kylin is reputed to have the power of an imperial censor, to distinguish honesty and corruption in officials. Its placement before an imperial audience hall serves as a warning to those who report to the emperor.

Guides and guidebooks tell you that in the Hall of Benevolence and Longevity, burnt to the ground by foreign troops in 1860 and rebuilt in 1888, the young Guangxu Emperor held court while Aunt Cixi "ruled the empire from behind a curtain." While a similar curtain can be seen in both the Forbidden City and here in the Summer Palace, the phrase is actually a classical expression for a female regency; the expression originated with the Empress Wu Zetian of the Tang dynasty, a dragon lady in her own right.

In this hall Cixi also entertained members of the Peking foreign diplomatic corps on several occasions in the first years of the 20th century. Today, the refurbished building contains some authentic *objets d'art* from the late Qing dynasty, but in the interest of conservation, visitors are no longer allowed to enter. The small chambers to the side of the throne area were lounges where the emperor and the dowager rested when not holding court.

Bear right around the north of this hall and proceed to the group of buildings called the **Garden of Harmonious Virtue** (*Dehe Yuan*) [德和园], including a multi-tiered theater (similar to the one in the Forbidden City) that is said to be one of the finest old opera houses in China. Inside you may see young women dressed up as Manchu palace maidens. Their gowns are polyester, the colors loud, their hair ornaments preponderantly plastic, but their clumsy tall Manchu shoes (Manchu women did not bind their feet) are authentic in design. Cixi would attend operatic performances here beginning on the second day after her arrival in the garden. On her birthday, performances by her troupe of 380 singers, actors, musicians, costumers and stage hands would last for as long as eight days. Each of the three stages is equipped with pulleys and traps in the floors and ceilings that made it possible for performers dressed up as immortals to drop down from heaven and ghosts to emerge suddenly from the underworld.

From the theater we backtrack a few steps, circumnavigate the large semi-circular planter, where there is a well from which Cixi drank before fleeing Peking for Xi'an in 1900 after the Boxer Uprising. Turn left just after the well and proceed north through an alley that separates the theater (on your left) from a complex of buildings, formerly the imperial kitchen. Turn right at the end of the alley, continue on the path (don't climb the stairs) until you come to the fortress-like gate tower, dubbed **Violet Vapors from the East** (Ziqi Donglai Chengguan) [紫气东来城关], one of several such towers in the Summer Palace that were "manned" by eunuch guards responsible for keeping the peace. Pass through the tower and down the slope until you come to the **Garden of Harmonious Interests** (*Xiequ Yuan*) [谐趣园], first built in 1754 by Qianlong in imitation of a garden favored by his father, Yongzheng, in Wuxi, Jiangsu Province. The present reincarnation dates from the 1860s.

This multi-tiered theatre, in the Garden of Harmonious Virtue, was popular with Cixi

Enter the garden to your right and bear right again to the small lake, which will be on your left. The "interests" referred to in the garden's name are:

1. *Water*: in the northwest corner of the garden, there is a stepped fountain with nine levels that produces gurgling background music, a highly desirable sound effect in a northern Chinese garden. The water is the overspill from the lakes to the north of Longevity Mountain, where the water level is more than two meters (seven feet) higher than that in this garden.

2. *Buildings*: one of the several halls built in the southern style, the **Fresh View Tower** (Shuxin Lou) [属新楼] (to the west of the pond) appears to have two stories when viewed from inside the garden, but only one when seen from outside.

3. *Bridges*: can you count five bridges in this compact garden? The longest one, **Knowing the Fish Bridge** (Zhiyu Qiao) [知鱼桥] stretches diagonally across the pond, and has a *pailou* named after a famous Taoist anecdote that is a fine example of Zen irreverence:

Suzhou Jie, or more prosaically Back Lake

The philosopher Zhuangzi (Chuang Tzu) was once standing on a bridge over the Hao River with his disciple Huizi.

Zhuangzi: Sir, do you see how the fish are enjoying themselves?

Huizi: You, sir, are not a fish. How dare you claim to know that the fish are enjoying themselves?

Zhuangzi: But sir, since you are not me, how do you know that I *don't* know the fish are enjoying themselves?

Huizi: Indeed I am not you, and cannot know what you are thinking. But I know that you are not a fish, and thus you cannot know how happy they are.

Zhuangzi: Do you recall when we began this discussion, you asked me how I knew the fish were happy? By saying that, you implied that I had this knowledge. Actually, I know that the fish are happy by virtue of the fact that I am now standing on the bridge over the River Hao.

We will come across another reference to the Hao River in another garden-within-a-garden in Beihai Park.

Walk counter-clockwise three-quarters of the way around the small lake, climb the steps behind the **Hall of Far Vistas** (Hanyuan

Tang) [涵远堂] and wind your way northwest past the walled compound of the **Pavilion of Clearing Skies** (*Jiqing Xuan*) [霁清轩], where Reginald Johnston, English tutor, tennis and bicycle instructor, and political advisor to the last emperor, Puyi, lived in 1919 after he was made the nominal supervisor of the Summer Palace and Jade Spring Mountain. In the 1980s, the residential compound was leased to the hotel group Club Med for a few years. You can try to talk your way in for a look around this day-dreamy place. Johnston's three-room flat on the top of the hill is worth a visit. Descend from here to the north shore of the easternmost section of the **Back Lake (Houhu)** [后湖], a large man-made extension of the waterways on the other side of the mountain.

The big hall on the right, the first that you come to, set against the north wall of the Summer Palace and facing north is the **Studio of Distant Views** (*Tiaoyuan Zhai*) [眺远斋], which overlooks the road that leads to the Western Hills and beyond. In her heyday, Cixi would arrange for command performances in the road by the stilt-walkers and other performing troupes passing by here on their way to the annual Taoist temple fair at Miaofeng Mountain.

Continue west on the smaller path along the north shore of the lake until you come to the second bridge that spans the lake. On your way you will pass a uniquely designed pavilion with a rectangular flat roof contiguous with another hexagonal pavilion. Cross this bridge, and when the path reaches a junction, turn right and walk about 120 steps to the first path on the left. Follow the path up and around in the direction of the **Porcelain Pagoda (Duobao Ta)** [多宝塔], an immaculate relic from the Qianlong period, despite the fact that a few of the original Buddhas are missing. The crescent-shaped promontory here, scattered with ruins and the plinths of buildings no longer extant, offers a fine view of the Western Hills.

Wind your way back down the mountain and follow the path west until you get to the **Hall of Pines** (*Song Tang*) [松堂], a large square patio at the foot of the Lama Temple. From here you can visit Suzhou Street (Suzhou Jie) [苏州街] (extra ticket required).

Rebuilt and opened for business in 1990, this area on the shores of the rear lakes is an idyllic reconstruction of the canals and shops of Suzhou, the Venice of China. Suzhou Street was a Qianlong brainstorm, one of the several souvenirs of his excursions to southern China that he brought back to Peking. Here the cloistered denizens of the palace would gather to enjoy a taste of the outside world. Eunuchs and palace maidens played the role of shopkeepers, hawking their wares at the top of their squeaky voices as the Son of Heaven walked by. The shops were fully stocked with luxury goods imported from southern China at great expense. The eunuch Li Lianying revived this entertainment in the late 19th century to relieve the boredom of the Empress Dowager Cixi. The shops today range from two-storey teahouses, wine shops and traditional Chinese snack bars to millinery shops, shoe makers, kite sellers and tobacconists. The young merchants are dressed in (polyester) traditional merchants' costumes. Beware that the pavement lining the water is treacherously narrow in places. This is wonderful place to break up the afternoon's trek and rest for a few moments with a cup of tea.

To the southwest of Suzhou Street further up the mountain here once stood a place called the **Porch of Gutters and Ditches**, described in *In Search of Old Peking*:

> There are numerous small water-courses running round and under this building. The floors are made of glass through which fish may be seen darting about, something after the style of the glass-boats on the Californian coast.[6:7]

But Chinese sources suggest that there was little left of this "Porch" even before *In Search of Old Peking* was written in the 1930s, and only its ruined foundation remains today.

Take the steps up to the vast **Lama Temple** (Xiangyan Zongyin Zhige) [香岩宗印之阁], looking as if it were pinned to the north face of the mountain and preventing it from collapsing, dates from the 18th century. In 1752 Qianlong sent a delegation of four—two officials, a painter and a draughtsman—to the Samye

(6:7) L.C. Arlington and William Lewisohn *In Search of Old Peking*, p. 290.

Top, Bottom: *The Hall of Pines, the former sacred precincts of Mount Sumeru and the Lama Temple on the north face of Longevity Hill*

Right: *Wisdom Temple high above Kunming Lake*

Monastery in Tibet, and upon their return, had them install smaller versions of the monastery here and at the **Mountain Retreat for Avoiding Summer Heat** (*Bishu Shanzhuang*) in Chengde (formerly Jehol), some 250 kilometers (155 miles) north of Beijing.

Much of the temple, including the building called the **Sacred Precincts of Mount Sumeru** (*Xumi Lingjing Zhi*) [须弥灵竟址], which once occupied the large courtyard at the lowest level of the temple, was destroyed in 1860 by English and French armies. What remains clinging to the hill today are the results of repairs made from 1888 to 1903 during Cixi's heyday. Buddhist images that had been brought here at that time from a temple Qianlong had built elsewhere for his mother were ravaged by Red Guards during the Cultural Revolution.

Nothing inside the temples on the north side of the hill is of much interest—most of the buildings are sealed up anyway—so after exploring the temple briefly you can follow the rather steep path leading up from the highest point in the southwest corner (facing the mountain, the upper right hand corner) of the temple complex to the **Sea of Wisdom Temple** (*Zhihui Hai*) [智慧海], the treasure-chest of a shrine covered entirely with green and yellow glazed tiles. The Sea of Wisdom Temple is built of brick and stone, and thus only suffered minor cosmetic defacement when the Summer Palace was occupied by foreign troops in 1900; for target practice they decapitated many of the 1,008 molded Buddha images in their niches. David Kidd, an American who lived in a spacious apartment in the north gatehouse of the Summer Palace between 1946 and 1950, mentions in his delightful memoir, *Peking Story*, that the three bronze Tibetan Buddhas originally in the Sea of Wisdom, one of them two stories tall, were victims of Red Guard fury in the Cultural Revolution.[6:8]

(6:8) David Kidd, *Peking Story: The Last Days of Old Peking*, pp. 70–80.
(6:9) Gilbert Collins *Extreme Oriental Mixture*, p. 96.
(6:10) John Dewey and Alice Chipman Dewey *Letters from China and Japan*, pp. 205–206.

An earlier visitor, Gilbert Collins of the British Navy, remarkably considerate of later tourists' interests, and somewhat full of hot air, found the Sea of Wisdom to be

> "…one of the most beautiful pieces of architecture I ever saw. Unfortunately, by reason of its inaccessible position one cannot snap it. My photograph …was disappointing in the extreme…. I mention this for the benefit of future travelers. The guide-book fails here, as it so often fails over a point of real importance. It doesn't so much as hint to the tourist what he will require to bring with him if he wants to secure a fair and square photograph of the most beautiful building on Wan Shou Shan. So I am supplying the deficiency. The tourist will require to bring a balloon with him. A scaffold would do in a pinch, but it would have to be a pretty tall one, and a balloon would be handier, anyway, and easier to pack.(6:9)

A still earlier visitor, the American educator and philosopher John Dewey, visited the palace in 1919 with his wife. In a letter to their children, they described the site as follows:

> Yesterday we went to the Western Hills where are the things you see in the pictures, including the stone boat, the base of which is really marble and as fine as the pictures. But all the rest of it is just theatrical fake, more or less peeling off at that. However, it is as wonderful as it is cracked up to be, and in some ways more systematic than Versailles, which is what you naturally compare it to. The finest thing architecturally is a Buddhist temple with big tiles [the Sea of Wisdom?], each of which has a Buddha on—for further details see movie or something…. The Manchu family seems to own the thing yet, and charge a big sum, or rather several sums, a la Niagara Falls, to get about—another evidence that China needs another revolution, or rather a revolution, the first one having got rid of a dynasty and left… a lot of corrupt governors in charge of chaos….(6:10)

Walk to the back of The Sea of Wisdom Temple. From here, the highest point in the Summer Palace, you obtain your first panoramic view of Kunming Lake and the surrounding countryside. On a clear day, you can see the skyscrapers of

Panoramic view of Kunming Lake and the surrounding countryside. On a clear day, you can see the skyscrapers of Beijing to the east

Beijing, as well as obtain a fine view of the Western Hills. Stake out a pavilion nearby for a picnic or a rest. If you are in a hurry, you may descend the south face of the mountain from here, skirting the giant pagoda (*Foxiang Ge*, the **Pagoda of Buddhist Virtue**) [佛香阁], and ending up in the **Hall of Dispelling Clouds** (Paiyun Dian) [排云殿] that encroaches onto the shore of the lake. Otherwise continue on the walk by working your way down the mountain by following the path that heads directly west, bearing right at the first intersection and left at the second until you descend to water level again.

By taking a left at the first intersection, a short climb brings you to the pavilion named **Strolling through Painted Scenery** (Huazhong You) [画中游], which offers a fine controlled view of **Jade Spring Mountain** (*Yuquan Shan*) [玉泉山].

Continuing your descent, within minutes you will come to an intersection where you will turn left and walk to the bottom of the

Cross the bridge over the inlet called Little Suzhou Creek and you have an excellent view of the lake and the famous Marble Boat

steps to another fortress gate, the **Eaves that Play Host to Clouds** (*Suyunyan*) [宿云檐], which rises up to your right. The area we are passing through is **Little Suzhou Street** and dates back to Qianlong times. On your right the lovely covered bridge, called **Floating-heart** (a water plant) **Bridge** (*Xing Qiao*) [荇桥], is another quaint reminder of that Yangtze-delta town. Cross the bridge over the inlet called Little Suzhou Creek. From here you can get an excellent view of the lake and the famous Marble Boat, which does not float.

It is a well-known story that Cixi, in carrying out a "pious fraud," used funds earmarked for the Chinese navy to renovate the Summer Palace in 1888, but only after her other sources of garden-building money dried up. Offering an anodyne to the endless harangues about the Old Buddha's evil ways, David Kidd wrote in her defense:

> *Chinese and Western historians [who] talk about it in tones of outrage . . . do not see that this navy, had it been built, today would be lying at the bottom of the China Sea, sunk on its first encounter with a foreign power, while the empress's extravagance still stands, a delight to all who see it . . . .*[6:11]

Admiral Collins also found a way to justify her actions:

> *The Chinese Navy of modern times has never really justified its existence; the only hostile act it ever managed to commit was to take that fearful thrashing from Japan in 1894... I have inspected samples of the Chinese Navy from time to time. It was always washing-day aboard when I arrived. Even when I didn't go aboard I could see from afar that it was washing-day . . .*[6:12]

The notorious yet thoroughly innocuous **Marble Boat** (*Qingyan Fang* or *Shi fang* 清宴舫 / 石舫)—only the hull is marble—was first built on this spot in 1755 by Qianlong (not by Cixi, as is often stated), who fitted it out with a Chinese-style naval superstructure. As a "ship of state" it symbolized the stability of the dynasty, yet as Qianlong reasoned in an essay on the subject: "Water (the people) keeps the boat (the empire) afloat; yet it can cause the boat to sink as well." In the Ming dynasty, this

(6:11) David Kidd *Peking Story*, p. 77.
(6:12) Gilbert Collins *Extreme Oriental Mixture*, p. 92.

had been the site of a Buddhist temple, where live animals were set free in an annual ritual for obtaining merit. Qianlong and his mother would perform this act of piety here with birds and fish. All the sinkable bits of Qianlong's ship were scuttled by the French and English armies in 1860, but not the marble hull.

Cixi rebuilt and modernized the boat in 1893, adding the (steam-driven) *faux* paddlewheels and a Western-style cabin and superstructure. Here she installed a large mirror before which she would sit on rainy days, sipping tea and gazing at the mirror, which reflected the image of the lake as if it were a painted scroll, thus producing the illusion that she was sailing in the midst of a vast ocean. She could also listen to the trickle of rain draining from the boat into the lake through the mouths of the four marble dragons chaperoning it through the seas. In 1903 a second storey with stained-glass windows was added to the superstructure, the model for the present refurbishment, and in Republican days (1911–49) it was open to the public as a European-style teahouse that was frequented by the Chinese middle classes.

Admiral Collins had the following to say about the boat. Due to his qualifications we quote his comments at length:

> *I regarded it and still regard it still as a sidelight on the character of the Empress Dowager. She had raised that appropriation-in-aid to build a modern navy, and she appears to have determined there should be at least one modern naval feature about the use to which she put the money. And this is it. The marble boat of Wan Shou Shan rests on the bottom of the lake and never rested anywhere else; it is moored to the bank with cement and in the circumstances can't be unmoored, and if it could be unmoored, all the tugs in the world couldn't heave it away off shore so as to get it there in one piece, and I'm practically certain it wouldn't float even then. Never mind, it's a boat. A reasonably up-to-date kind of boat with a pair of paddle-wheels; and the whole structure proves to my satisfaction that Dowager Empress Tzu Hsi kept, somewhere or other deep down inside of her, a conscience. Or a sense of humor at all events....* [6:13]

(6:13) Gilbert Collins *Extreme Oriental Mixture*, p. 98.

From the Pagoda of Buddhist Virtue, the Hall of Dispelling Clouds and the lake shore

Retrace your steps over the **Floating-heart Bridge** and continue south until you come to the western end of the **Long Corridor** (*Chang Lang*) [长廊], erected by the Qianlong emperor to enable his mother to enjoy the scenery on the lake protected from the rain. Burned to the ground by foreign troops in 1860, it was reconstructed in 1888, and restored by the Japanese during their occupation of Peiping (1937–45), and then restored again by the communists in 1959 and again in the early 1980s. The corridor links up the many buildings scattered along the south face of the

mountain, and frames the **Hall of Dispelling Clouds** (*Paiyun Dian*) [排云殿] like a pair of lengthy neatly plucked eyebrows as it skirts the delicately arched contour of the lake. In tourist season both railings of the Long Corridor are normally full up with 2 x 728 meters of tourists munching or resting or just looking up. Inspired by a bad case of *horror vacui*, the overhead beams are decorated with a total of 14,000 Chinese landscapes and scenes from Chinese myths, fiction, drama and the lives of famous people, for the most part rather mechanically painted by art academy students. The large painted panels in the four midway gazebos display brushwork of a much higher quality. During the Cultural Revolution, all the bourgeoisie reactionary figures and scenes in the Long Corridor were painted over with white paint in anticipation of replacing them with images of revolutionary heroes, but this was not carried out.

As you proceed east along the corridor (or alongside it if the human traffic is too heavy), the first set of buildings on your left up on the hill is the **Hall for Listening to Orioles Sing** (*Tingli Guan*) [听鹂馆], formerly a small-scale concert hall that Cixi built in 1892 especially for ballad performances. It now houses a large tourist restaurant of the same name that serves dishes based on imperial palace cuisine.

During the Qing dynasty, thoroughbred carp destined for the imperial dining table were raised in the Summer Palace lakes. As late as the early 1950s, a huge grass carp, a favorite Chinese fish, with a gold ring inscribed with the Empress Dowager's name clipped to its gills, was allegedly discovered in the lake, and in recent years a privileged few have continued to savor the scions of this imperial school.

Continuing along the Long Corridor you come to the **Hall of Dispelling Clouds** (*Paiyun Dian*) [排云殿] complex and its crowning glory, the **Pagoda of Buddhist Virtue** (*Foxiang Ge*) [佛香阁], one of the tallest wooden buildings in China. As stated above, this is the site on which Qianlong chose to build a temple for his mother's 60th birthday in 1750. Here too, in 1894, Cixi celebrated her own 60th birthday by rebuilding the entire complex at immense cost (5.4 million ounces of silver). To decorate the Hall of Benevolence and Longevity (near the Summer Palace entrance) alone, a tent of silk was erected comprised of 17,500 bolts of silk, which if laid end to end would have extended 230 kilometers (144 miles). As the contents of the Hall of Dispelling Clouds were sacked in 1900, the present display here consists mostly of gifts Cixi received on her 70th birthday in 1904.

You can now climb to the top of the pagoda, rebuilt in its present form in 1891–94, for a glance at the lake, but if you made it up to the Sea of Wisdom when exploring the other side of the hill, you have already enjoyed the superb view from the top. On the first and 15th day of the first lunar month, Cixi would burn incense in this 41-meter (135-foot)-tall pagoda and make obeisance to the huge Buddha image housed here. The Buddha with 1,000 eyes and 1,000 hands now on display on the first interior level is not the original inhabitant of the pagoda, but was discovered in a dusty store room in a temple near the Rear Lakes, and moved here to fill the void. The second storey houses three Buddha images dating from the Qianlong period. To the west of the pagoda is the famous **Bronze Pavilion** (Baoyun Tongting) [宝云铜亭], weighing 207 tons, cast by the lost wax method by the Jesuits in Qianlong's day. Ten doors and windows from the pavilion were spirited away in 1900, and only discovered in Paris in 1992. One year later, the American insurance company AIG purchased them for more than half a million U.S. dollars and restored them to their rightful place in the Summer Palace. The origins of the Bronze Pavilion proved puzzling to the visitor Gilbert Collins:

> A little way down from the crest you come upon a pagoda twenty feet high and exactly copying the ornate roofs and bristling eaves of a hundred and one pagodas elsewhere on the hill; the only difference, this one is all solid bronze. It must not be charged as an item of extravagance against Tzu Hsi [Cixi], however, for this pagoda formed part of the embellishments of the original Summer Palace. . . . I cannot at all conceive how the pagoda was originally erected. The hoisting into position must have been an operation of prime magnitude, and it to me it is a matter of prime mystery—one of those riddles like Stonehenge, which are usually explained away with a long ramp of earth, and rollers, and unlimited human beasts of burden. Even when I have postulated all this the bronze pagoda of the New Summer Palace leaves me skeptic and unsatisfied. Yet there it undoubtedly is.[6.14]

(6:14) Gilbert Collins. *Extreme Oriental Mixture*, p. 97.

Top: *The Hall of Dispelling Clouds towers above the Marble Boat*

Above: *The east section of the Long Corridor*

Right: *At the Pagoda of Buddhist Virtue, the Hall of Dispelling Clouds*

Facing page: *The freshly painted West Pailou at the entrance to the Hall of Dispelling Clouds*

To the east of the pavilion is a group of buildings centered around a **Tibetan Prayer Wheel** (Zhuanlun Zang) [转轮藏].

We now proceed along the east section of the Long Corridor. On your left you will pass several self-contained residential courtyards closed to the casual public, but in recent years rented out to foreign companies, as they had been before 1949. The painter Zhang Daqian stayed here at one time, as did Chiang Kai-shek, although his visit only lasted three days. Two other groups of courtyards that have been converted into hotels flank the Hall of Dispelling Clouds. During the Cultural Revolution, Peng Zhen, the mayor of Beijing, and Chairman Mao's wife Jiang Qing lived here in the Summer Palace. Madame Jiang supposedly rode her pony up and down the Long Corridor on rainy days, but as the Summer Palace was closed to the public then, evidence for this is hard to come by.

The end of the east section of the Long Corridor is marked by the **Gate of Welcoming the Moon** (*Yaoyue Men*) [邀月门], after which the corridor takes a sharp turn to the right and cleaves to the shore of the lake for a few meters from where in summer, a dense crop of lotuses can be viewed through the curiously shaped windows. These pedigree lotuses on view today were transplanted from the Chengde Retreat for Avoiding Summer Heat in 1976. Presumably the former stock had died of neglect during the Cultural Revolution. Here too is the dock, marked by two tall flagpoles, where Cixi landed after her journey from the city. George Kates (né Katz) records an exquisite vignette of imperial refinement set in these precincts:

> *I once heard a story of how, during the season of the lotus, the Empress had her tea perfumed in this place. The large rose flowers, when first they come to bloom, close their petals each night, to open them the next morning. At dusk, therefore, ladies-in-waiting, from shallow skiffs that could make headway through the thick round leaves, deftly placed within them little packages of tea wrapped in soft paper. These were left during the night in the hearts of the flowers, to be gathered when they opened at dawn again. They then*

would be delicately perfumed with that scent so difficult to describe, and yet so fragrant that it almost may be said to represent by itself the dignity, display and beauty of the Chinese ideal of life.[(6:15)]

The adjacent courtyard belongs to the **Hall of Happiness in Old Age** (*Leshou Tang*) [乐寿堂], Cixi's private residence, where she was served by a staff of 48.

The largest of the gewgaws on display in the courtyard is a giant hunk of gnarled Taihu stone that Qianlong was only able to transport here by having the doorway to the courtyard broken down, an act that incited his mother's displeasure because she believed that destroying anything in the palace was inauspicious. The rock is inscribed with Qianlong's own calligraphy and that of several other famous scholars of the day. In this courtyard Cixi planted her favorite flowers, movingly described by Juliet Bredon:

Oleanders, pink as painted lips, pomegranates, red as wounds, and chrysanthemums, like groups of ambassadors in full dress, stood outside the latticed windows of the Dowager's own pavilions.[(6:16)]

In 1903, despite Cixi's initial objections, a German firm installed electric lights in the Hall of Happiness in Old Age, and a generator to power them. It is said that Li Lianying (1848–1917), the immensely wealthy (according to one source, three million taels in gold bullion, or about US$50 million in today's money, was found under his bed after his death) and corrupt eunuch who for years was Cixi's favorite, gave the go-ahead for the project after accepting a bribe from the Germans. Li's own courtyard residence stands immediately to the east of Cixi's, and he owned another larger but no longer extant residence to the north of the Summer Palace on the present-day campus of the Institute of International Relations, reputedly a school for spies.

Continuing east the corridor runs into the **House of Fragrant Herbs** (*Yiyun Guan*) [宜芸馆], the living quarters of Guangxu's empress. Attached to it to the south is the **Hall of Jade Ripples**

(6:15) George N. Kates *The Years that Were Fat: The Last of Old China*, pp. 207–8.
(6:16) Juliet Bredon *Peking*, p. 299.

The Seventeen-arch Bridge to South Lake Island, according to the Dutchman

(*Yulan Tang*) [玉澜堂]. This is where Aunt Cixi notoriously held Guangxu under house arrest after he had lent his support to the Reform Movement of 1898. The brick walls she built between several formerly unattached buildings to make him stay put can still be seen. The Hall of Jade Ripples contains a number of authentic relics from the Qianlong and Guangxu periods. Between the two imperial residences is a spacious courtyard containing a large walk-through maze, constructed of Lake Taihu stones, called

Henri Borel, is "to be trodden by none but shining angels and beatified souls".

the Forest of Lions. One easily imagines the emperor and empress of China playing hide-and-seek here on a summer night. There is a more elaborate Forest of Lions in a garden of the same name (*Shizi Lin*) in Suzhou, once the property of the family of the noted Chinese-American architect, I.M. Pei.

Proceed south from here past the boat docks towards the pavilion on the water, and you will walk past the **Memorial Temple to Yelüchucai Ci** [耶律楚材祠] on your left, which is no longer open to the public. The Khitan Yelüchucai (1190–1244), personal astrologer to Genghis Khan, successfully advised the Mongol emperor on economic and political matters. His tomb, a giant inverted wok-like mound now squeezed into a room on the north side of the temple, disappeared during the Cultural Revolution, though one wonders where it could have gone. There is some lovely stone carving on the marble stands here which once held bronze incense burners.

Continuing south along the shore, pass the **Pavilion for Knowing Spring** (*Zhichun Ting*) [知春亭], where impromptu performances of Peking opera and ballads can sometimes be heard on summer evenings. Pass through the tall fortified gate called the **Pavilion of Flourishing Culture** (*Wenchang Ge*), [文昌阁] where eunuchs kept watch over the lake. Approaching the **Seventeen-arch Bridge**, (*Shiqi Kong Qiao*) [十七孔桥] you will see the famous **Bronze Ox** (*tongniu*) [铜牛] reclining on a stone platform. In the imperial inscription on its back (1755), Qianlong commemorates the completion of the dredging of the lake and immodestly compares himself to the ancient mythological emperor Yu, who had once recorded his own success in quelling a flood on the back of an ox. The Dutchman Borel, who perhaps had been eating lotuses, had a near-religious experience here when he encountered this massive bovine paperweight:

> It is an ox of bronze; but a marvel, a marvel on the border between life and death. . . . There is life in each curve, in each flexure; but it is more beautiful than life, because it is art and cannot die. Nothing brutal is left: it is life made divine, immortalized in bronze. I saw many superb bronzes in China, but this one is the masterpiece. Softly and discreetly I stroked the smooth bronze, as if I touched sacred life.[6:17]

Stroll past the octagonal pavilion and across the **Seventeen-arch Bridge** (Borel again: "It is not like a bridge for human beings, rather for the Elysian Fields, to be trodden by none but shining angels and beatified souls") onto the **South Lake Island** (*Nanhu Dao*) [南湖岛]; in winter you may walk or skate to the island on the ice. The **Temple of the Dragon King** (*Longwang Miao*) [龙王庙], the first building on your right, dates from the Ming dynasty, when it stood on the shore of the lake. When Qianlong expanded that body of water and created Kunming Lake, he left the temple in its original place, formed an island around it, and connected the island to the shore by constructing the Seventeen-arch Bridge. Legend has it that Qianlong's son, the Jiaqing emperor-to-be, once came here from the Yuanming Yuan to pray for rain. His appeal was answered, and he left an inscription that now appears on the plaque hanging over the temple:

"The Shrine for Plenteous and Beneficent Rain from Heaven."

Qianlong also built a tower on the north shore of the island where he and his mother would go fishing and review naval exercises conducted on the lake. Cixi followed suit and in 1899 organized similar exercises. But the miniature battleships stirred up so much mud in the shallow lake that she cancelled the entire show before it had hardly begun. The present building, the **Hall of Infinite Space** (*Hanxu Tang*) [涵虚堂], where Guangxu would spend time in the summer, offers a superb view of Longevity Mountain.

In Republican times, the Society for the Prevention of Vandalism held meetings in the buildings on this island, and the courtyard complexes on the west were used by the Chinese Nature Society in the 1920s and 1930s as a spa.

There are two more sections of the lake to the west of the long causeway, both with small islands in their centers. The island in the southernmost lake conceals a complex of buildings called the **Seaweed-viewing Hall**, property of the Beijing Communist Party headquarters. Strangely enough, some contemporary maps omit the recently-built short causeway that enables VIPs to be drive there by car. A few other buildings in this section of the Summer Palace remain off limits to common mortals. The island in the west lake was once the site of a round fortress-like tower, but that is now in ruins.

Bridge of Embroidered Ripples, forming an elegant oval with its reflection in the lake. A nearby dock is the terminus for excursion boats that ply between Wanshou Si (万寿寺) and the Summer Palace

To leave the Summer Palace you backtrack along the west shore of the lake, while the setting sun puts its finishing touches on the day. We conclude this walk with Borel's parting meditation.

> *I knew now that I had felt the soul of the Summer Palace. The truest beauty was not in the marvels of architecture, the jewel-like dwellings on the hill: it was in the silent, deep blue lake mirroring the azure sky, in the clear spaces of air and light, in the mountains that seemed to lift their heads in worship. In this holy solitude all that is eternal sinks away.*[6:18]

(6:18) Henri Borel *The New China*, p. 242.

Qianlong's Bronze Ox, just a stone's throw from the Seventeen-arch Bridge, Longevity Hill is on the horizon

ADDITIONAL INFORMATION
BEIJING AND CHINA ON THE WEB

The internet has changed forever the way we read, communicate and learn—even the way we think. The internet also changes the way we travel, supplying vast amounts of instant, yet not necessarily up-to-date, information on transportation, accommodation and sightseeing, often with commercial strings attached. Yet with all its virtues, the internet cannot replace this book, although you now may be reading it on a cell phone, personal organizer device, or some form of magic paper not yet invented as of this writing.

The following websites provide (in English) endless details and virtual touring:

Courtesy of the United States Government, see the Consular Information Sheet on China at http://www.travel.state.gov/travel/china.html (best and deepest "non-commercial" background coverage available) and also the Tips for Travelers to the People's Republic of China, accessible from the same site.

The government of the United Kingdom offers similar parcels of fresh information at www.fco.gov.uk and then search China.

The Australian equivalent can be found at www.smartraveller.gov.au and then search China.

Commercial websites for consideration include:

www.beijingpage.com

www.beijingtraveltips.com

www.thatsbj.com

www.thebeijingguide.com

www.travelchinaguide.com

www.btmbeijing.com (official web site of the Beijing Tourism Authority)

www.economist.com/cities/citiesmain.cfm?city_id=BJS (An online guide to travel in Beijing, including tourist sites, restaurants, nightlife, travel information and the latest news about the capital. An extraordinary satellite map of Beijing can be found on http://maps.google.com/maps).

For excellent customized tours of Beijing's colorful *hutongs* and excursions to other off the beaten track locations, check out www.stretchaleg.com.

VISAS

Go to www.china-embassy.org/eng (Chinese government site for visa information)

www.travel.state.gov/travel/china.html

Most holders of foreign passports must have a visa in their passports in order to enter China. Visas can be obtained at Chinese embassies and consulates abroad and through travel agents. At present, Japanese tourists do not need visas for entry.

Tourist visas are generally valid for six months after the day of issue, for a single visit of one month's duration. Tourist visas can be extended for an additional month at the Foreign Affairs section of any office of the Public Security Bureau. Visitors in Beijing must go to the Exit and Entry Management Section, Beijing Municipal Public Security Bureau, No. 2 Dong Da Jie, Andingmen, Dongcheng District, tel: 8402 0101. Multiple-entry visas valid for one or two years are also available from Chinese embassies and consulates. Passport photographs and fees are required for citizens of most countries.

If you are traveling to China with a group of ten or more people who will enter and exit China together, the travel agent may obtain a group visa. With group visas, individual passports will be sighted but not stamped by Immigration officials upon entry and exit.

CLIMATE, DRESS AND TIME OF TRAVEL

Although Beijing can claim to have four seasons, the finest days of the year are limited to a few fleeting weeks in spring and fall. Winters are very cold and dry, summers hot and sometimes rainy with varying humidity. The famous dust storms of March and April that have plagued the city for centuries color the atmosphere yellow and sometimes orange with silt from the Mongolian plains and dirt from the many construction sites. The storms can be depressing, terrifying and choking, as well as a great bother, as the dust lands everywhere, even seeping its way into sealed closets. Peking dust is so fine it seems to be able to penetrate glass, and your lips.

For the winter, a hat, gloves, and long underwear are strongly recommended in addition to warm outerwear. The interiors of some buildings may be barely heated in winter and are sometimes uncomfortably cold by Western standards. Many Chinese office and factory workers still wear their overcoats inside at work.

For fall and spring the best advice is to bring layers that can be peeled off and replaced as necessary. Shoes should be light and sturdy. Running shoes or good walking shoes are a fine choice.

Informal dress is the rule except for business meetings and formal banquets, where you will be judged by what you wear as much as by your title. Business cards in Chinese giving your name in translation or transliteration, and stating your title are essential accessories in such situations.

In recent years, air pollution has become a major factor in the climate of Beijing. September/October and May/June were traditionally the finest time of year weather-wise to visit Beijing, but nowadays no season is exempt from the city's off-the-charts pollution. The government has taken steps to alleviate the plague by removing dirty industries from the immediate suburbs, but the vast population of motorized vehicles, growing at a rate as fast as 1,000 units per day, the cheap petroleum they burn, and carelessly managed construction sites easily cancel out any benefits gained from shutting down factories. In addition to providing some psychological comfort, surgical-type face masks are only effective in keeping the largest airborne particles out of your system.

When to come? Avoiding the peak months of September, October, April, and May will mean jostling fewer tourists, but be prepared for correspondingly warmer or cold weather. The intense blue sky on a clear chilling winter day is miraculous to behold but, alas, increasingly rare. In June, July and most of August you bake, fry or steam in the radiant sun in the afternoon and can be swallowed up by the army of increasingly mobile Chinese travelers who swarm to the capital as soon as the kids get out of school. Each to his/her own but as elsewhere, the experienced traveler will be well rewarded when he or she rises really early and beats not only the rush but also the heat.

Perhaps as important as when to come is when in the day to travel, once you get to Beijing. Rush hours, from 7:30–9:30 am and 4:00–8:00 pm are best avoided. But they are to be especially avoided on Monday morning and Friday afternoon.

Staying Healthy

wwwn.cdc.gov/travel/destinationchina.aspx is the U.S. Center for Contagious Diseases' excellent site with up-to-date information on possible health hazards in China.

The following suggestions may sound fussbudgety, but when it comes to your health it makes sense to err on the side of caution. In fact, few foreign tourists get sick in China, and those who do usually contract a relatively small range of illnesses. The most common ailments in dry, dusty, and polluted Beijing is the upper respiratory infection (URI) or throat cold.

Two cardinal health rules for travel in China:
1. Never drink unboiled water and don't sing in the shower.
2. Wash your hands before meals, especially after flea-marketing or visiting a crowded site.

When you brush your teeth, try to rinse your mouth with bottled or boiled water rather than tap water. Most hotels supply complimentary bottled water in the rooms, and it is suggested that you keep a supply with you at all times.

While human night-soil fertilizer is no longer widely used on Chinese farms that supply the capital, food transport and handling may not always be up to Western standards. Peel all fruit (even so-called Delicious apples imported from the U.S.), and avoid raw vegetables unless they are scrupulously washed and dried. At the top hotels, salads and cut fruit are unlikely to cause problems.

In restaurants avoid recycled washable wooden chopsticks that could be carrying germs from a previous user. Painted (with unscratched tips) or heavy plastic chopsticks that can be dried completely are preferable to absorbent bamboo chopsticks that have been used and washed. Consider acquiring your own set of chopsticks or bring along a few dozen pair of disposables, available in department and convenience stores. Many fast food restaurants and noodle shops provide disposable chopsticks and plastic utensils.

In very hot weather, avoid cold dishes in all but the finest restaurants. Anything that is cooked and still hot is likely to be safe to eat.

The U.S. State Department and Center for Contagious Diseases have at various times recommended a long list of vaccinations for long-term residents and/or travelers to some of the border districts, particularly in southwest and northwest China: gamma globulin (for hepatitis A), hepatitis B, Japanese B encephalitis (not recommended by the CDC for tourists), cholera, tetanus, polio and malaria. Consult the excellent CDC website given above, the appropriate health authority, a travel medicine specialist who knows Asia well or your personal physician concerning these vaccinations.

EMERGENCIES

In case of medical emergencies of a life threatening nature, call 120 for the Beijing Emergency Center, which operates a fleet of ambulances. You will naturally save time if a Chinese speaker makes the first contact, but if none is available, you could begin with "Speak English?" and wait until someone who does comes on the line.

If you are staying in a hotel, the front desk or assistant manager is likely to be able to call an ambulance faster than you could. If an ambulance seems unnecessary or is unavailable, take a taxi to the emergency room of one of the following hospitals:

Beijing United Family Hospital (*Beijing Hemu Jia Yiyuan*) 北京和睦家医院
—comprehensive care
2 Jiangtai Lu (near the Holiday Inn Lido in the northeast corner of the city)
Tel. 6433 3960

Peking Union Medical College Hospital (P.U.M.C.) (*Xiehe Yiyuan*) 协和医院
—a comprehensive hospital with a large clinic for foreigners
Dongdan Beidajie (one block east of Wangfujing). Tel. 6529 5284

Sino-Japanese Friendship Hospital (*Zhong Ri Youhao Yiyuan*) 中日友好医院
Yinghua Yuan Dong Jie. Tel. 6422 2949

Beijing International SOS Clinic 北京国际救援中心诊所
—offers a wide variety of services, including emergency evacuation plans
No. 5 Sanlitun Xiwujie. Tel. 6462 9112 (24-hour emergency, Tel. 6462 9100)

Hong Kong International Medical Clinic 香港国际医务诊所
3/F, Office Tower, Swissotel Hong Kong Macao Center
Chaoyangmen Beidajie. Tel. 6553 2288 (ext, 2345, 2346, 2347)

Bayley & Jackson Beijing Medical Center 庇利积臣医疗中心
7 Ritan Dong Lu (east side of Ritan Park). Tel. 8562 9998

It is impossible to generalize about the quality of local medical services, but in Beijing doctors tend to be thorough and reliable. Most foreign residents prefer to travel abroad for major medical and dental treatments and surgery, while at the same time, some patients from other parts of Asia travel to China to save money on hospital and surgical costs.

Money

The principal unit of currency is the *yuan* (pronounced like the letters UN sounded in quick succession) which is divided into 100 *fen* ("fun") or ten *jiao* or *mao*.

The RMB (*renminbi* or "people's money"), or *yuan*, is the principal unit of currency. It is issued in bills in denominations of 10 and 50 *fen*, and 1, 2, 5, 10, 50 and 100 *yuan*. The coins are in denominations of 1 fen, 2 fen, 5 fen, 1 mao, 5 mao, and 1 yuan.

You will enjoy precisely the same exchange rate everywhere in China—at banks, stores, and hotels. Traveler's checks will fetch you about one percent more than cash.

When you leave the country, an exchange memo must be presented to the bank when exchanging RMB back into foreign currency. The most convenient place to do this is at the Bank of China counters at international airports. At the Beijing airport there are exchange counters on both sides of customs and immigration.

Transport

The six walks described in this book will take you to some of the far corners of Beijing. Taxis are the fastest way to get around the city, especially if you time your movements in an attempt—often in vain—to avoid rush-hour traffic jams, particularly on Chang'an Boulevard, the main east-west thoroughfare in the center of the city. Taxis can be hailed virtually anywhere in the street, and most hotels have their own designated queues. Taxis can be booked for half a day, an entire day, or for longer durations. Extra charges are assessed for overtime, going beyond the city limits or waiting. Individual drivers are always happy to make deals for extended use. Hotel taxis booked through the hotel usually charge the highest possible rates. Fares cost 2 *yuan* per kilometer, with a 3 km, RMB10 flagfall charge. A taxi between the city and the airport will cost about 80–120 *yuan*. At the airport, go out of your way to avoid the obnoxious drivers who stalk their prey in the arrivals hall, and line up at the fast-moving taxi queue.

The Beijing Underground (metro), built originally beneath the scars remaining when the city walls were demolished, is useful for most of the walks (see end-paper map). Buses—air conditioned and windowed—and trolley-buses can be extremely crowded and are somewhat slower than taxis, but they are cheap and convenient and often as fast as taxis in bad traffic. Beijing, which is monotonously flat (otherwise the emperors would not have built their own mountains in the city), is ideal for bicycle riding, and most major thoroughfares have bicycle lanes. Bicycles can be rented in many places. With the monstrous increase in bourgeoisie cars and taxis (60 taxis in Beijing in 1980, 75,000 in 2006), proletarian bicycles have been relegated to a position of passive inferiority. Cars now rule the roads, absolutely.

SAFETY, SECURITY, NUISANCES

The explosive growth of automobile culture in Beijing has made traffic safety a major health concern for drivers, pedestrians and cyclists. With thousands of new vehicles and inexperienced drivers hitting the roads everyday, road accidents are common. In fact, in per capita and per vehicle terms, China has one of the world's worst road safety records.

Traffic aside, Beijing is a very safe city for visitors. Muggings, robbery, rape and other crimes against the person are rare occurrences for foreigners. The most widespread risk for travel in *any* foreign country, especially China, is pickpocketing, a highly developed art in the main tourist sites in China, although today local Chinese tourists are as likely to be the victims as foreign tourists. Pickpockets come in all sizes and shapes. Women carrying a baby (rented?) have been active recently at the Beijing Train Station, stealing cell phones out of belt holders by leaning up against you for two seconds while passing you on the escalator.

Tourists in China can be prime targets for all sorts of commercial inducements, traps and scams. At the light end are the "art students" who draw the gullible into painting shops where they sell overpriced mediocre Chinese paintings by unknown artists. Or the touts in Liulichang antiques street, or at the Panjiayuan market who hold up a small wrinkled color picture of a piece of porcelain cut out of a magazine and say "on-tee-cuss; very old... very cheap." And then there are the "students" who frequent Wangfujing and Tiananmen Square, who want to practice English with you over a pot of tea. Be on your guard. They work with the tea houses and that cuppa could end up costing you $200.

BRIGANDS, PIRATES AND ...

For the benefit of timid persons who may forego the pleasure of a visit to China because of alarming stories it may be well to point out that these dangers are very small. It should be remembered that China covers a very large territory, and brigands may ravage some parts of it without in any way disturbing the sections ordinarily visited by foreigners. All in all, travel is as safe in China as in any other part of the world. Robbers and pirates exist, of course, and there is usually a revolution or rebellion going on in some part of the country, but these things add zest rather than danger to the journey.[7:1]

This sanguine appraisal suggests that tourists in 1920 were made of considerably stronger stuff than many of their counterparts 87 years later.

TIPPING AND COMMISSIONS

Tipping is officially discouraged in China's "socialist market economy with Chinese characteristics" but with the tipping of the balance in the direction of the market, tipping has become a way of life on the tourist circuit: tourist guides and bus drivers expect tips from foreign tourists traveling in groups, as do hotel bellboys who deliver your bags to your room. For the bellboys, RMB5 for one bag or RMB10/US$1 for a single delivery of 2-3 bags should suffice.

(7:1) Carl Crow *The Travelers' Handbook for China (Including Hongkong)*, p. 26.

Most hotels and some upscale restaurants add a "service charge" to the bill that goes right to the management and no tipping is necessary above and beyond that, although there is no reason not to reward extraordinary service. Beijing taxi drivers do *not* expect tips. On the other hand, if you book a taxi for the day or if the driver is extraordinarily helpful, or if you have a long wait in traffic for which the driver is barely compensated, you might throw in a few *yuan* beyond the fixed rate.

Carl Crow's 1921 warning on the practice of tour guides earning commissions is still, remarkably, valid today:

> The advice of any [tour] guide as to purchases should be accepted with a great deal of caution, for according to universal custom he is entitled to a commission on sales and it is to his interest to lead to shops where the commission is the highest. It is not an unknown occurrence for the guide and the shopkeeper to take advantage of the tourist's ignorance of the language and arrange the terms of the commission in his presence while pretending to be haggling over the price.[7:2]

In some cases, tour guides and bus drivers in Beijing working as independent contractors actually pay travel agencies for the "privilege" of taking tour groups around the city. To pay off these fees and fill their rice bowls, the guides cajole tourists into dining, shopping and touring in places where they and the drivers can collect fat kickbacks.

TELEPHONES

Beijing is now a wireless city, inasmuch as urban China has one of the world's highest densities of cell phone users. China Mobile and China Telecom are the local providers for international roaming services, which are usually trouble free. You can purchase second hand local phones and a local phone number for as little as US$10–20 and charge them up with stored value phone cards, which require no registration. International calls can be placed from fixed line phones for as little as 15 US cents per minute using IP (internet phone) cards, with optional English prompts and some very lengthy PINs, sold at newspaper kiosks and commercial centers (be sure to purchase at a sharp discount, sometimes up to 75 per cent off the face value; stored value cards for cell phones are at most discounted 2 per cent). Some hotels (usually not the top hotels, strange as it seems) block the IP access numbers to squeeze a few more dollars out of their guests.

(7:2) Carl Crow *The Travelers' Handbook for China (Including Hongkong)*, p. 27.

INTERNET ACCESS

Many Beijing hotels offer in-room broadband access, but often charge a per diem maximum of $10–20, for sometimes slow access. An alternative means of getting online is to use one of several low-priced local dial-up connections. Check with the hotel business center or front desk for the latest numbers, but username/password 169 and local number 16900 (preceded by the hotel's local outside line prefix) can usually deliver a 52 bps connection. The cost of 30 *fen* (US 4 cents) per minute will be charged to your hotel phone bill. Many information-providing websites are blocked in China, but personal email flows freely, although it may be monitored. Internet bars offer inexpensive online time, sometimes as little as RMB 3 per hour. A growing number of places in Beijing, from high-end restaurants to hole-in-the-wall coffee shops and bars, offer free WIFI. Most branches of Starbucks, Pacific Coffee Company and SPR Coffee offer free wireless. For more locations, go to www.chinapulse.com

ESSENTIAL TELEPHONE NUMBERS

Note: When calling or faxing to Beijing from abroad, the international dialing code for Beijing is 86–10 (86 is the country code and 10 is the city code for Beijing). When dialing from other cities in China, 010 is the Beijing dialing code. When dialing internationally in China, 00 comes before the country code.

Important numbers in China:

Beijing Tourist Hotline	6513 0828
Police	110
Beijing Emergency Center	120
Time	117
Weather	121
Visa Department, Public Security Bureau	8402 0101
(Anding Men Dong Da Jie)	

Embassies

(Office hours are generally 9.00am–12.00noon; 1.30–4.00pm, but emergency calls are put through 24 hours a day.

United States	6532 3831
United Kingdom	6532 1961
Australia	6532 2331

Canada	6532 3536
New Zealand	6532 2731
France	6532 1331
Germany	6532 2161
Italy	6532 2131
Japan	6532 2361
India	6532 1908
Russia	6532 1381

ENTERTAINMENT

"Beijing nightlife" was once an oxymoron. The situation has changed radically since the early 1980s to the point where you can drink, dance, get tattooed or have your tongue pierced at any time of day or night in Beijing. It is apparent that most commercial forms of pleasure known to mankind since the dawn of civilization are available for the asking, at a price.

The bar districts of Sanlitun (Bar Street = *jiuba jie*), Shichahai, Chaoyang Park, Workers' Stadium and Nan Luogu Xiang are popular hangouts for locals and expatriates in their 20s and 30s. There is a relatively quiet gay scene which can be accessed via the Web or expat magazines.

For listings of cultural events in the city, consult *Time Out, That's Beijing* or *City Weekend*, or their web sites. Standard fare served up mostly for tour groups and Chinese families includes Peking opera, acrobatics, magic shows, and kitschy dance performances. Almost all public entertainment in China is kosher for children, and thus may seem surprisingly naïve to patrons of Off-Broadway plays and American television. There are many new cinemas in Beijing, and the best venues, such as in Oriental Plaza and Wanda Plaza, also screen Western movies in their original languages. To protect the local film industry, China only imports a limited number of foreign films for display each year. However thanks to the internet and express mail, DVDs of the latest international films are peddled illegally at street corners throughout the city, and cost less than RMB10 per disc. Ethics aside, compatibility is sometimes a problem.

International concert artists, from Italian opera to the pop divas, show up in Beijing from time to time; the best tickets sell for over RMB1,000. Don't forget the jetlag the performers may be suffering from.

International programming in English, including local news and other programs for foreigners, can be found on CCTV 9. Most four and five star hotels have international satellite broadcasting.

Walking around the city at night is generally safe and pleasant. The parks are open until sundown in summer, and are popular among the locals. The night food market at Donghua Men Da Jie (a far better photo opportunity than a culinary one, unless you crave fried scorpions, silkworms or starfish on a stick) and the Shichahai district are good destinations for a late night stroll. The bar areas stay open until the wee hours.

SHOPPING

Beijing can now claim the distinction, dubious to some, of being one of the "shopping capitals" of Asia (if not the universe), and offers visitors a greater range of items than any other city in China. While shops today fill virtually every square inch of street space, it is important to remember that as recently as 1980 there were virtually no private businesses or non-state commerce in China, and retirees had just obtained the "right" to offer minimal survival services on the streets, such as repairing bicycles or cutting hair. Five years earlier they would have been condemned as capitalist running dogs for patching a tire.

The same Chinese products that now fill the shelves of department stores and the pages of mail order catalogs all over the world are sold at even lower prices in department stores and commercial centers such as the **Hongqiao** shopping center near the east entrance of the Temple of Heaven. The bustling **Silk Street Market** near Xiushui Jie and the American consulate, dear to foreign visitors and locals alike since the mid-1980s for fake brand-name clothing and accessories, has been forced indoors and upstairs price wise by the unpopular machinations of local authorities.

The juiciest slice of **Wangfujing**, long a prime commercial center, has been converted into a pedestrian-shoppers-only uncovered mall, taking after Nanjing Road in Shanghai. Wangfujing is a fascinating place to walk, and boasts some of the most venerable food, tea, hat, shoe, book, watch, fur and medicine shops in China, including the classical Number One Department Store, which proves how difficult it is to beat state commerce. The Xinhua Book Store has a modest but interesting section featuring books in English, from the most recent best-sellers to books on China. Beware of innocent-looking young "students" and "artists," mostly female, who prey on foreign tourists in this crowded tourist area. The **Xidan** commercial district is known for clothing the youth of the capital, but it is also home to **Beijing Book City** (*Beijing Shu Cheng*), a vast emporium of the printed word (mostly in Chinese). On weekends the sight of young children and their mothers browsing eagerly in the juvenile section can bring tears to your eyes.

Contemporary Chinese arts and crafts are not to everyone's taste, but there seems to be a bottomless inventory of these products, which show up at stalls at the Great Wall, hotel gift shops, and almost every place in between. The goods include cloisonné, cork carvings, papercuts, stuffed pandas, puppets, kites, hand-exercise balls, Olympics souvenirs, embroidered blouses, crocheted table cloths, batik printed cottons, toys, combs, artists' materials, jewelry, bamboo ware and lacquer ware.

The Beijing Friendship Store (*Youyi Shangdian*) [友谊商店] occupies four floors of a building near the embassy quarter in Jianguo Menwai. Modeled originally on Soviet-era hard currency stores, an idea that was "buried" in the mid-1980s, the Friendship Store has failed to keep up with the other department stores in the city, but is a good if stodgy standby if you are in the neighborhood. While the atmosphere is not always remarkably friendly, it is an efficient place to shop for gifts, practical items, food and drink. It also has a good selection of foreign newspapers and magazines, books on China and maps.

There are numerous opportunities in the antiques markets and curios shops but caution is advised. Buying antiques in China is a serious business for many, so unless you are well educated in the field it pays to take much time and care with large purchases. A post-Cultural Revolution generation of antiques traders, some of them the offspring of old time dealers, subscribe to all the latest Sotheby's and Christie's sales catalogues and have their in-shop computers tuned into the auction houses' websites; a dozen or so auction houses in Beijing and Shanghai turn over tens of millions of US dollars in sales every few months, and have deprived Sotheby's and Christie's of a highly lucrative market. On occasion rare Chinese works of art in overseas collections are shipped back to China and auctioned at prices they could not fetch in London or New York, although mainland buyers are now prominent buyers internationally as well. Chinese crowd out the overseas buyers of most categories of Chinese works of art in China as well; a natural outcome of present economic conditions and long tradition.

Taken literally, Chinese customs regulations forbids the export of a remarkably broad range of "cultural relics," including anything manufactured before 1949 that does not bear a Customs seal, although such rules are impossible to enforce. It can be argued that anything sold openly in the curios markets and shops in Beijing can be exported. Refer to Walk Two (see page 141) for **Liulichang**, sometimes called Antiques Street, where both official and privately-run stores sell real and fake antiques—not necessarily in that order.

For lovers of flea markets, Beijing boasts one of the largest in the world, the weekend market at **Panjiayuan** in the southeast quarter of the city. Go early, as the market opens at sunrise and closes by around 4.00pm. Another market, **Baoguosi** in the southwest quadrant, operates on Thursdays and on the weekends. **Hongqiao Market** near the Temple of Heaven has a small area of curios dealers.

RESTAURANTS

Beijing's restaurants offer the greatest variety of cuisines, venues and prices in the country, and the city is a paradise for gourmets and gourmands of every stripe. From the humblest dumpling and noodle joint, to the hundreds of McDonald's, Kentucky Fried Chicken and Pizza Hut outlets, to flashy and serious banquet houses offering regional cuisines, the food scene in Beijing is highly competitive, and it might be said that it is relatively difficult to have a truly bad meal.

Virtually all Asian cuisines and both popular and highly rarified Chinese regional cuisines are authentically represented in Beijing, remembering that there are now many more Taiwanese, Japanese, Korean, Hong Kong and Southeast Asian residents and tourists in Beijing—not to mention tourists from other parts of China—than their counterparts from Europe, North America, Australia, etc.

Even the smallest restaurants in the city are accustomed to serving foreigners who don't speak or read the language. English-language menus in Beijing are sometimes grotesque parodies of their Chinese originals ("diligent right rabbit's leg," "bite the scalloped pork," "lamb kidneys of head explosion," "mix the sea intestines warmly" and "seafood's hang-up soup" complemented by a wine list for Great Wall brand dry red wine listed as "Long City fuck red"). But even without such amusing linguistic aids, friendly managers, waiters or fellow diners will assist the hungry stranger to order something to eat.

Chinese people have a profound reverence for food and eating. When choosing restaurants, follow the crowd. The culinary less adventurous may follow the expatriates, while those with a more curious tongue may safely go native. Kitchen sanitation is hard to judge from a restaurant's public areas, but if you have any doubts, move on. When this is not possible, avoid cold dishes and eat only steaming hot food. Avoid multi-use wood and bamboo chopsticks, which may fail to dry thoroughly between the last customer and you. Use one-time or plastic chopsticks that can be dried thoroughly.

Home-style Chinese food (*jiachang cai*), served at many low priced restaurants, resembles to some degree the Chinese food served in restaurants throughout the world, but is likely to differ in terms of more intense flavors and more obvious wok-flavor (*guo wei'r*), the magic quality imparted to freshly cut ingredients seared in seconds by stir-frying in a red-hot iron pan.

Beijing food and Northern Chinese cuisine in general tends to be considerably more salty and heavily seasoned, though not spicy-hot, than, say, Cantonese cuisine. Per capita salt consumption in Beijing is around four times higher than that of Guangzhou (Canton). You can ask to have less salt used (*Bu yao tai xian*) and to eliminate sodium-rich MSG (*bu yao weijing*), but even when a Beijing local requests the waiter to do this, the appeal to sane non-salinity rarely succeeds in restraining the salt-heavy hand of the chef.

The classic local dish, Peking roast duck, is served at dozens of restaurants in Beijing. Most of the specialized roast duck restaurants in Beijing serve an all duck banquet that includes the liver, heart, brain and webs as well as a soup of duck broth and (cow's) milk.

In residential neighborhoods, Chinese on their way to work often buy and consume their breakfast in the street. Peddlers sell hunks of deep-fried bread that resembles an elephant's ear, long deep-fried crullers, and freshly made crepes wrapped around a fried egg, for 2 RMB.

In 1950, there were fewer than 1,000 restaurants in Beijing. Today there are some 40,000, serving food from all over the world, and from every corner of China. While American chains like McDonald's, KFC, Pizza Hut and Starbucks have made impressive inroads into the Chinese diet and pocketbook by their seeming omnipresence, these purveyors of exotic snack food present no serious challenge to the primacy of Chinese cuisine, which years ago recovered from the proletarian mediocrity of the Cultural Revolution. In fact, Chinese cooking is alive and well in Beijing, thanks to intense competition among restaurants on the one hand, and rapidly rising standards of living and mobility on the other.

Commercial openness has encouraged foreigners from every corner of the earth to open restaurants featuring their native cuisines in Beijing: Brazilian barbecue, bagels/deli, Indian, Indonesian, Indochinese, Italian, Israeli, Korean, Japanese, Thai, Tibetan, Vietnamese, Fusion (Chinese food in nature but using Western ingredients), French and Belgian, North African, Serbian and Russian restaurants, from the proletarian to the pretentious, blend right into the local dining landscape. But if you are in Beijing for less than five days, and have only ten lunches and dinners on your calendar, does it make sense to eat the kind of non-Chinese food you can get at home? The author of this book adheres to the anthropological view: when in Beijing, eat as the Beijingers eat, eliminating such adolescent lapses as McDonald's et al. Also, the Chinese food in Beijing is generally unlike, no, actually better than, most of the Chinese food available, even in Chinatown, outside of China/ Taiwan/Hong Kong. Another anthropological suggestion: one of the best ways to quickly judge, or pre-judge, any restaurant in China is by the number of empty seats at meal time; if possible—and sometimes it's not—stay away from restaurants packed with large tourist groups.

Given the volatile nature of the restaurant trade in China today, and the overwhelming number of not only decent but excellent places to eat in Beijing, the following walk-related list contains both restaurants with relatively long histories that have more or less maintained their reputations and the quality of their food over many years, as well as some newer creative upstarts. No hotel restaurants are listed here (lists of the "best" Beijing restaurants in every category can be found in free tourist magazines and guidebooks), although in terms of food and especially service, décor and ambiance, these certainly count among the best places to eat in the city. By definition, four- and five-star hotels in Beijing are home to at least one Chinese and at least one other Asian or Western restaurant. Most of the top hotels offer vast international buffets three meals a day, a wonderful way to overcome any food hang-ups you might have in China.

RESTAURANTS

WALK 1—FORBIDDEN CITY

Da San Yuan 大三元酒家

50 Jingshan Xijie, Xicheng District. Tel. 6401 3920; open 7:30 am–2:30 pm;
5:00–9:00 pm

西城区景山西街50号

Da San Yuan, the first Cantonese restaurant to set foot in Beijing, specializes in
Cantonese cuisine with a limited dim sum menu offered in the morning from
7.30–10am. The mouth-watering crispy skin roasted pork is fantastic; served
with delectable fermented wheat dipping sauce.

Dong Lai Shun 东来顺

5F Xing Dong An Plaza, Wangfujing Dajie, Dongcheng District
Tel. 6528 0932; open 11:00 am–10:00 pm

东城王府井大街138号

Relocated, or perhaps relegated, to an upper floor of the Sun Dong An Plaza in
Wangfujing, this is a famed classic Muslim restaurant serving the second most
famous dish in Beijing, mutton hot pot, aka rinsed mutton. Best in autumn and
winter, but available year round.

Laijin Yuxuan 来今雨轩

On the west side of Zhongshan Park, Dongcheng District
Tel. 6605 6676; open 10:30 am–7:00 pm daily

中山公园内西侧

Laijin Yuxuan is know for the '*Dream of the Red Mansion*' cuisine, based on
foods introduced in the Chinese classic by the same name. An advance
reservation is required to enjoy a full Red Mansion banquet, which runs from
RMB300–500 per person with a minimum of eight people. However, *qiexiang*,
an eggplant dish, and *jisi haozi gan*, stir fried chicken with crown daisy
chrysanthemums, are two simple dishes that are available daily. The restaurant
also has a wide variety of other dishes and is famous for its tasty *baozi*, or
buns filled with minced pork and preserved vegetables.

The nearby Laijin Yuxuan Teahouse, a short walk away, is a lovely spot for a
cup of tea and light traditional snacks such as red bean pastry, haw cakes,
almond cookies, nuts, watermelon seeds, dried fruits and the famous *baozi*.

Shudu Binguan 蜀都宾馆

30 Shatan Hou Jie, Dongcheng District

Tel. 6403 4440; open 11:00 am–2:00 pm, 5:00–9:00 pm

东城区沙滩后街 30 号景山公园东街斜对面 50 米

Shu Bin is operated by the Chengdu city government and specializes in Sichuan fare, serving some of the best and most authentic Sichuan cuisine at amazingly low prices. Start with *Chuanbei liangfen,* a jelly starch appetizer, to whet your appetite. Shu Bin serves all your favorite Sichuan dishes, and the gongbao chicken, mapo beancurd, twice-cooked pork, and stir-fried beans are all terrific. The *hongyou chaoshou,* a traditional tiny Sichuan wonton boiled and served in a wonderful chilli sauce, are the best in Beijing.

WALK 2—LEGATION QUARTER

Peking Duck This famously fatty local specialty is best ordered alongside a variety of other dishes, duck- or non. At the best of times the roasted flesh and crispy skin wrapped in a freshly baked pancake with raw scallions and bean sauce (made primarily of fermented soybeans and wheat flour, the authentic non-sweet sauce is neither plum sauce, nor "duck sauce" nor hoisin sauce) rivals in sensuousness the pleasures of *fois gras* or caviar on toast, suggesting that rich Peking duck is best appreciated *not* as a main course. The finest ducks are raised near the Summer Palace in the northwest outskirts of the city. Legend has it the breed of bird popularly used for the dish descends directly from the Long Island (New York) duck.

Hepingmen Quanjude 和平门全聚德

14 Qianmen Xi Da Jie, Chongwen District

Tel. 6403 4440; open 10:30 am–2:00 pm, 4:30–8:30 pm

崇文区前门西大街 14 号

The world's largest duckery, called the Wall Street Duck, as Hepingmen was the site of a gate in the former city wall, or McDonald Duck due to its size. Claims to serve 1,500 ducks a day. Innumerable public and private dining rooms, and a sometimes bewildering set of prices.

Li Qun Kaoya Dian 利群烤鸭店

11 Beixiangfeng, Qianmen Dong Da Jie (south of Zhengyi Lu), Chongwen District. Tel. 6702 5681; open noon–10:00 pm daily

崇文区前门东大街北翔风胡同 11 号 (正义路南口)

An alternative to sample Peking Duck other than Beijing's most well-known and too commercial Quanjude. Li Qun is located in a somewhat dilapidated old courtyard house full of Beijing flavor. In the warmer months take a seat in the open courtyard.

WALK 3—BEIHAI PARK

Fangshan 仿膳

1 Wenjin Lu (inside Beihai Park), Xicheng District

Tel. 6401 1879; open 11:00 am–1:30 pm, 5:00–10:00 pm daily

西城区文津街1号北海公园内

"House of Beijing Flavors," Fangshan, located on the north shore of Qionghua Island in Beihai Park, is the most famous imperial-heritage restaurant in China, specializing in the imperial court food that had its origins in the palace kitchens. Situated in a superb and unique setting, with staff dressed in Manchu outfits, it reminds one of a costume drama. The service and food are usually not up to the location, but you might take lunch here if you are visiting Beihai (see page 173) in the middle of the day or complete your walk toward the late afternoon. The set meals, starting from RMB200 per person, give you a taste of what imperial food was like. The full "Man-Han Banquet," consists of 108 imperial dishes and goes for as much as RMB10,800.

Han Cang 汉仓

Shichahai Dongan, Houhai, Xicheng District

Tel. 6404 2259; open 11:30 am–3:00 pm, 5:00–10:30 pm daily

西城区后海什刹海东岸

The Hakkas, or Guest People, settled in Guangdong and Fujian provinces, bringing with them their earthy and hearty food—honest and good grub. Book a table on the second floor by the window overlooking the lake.

Jing Wei Lou 京味楼

181 A Dianmen Xi Da Jie, Xicheng District

Tel. 6617 6514; open 11:00 am–2:00 pm, 4:30–9:30 pm daily

西城区地安门西大街181号甲

Aptly named as the 'House of Beijing Flavors,' the menu is full of traditional Beijing favorites such as mung bean pulp, mung bean fries, eggplant puree as well as Peking duck.

Jiumen Xiaochi 九门小吃

1 Xiaoyou Hutong, Xicheng District

Tel. 6402 5858; open 10:30 am–1:30 pm, 5:30–9:00 pm

西城区孝友胡同1号

An Old Peking repertoire from sour bean juice, donkey rolling on the ground, a sweet snack, pot stickers and boiled tripe served in a cafeteria-like setting.

Kaorou Ji 烤肉季

14 Qianhai Dongyan, Xicheng District. Tel. 6404 2554; open 11:00 am–11:00 pm
西城区前海东沿 14 号

On the shores of Qianhai in the Rear Lakes (Houhai) area. Roast mutton along with an entire range of Chinese Muslim (Hui) halal dishes, a highly underrated cuisine. Everything but pork is served in a pleasant setting. In the warmer months, you can hire a small boat and stop by here for plates of kebabs and other food to be eaten on the boat.

Kong Yiji 孔乙己

Deshengmennei Da Jie (South shore of Shichahai), Xicheng District
Tel. 6618 4915; open 10:00 am–2:00 pm, 4:30–10:00 pm daily
西城区德胜门内大街什刹海南岸

This restaurant, serving the specialties of Zhejiang province, is named for the down-and-out protagonist of a short story by Lu Xun. Fennel-flavored broad beans and Shaoxing wine were the only items that the poor protagonist could afforded. Try the fatty pork slow cooked for hours in a casserole.

South Silk Road 茶马古道

19A Shichahai Qian Hai Xi Yan, Xicheng District
Tel. 6615 5515; open 11:00 am–midnight
西城区什刹海前海西沿 19 号甲

South Silk Road made ethnic eating chic. Sample Yunnan's exotic wild mushrooms and vegetables, and uniquely flavored sausages while looking across the lake.

Zhang Qun Jia 张群家

5 Yandai Xiejie, Houhai, Xicheng District. Tel. 8404 6662
西城区后海烟袋斜街 5 号

A home-style set meal featuring Suzhou specialties selected by owner Zhang Qun. The set meal, served in a small shop front, starts from RMB200–500 per person. Reservations are essential, because this restaurant essentially has just one table. Zhang Qun Jia can accommodate anywhere from two to eight diners.

WALK 4—TEMPLE OF HEAVEN

Old Beijing Noodle King 北京炸酱面大王 *(Lao Beijing Zhajijang Mian Dawang)*

29 Chongwenmenwai Da Jie, Chongwen District
Tel. 6705 6705; open 11:00 am–10:00 pm
崇文区崇文门外大街29号

Known for the noodle that made Beijing famous—*zhajiang mian*. The noodles are hand-pulled and served with several vegetables and a delectable meat sauce.

Jinyang Fanzhuang 晋阳饭庄

241 Zhushikou Xi Da Jie, Xuanwu District. Tel. 6354 1107
宣武区珠市口西大街241号

A time-honored restaurant serving Shanxi classic dishes such as *guoyou rou*, oil-passing meat, *xiangsu ya*, or crispy duck, and cat's ears, stir-fried tiny morsel pasta shaped like a cat's ear and cooked with vegetables and meat. Attached to the residence of Ji Xiaolan, a Qing dynasty scholar who compiled the Complete Library of the Four Branches of Literature during the years 1773–1782. While you're there take a tour of this historical house.

Guilin Ren Sijia Cai 桂林人私家菜

2 Qisheng Xiang, Wanming Lu, Xuanwu District
Tel. 6304 5269; open 10:00 am–11:00 pm
宣武区齐胜巷2号

This small hole-in-the-wall place serves the big flavor of Guilin, Guangxi province, a little-known provincial cuisine. Go for dry-pot duck cooked with beer, stir-fried sour bamboo shoots with shredded beef and grilled streaky pork. They are heavenly delicious.

WALK 5—LAMA AND CONFUCIUS TEMPLES

Xu Xiang Zhai 叙香斋素食餐厅

26 Guozijian Jie, Dongcheng District
Tel. 6404 6568; open 11:30 am–10:00 pm
东城区国子监大街甲26孔对庙面

Located directly opposite the Confucius Temple, this is one of the few vegetarian restaurants that serve a vegetarian buffet meal with an impressive spread of dishes, including soups (three different kinds), stir-fried vegetables, *liangban*, or vegetables tossed in delectable seasonings, mock meat dishes, and even sushi platters.

Vineyard Café 葡萄院儿 31 Wudaoying Hutong, Dongcheng District
Tel. 6402 7961; open 11:00 am–11:00 pm daily
东城区五道营胡同 31 号

Hidden in an obscure *hutong* not far from the Lama Temple, the contemporary Vineyard Café, set up in an old courtyard house, serves typical Western dishes, and also a wonderful hearty British brunch on the weekends: eggs, bangers, sautéed mushrooms, fried potatoes, baked beans, a glass of freshly squeezed apple juice and coffee or tea. Outdoor courtyard seating in the warmer months.

Café de la Poste 云游驿　58 Yonghegong Da Jie, Dongcheng District
Tel. 6402 7047; open 9:30 am–late, closed Mondays
东城区雍和宫大街 58 号

Café de la Poste is about 15 minutes walk from the Lama Temple. This French bistro offers a simple classic quiche and steaks, from thin-cut to a normal 400 grams steak. Decent house wine available by the glass or bottle at moderate prices.

Courtyard No. 28 二十八号院
1 Xilou Hutong, south corner of the Lama Temple, Dongcheng District
Tel. 8401 6788; open 10:00 am–10:00 pm
东城区雍和宫南侧戏楼胡同 1 号南侧

Set in a small traditional courtyard house, Courtyard No. 28 specializes in Guangxi cuisine. Highly recommended is Zhuang's bean curd, stir-fried Chinese cabbage, and stir-fried sour bamboo shoots with shredded beef.

Guo Yao Xiaoju 国肴小居
58 Bei Santiao, Jiaodaokou, Andingmennei Da Jie, Dongcheng District
Tel. 6403 1940; open 10:00 am–2:30 pm, 4:30–9:00 pm
东城区安定门内大街交道口北三条 58 号

The family run Guo Yao Xiaoju deserves a Michelin star for its fantastic Tan cuisine (*tanjia cai*) set meal which includes braised shark fin soup, sea cucumber, fish maw, baked cod fish, and a variety of cold dishes. Guests can select from several set meals (RMB300–1,500 per person) with varying number of dishes. Highly recommended is the RMB800–1,000 set meal for a one-time experience. Bookings are required for a Tan set meal. This is the only dining venue offering quality delicacies without exploitative exorbitant prices. À la carte ordering is also available and reasonable, with a meal for two costing as little as RMB200. This is definitely one of the best Chinese restaurants in Beijing.

WALK 6—SUMMER PALACE

Baijia Dazhaimen 白家大宅门食府

29 Suzhou Jie, Haidian District. Tel. 6265 4186; open 11:00 am–9:30 pm
海淀区苏州街 29 号

Huge yet unpretentious imperial garden-style venue dating back to the Qing
dynasty, with costumed waitresses, numerous rooms and lovely outdoor
dining in season. In the Haidian district, this is a perfect place to eat after a
visit to the Summer Palace. The cuisine is similar to Fangshan (see above) but
the menu is more user-friendly and less expensive.

Ting Li Guan 听鹂馆

Beneath the Wanshou Mountains, Summer Palace
Tel. 6288 1608; open 11:00 am–2:30 pm (must book in advance for dinner)
颐和园内万寿山南麓

Overpriced imperial-style food in a pleasant setting is available at the Tingli
Guan Restaurant, at the western end of the Long Corridor. Spots around the
lake are perfect for picnics, and Kunming Lake is ideal for skating in the
depths of winter.

Najia Xiaoguan 那家小馆

South of the Fragrant Hills Botanical Garden crossroad, Haidian District
Tel. 8259 8588; open 11:00 am–10:00 pm
海淀区香山一棵松 29 号，北京植物园正门向南 100 米路西

Opened by a Beijinger to focus his family's Manchu cooking without the
hoopla of those restaurants specializing in court dishes. Huangtanzi, or royal
chicken broth, is a signature dish. Another recommended dish is *cuipi xia* 脆皮
虾, a sweet and crispy shrimp dish. Also try one of the *tanzi*, or dishes served
in a crock.

HOTELS

The number of hotels in Beijing has increased over the past decade, most dramatically in the last few years as the city began to gear up for the 2008 Olympics, with big-name 5-star hotels opening their doors all over the city. Lower budget travelers also have more of a choice today, as entrepreneurs rushed in to open more moderately priced places to stay, such as Home Inns and Super 8 chains.

Electricity in China is 220 volts, and in the hotels of lesser repute the power supply, and the hot water, can wobble and disappear entirely at times without warning. Plug compatibility can be a problem, and as there is no consistent standard in Chinese hotels. Most hotels can lend you an adapter, but sometimes the supply runs out, and so to be safe you should bring along a conversion device that accommodates American, British and Australian types of plugs. Adaptors can be bought at the Hongqiao Market, in department stores and at small electronics shops throughout the city. Hair dryers are supplied in the room in most three-star-and-up hotels.

Security is not a common problem in hotels, but the isolated incidents that do occur can spoil a trip. It is wise to leave no visible temptations in the rooms, such as cameras or novel electronic devices, not to mention wallets, passports, watches and jewelry. Cash and valuables should be placed in a safety deposit box in your room or at the front desk if you don't plan to keep them on your person during your stay.

Hôtel de Pekin, 1900

Hotels are listed in alphabetic order; by and large we have inclined toward the more comfortable but in some cases proximity to a given Walk has meant inclusion of budget hotels. For those seeking more modest accommodation the internet (see page 336) offers numerous additional choices.

WALK 1, 2, 3 and 4

Beijing Hotel

北京饭店　东城区东长安街 33 号

33 Dong Chang'an Da Jie, Dongcheng District

Tel. 6513 7766; Fax. 6523 2395; www.chinabeijinghotel.com.cn

Beijing Park Hyatt

北京柏悦饭店　朝阳区建国门外大街 2 号

2 Jianguomenwai Da Jie, Chaoyang District

Tel. 8567 1234; www.park.hyatt.com

China World Hotel, Beijing

北京中国大饭店　朝阳区建国门外大街 1 号

1 Jianguomenwai Da Jie, Chaoyang District

Tel. 6505 226; Fax. 6505 0828; www.shangri-la.com

Courtyard Beijing Hotel

万怡酒店　崇文区崇文门外大街 3–18 号

3–18 Chongwenmenwai Da Jie, Chongwen District

Tel. 6708 1188; Fax. 6708 1808; www.courtyard.com

Grand Hotel Beijing

北京贵宾楼饭店　东城区东长安街 35 号

35 Dong Chang'an Da Jie, Dongcheng District

Tel. 6513 7788; Fax. 6513 0048; www.grandhotelbeijing.com

Grand Hyatt Beijing

北京东方君悦大酒店　东城区东长安街 1 号东方广场

1 Dong Chang'an Da Jie, Dongcheng District

Tel. 8518 1234; Fax. 8518 0000; www.beijing.grand.hyatt.com

Grand Mercure Xidan Beijing

北京西单美爵酒店　西城区宣武门内大街 6 号

6 Xuanwumennei Da Jie, Xicheng District

Tel. 6603 6688; Fax. 6603 1481; Email: reservations@grandmercurexidanbeijing.com

Hilton Hotel

北京希顿酒店　朝阳区东三还北路东方路 1 号

1 Dongfang Road, North Dong Sanhuan Road, Chaoyang District
Tel. 5865 5000; Fax. 5865 5800; www.hilton.com

Holiday Inn Crowne Plaza
国际艺苑皇冠假日酒店 东城区王府井大街 48 号
48 Wangfujing Da Jie, Dongcheng District
Tel. 6513 3388; Fax. 6513 2513; www.ichotelsgroup.com

Huafeng Hotel
华风饭店 东城区前门东大街 5 号
5 Qianmen Dong Da Jie, Dongcheng District. Tel. 6524 7311; Fax. 6524 7495

Jianguo Hotel
北京建国饭店 朝阳区建国外大街 5 号
5 Jianguomenwai Da Jie, Chaoyang District
Tel. 6500 2233; Fax. 6500 2871; www.hoteljianguo.com

Kerry Centre Hotel, Beijing
北京嘉里中心饭店 朝阳区光华路 1 号
1 Guanghua Lu, Chaoyang District
Tel. 6561 8833; Fax. 6561 2626; www.shangri-la.com

New Otani Chang Fu Gong Hotel
北京长富宫饭店 朝阳区建国外大街 26 号
26 Jianguomenwai Da Jie, Chaoyang District
Tel. 6512 5555; Fax. 6512 9813; www.cfgbj.com

Novotel Peace Hotel
北京诺富特和平宾馆 东城区王府井金鱼胡同 3 号
3 Jinyu Hutong, Wangfujing, Dongcheng District
Tel. 6512 8833; Fax. 6512 6863; www.novotel.com

Novotel Xin Qiao Beijing
北京诺富特新桥饭店 东城区东交民巷 2 号
2 Dong Jiao Min Xiang, Dongcheng District
Tel. 6513 3366; Fax. 6512 5126; www.novotel.com

Peninsula Beijing
北京王府半岛酒店 东城区王府井金鱼胡同 8 号
8 Jinyu Hutong, Wangfujing, Dongcheng District
Tel. 8516-2888; Fax. 6510 6311; www.beijing.peninsula.com

Raffles Beijing Hotel
北京饭店莱佛士酒店 东城区东长安街 33 号
33 Dong Chang'an Da Jie, Dongcheng District
Tel. 6526 3388; Fax. 8500 4380; www.beijing.raffles.com

The Regent Beijing

北京丽晶酒店　东城区金宝街 99 号

99 Jinbao Street, Dongcheng District

Tel. 8522; 1888 Fax. 8522 1818; www.regenthotels.com

Sofitel Wanda Beijing

北京万达索菲特大饭店　朝阳区建国路 93 号万达广场 C 座

93 Jianguo Lu, Buildng C, Wanda Plaza, Chaoyang District

Tel. 8599 6666; Fax. 8599 6686; www.sofitel-asia.com

St. Regis Beijing

北京国际俱乐部饭店　朝阳区建国门外大街 21 号

21 Jianguomenwai Da Jie, Chaoyang District

Tel. 6460 6688; Fax. 6460 3299; www.starwoodhotels.com/stregis

Tiantan Hotel

北京天坛饭店　崇文区体育馆路 1 号

1 Tiyuguan Lu, Chongwen District

Tel. 6719 0666; Fax. 6719 0388; www.tiantanhotel.com

Traders Hotel, Beijing

北京国贸饭店　朝阳区建国外大街 1 号

1 Jianguomenwai Avenue, Chaoyang District

Tel. 6505 2277; Fax. 6505 0838; www.shangri-la.com

WALK 5

Bamboo Garden Hotel

北京竹园宾馆　西城区旧鼓楼大街小石桥胡同 24 号

24 Xiaoshiqiao Hutong, Jiu Gulou Da Jie, Xicheng District

Tel. 5852 0088; Fax. 5852 0066; www.bbgh.com.cn

Beijing Guxiang 20

古乡 20 号商务会所　东城区南锣鼓乡 20 号

20 Nan Luogu Xiang, Dongcheng District

Tel 6400 5566; Fax. 6400 3658; www.guxiang20.com

Hotel Cote Cour S.L.

朋院四和宾馆　东城区演乐胡同 70 号

70 Yanyue Hutong, Dongcheng District

Tel. 6512 8020; Fax. 6512 7295; www.hotelcotecoursl.com

Kempinski Hotel Beijing Lufthansa Center

凯宾斯基饭店　朝阳区亮马桥路 50 号

50 Liangmaqiao Lu, Chaoyang District
Tel. 6465 3388; Fax. 6465 3366; www.kempinski-beijing.com

Kunlun Hotel

北京昆仑饭店　朝阳区新源南路 2 号
2 Xinyuan Nanlu, Chaoyang District
Tel. 6590 3388; Fax. 6590 3228; www.hotelkunlun.com

Lu Song Yuan Hotel

北京侣松园宾馆　北京宽街板厂胡同 22 号
22, Banchang Lane, Kuan Jie
Tel. 6404 0436; Fax. 6403 0418; webmaster@the-silk-road.com

Swissotel Beijing

北京港澳中心　东城区朝阳门北大街 2 号
Hong Kong Macau Center, 2 Chaoyangmen Bei Da Jie, Dongcheng District
Tel. 6553 2288; Fax. 6501 2501; www.swissotel-beijing.com

Traveler Inn Hua Qiao Beijing

北京旅居华桥饭店　东城区北新桥三条 5 号
5 Santiao Beixinqiao, Dongcheng District
Tel 6404 5784; Fax. 6402 0139; www.travelerinn.com.cn

WALK 6

Holiday Inn Downtown

北京金都假日饭店　西城区北礼士路 98 号
98 Beilishi Lu, Xicheng District
Tel. 6833 8822; Fax. 6834 0696; www.holiday-inn.com

InterContinental Financial Street Beijing

金融街洲际酒店　西城区金融街 11 号
11 Financial Street, Xicheng District
Tel 5852 5888; Fax. 5852 5999; www.intercontinental.com

Shangri-La Hotel

北京香格里拉饭店　海淀区紫竹院 29 号
29 Zizhuyuan Lu, Haidian District
Tel. 6841-2211; Fax. 6841-8006; www.shangri-la.com

The Ritz-Carlton

北京金融街丽思卡尔顿酒店　西城区金融街金城坊东街 1 号
1 Financial Street, Xicheng District
Tel. 6601 6666; Fax. 6601 6029; www.ritzcarlton.com

In 1931 the Grand Hotel de Pekin was indeed the grandest hotel in Peking,
located on Chang'an Boulevard conveniently close to both the Forbidden City and the Legation Quarter

BIBLIOGRAPHY

There are enough books on Peking in Chinese, Japanese, Korean, English, French, and German to fill a Great Wall of bookshelves, and enough information to compile a vast encyclopedia of the city. The wealth of available data begins with early Chinese gazetteers and includes Marco Polo, Ming-dynasty novels, Korean travelers' tales, Japanese maps, Jesuits' letters to the Vatican, Manchu stone inscriptions, *risqué* ballads, imperial rescripts, *hutong* rumors, BBC broadcasts, journalists' and businessmen's memoirs, opera playbills and Peking duck menus.

Quotes from early works by European and American writers suggest the seductive effect Old Peking could have on people. Reading classics like Juliet Bredon's *Peking*, Arlington and Lewisohn's *In Search of Old Peking*, and George Kates' *The Years That Were Fat* makes one impatient for the invention of the backwards-oriented time machine.

Chinese-language sources, of which many hundreds have been published and reprinted in China since the late 1970s, have been particularly helpful. Guidebooks, specialized treatises, scholarly journals, and maps were essential in assembling the unfinished jigsaw puzzle of this book. The list below is limited to books in English and French.

Acton, Harold. *Memoirs of an Aesthete* (London: Methuen, 1948)

Aldrich, Michael. *Search for a Vanishing Beijing: A Guide to China's Capital Through the Ages* (London: Oxford, 2006)

Arlington, L.C. & Lewisohn. *In Search of Old Peking* (Peking: Henri Vetch, 1935; Oxford reprint, 1988)

Becker, Jasper. *City of Heavenly Tranquility* (Penguin 2008)

Blofeld, John. *City of Lingering Splendour* (London: Hutchinson, 1961)

Bodde, Derk. *Peking Diary: A Year of Revolution* (New York: Abelard-Schuman, 1950; reprinted by Fawcett World Library, 1967)

Bodde, Derk. (trans.) *Annual Customs and Festivals in Peking* (Peking: Henri Vetch, 1936; Hong Kong: 1965)

Bonnard, Abel. *In China 1920–1921* (New York: E. P. Dutton, 1927)

Borel, Henri. *The New China: A Traveller's Impressions* (London: T Fisher Unwin, 1912)

Bouillard, G. *Le Temple de Ciel* (Paris: 1930)

Bredon, Juliet. *Peking* (Shanghai: Kelly and Walsh, 1931; Oxford reprinted, 1982)

Bredon, Juliet and Igor Mitrophanow. *The Moon Year* (Shanghai: Kelly and Walsh; Oxford reprint, 1982)

Bridge, Ann. *Peking Picnic* (Boston: Little, Brown & Company, 1932)

Broudehoux, Anne-Marie. *The Making and Selling of Post-Mao Beijing* (New York and London: Routledge, 2004)

Buxton, L.H. Dudley. *The Eastern Road* (London: Kegan Paul, 1924)

Cameron, Nigel and Brian Brake. *Peking: A Tale of Three Cities* (New York: Harper and Row, 1965)

Carl, Katherine *With the Empress Dowager of China* (1906; KPI Limited reprint, 1986)

Chang, Jung and Jon Halliday. *Mao: The Unknown Story* (New York: Alfred A. Knopf, 2005)

Collins, Gilbert. *Extreme Oriental Mixture* (London: Methuen & Co. Ltd., 1925)

Cook, Thomas & Son. *Peking and the Overland Route* (London: Thomas Cook & Son, 1917)

Crow, Carl. *The Travelers' Handbook for China (Including Hongkong)* Shanghai: Carl Crow, 1921)

Cumming, C.F. Gordon. *Wanderings in China* (Edinburgh & London: William Blackwood & Sons, 1888)

Der Ling, Princess. *Two Years in the Forbidden City* (New York: Uoffat, Yard and Company, 1911)

Dewey, John and Alice Chipman. Dewey *Letters from China and Japan* (New York: E. P. Dutton, 1920)

Dorn, Frank. *The Forbidden City: The Biography of a Palace* (New York: Charles Scribner's Sons, 1970)

The Economist Business Traveller's Guides: China (New York: Prentice Hall, 1988)

Edkins, Joseph. *Peking*, in Alexander Williamson, *Journeys in North China, Manchuria and Eastern Mongolia with Some Account of Korea* (London: Smith, Elden & Co., 1870)

Elder, Chris. *Old Peking: City of the Ruler of the World* (Hong Kong: Oxford University Press, 1997)

Fei-shi [Emil Fisher]. *Guide to Peking and its Environs* (Tientsin: Tientsin Press, 1909)

Fitzgerald, C.P. *Flood Tide in China* (London: The Cresset Press, 1958)

Fleming, Peter. *The Siege at Peking* (London: Rupert Hart-Davis, 1950; reprint, Birlinn, 2001)

Goodman, David S.G. *Beijing Street Voices* (London and Boston: Marion Boyars, 1981)

Harper, Damian. *Beijing City Guide* (Melbourne: Lonely Planet Publications, 2005)

Hibbard, Peter, Paul Mooney, and Steven Schwankert. *Beijing & Shanghai: China's Hottest Cities* (Odyssey, 2008)

Hsü, Immanuel C.Y. *The Rise of Modern China*, 3rd edition (Hong Kong: Oxford University Press, 1983)

Japanese Government Railways *Guide to China* (Tokyo: Japanese Government Railways, 1924)

Johnston, Reginald. *Twilight in the Forbidden City* (London: Victor Gollancz, 1934; Oxford reprint, 1985)

Kates, George N. *The Years that Were Fat: The Last of Old China* (New York: Harper & Brothers, 1952; Cambridge: Massachusetts Institute of Technology Press reprint, 1967 and 1976; Oxford reprint 1988)

Kidd, David. *Peking Story: The Last Days of Old China* (New York: Clarkson N Potter, 1988)

Lao She. *Crescent Moon and Other Stories* (Beijing: Panda Books, 1987)

Lewis, Simon. *The Rough Guide to Beijing* (New York and London: Rough Guides, 2004)

Leys, Simon. *Chinese Shadows* (Beltimore: Viking, 1978)

Li, Zhisui. *The Private Life of Chairman Mao* (New York: Random House, 1994)

Little, Mrs Archibald. *Guide to Peking* (Tientsin: Tientsin Press, 1904)

Loti, Pierre. (tr. Myrta L. Jones) *The Last Days of Pekin* (Boston: Little, Brown, 1902)

Lowe, H.Y. *The Adventures of Wu: The Life Cycle of a Peking Man* (Peking: The Peking Chronicle Press, 1940-41; Princeton University Press reprint, 1983)

Madrolle. *A Handbook for Travellers in Northern China and Korea* (Paris and London: Hachete & Company, 1912)

Malone, Carroll Brown. *History of the Peking Summer Palaces Under the Ch'ing Dynasty* (Urbana: University of Illinois, 1934)

Marcuse, Jacques. *The Peking Papers* (New York: E.P. Dutton, 1967)

Martin W.A.P. *A Cycle of Cathay or China, South and North* (New York: Fleming H. Revell, 1897)

Michie, Alexander. *The Englishman in China during the Victorian Era* (Edinburgh and London: William Blackwood & Sons, 1900)

Mirams, D.G. *A Brief History of Chinese Architecture* (Shanghai: Kelly and Walsh, 1940)

Morrison, Hedda Hammer. *A Photographer in Old Peking* (Hong Kong: Oxford University Press, 1985)

Myron, Paul. *Our Chinese Chances through Europe's Eyes* (Chicago: Linebarge Brothers, 1915)

Nagel's *Encyclopedia Guide to China* (Geneva: Nagel Verlag, several editions)

Naquin, Susan. *Peking: Temples and City Life, 1400-1900* (Berkeley: University of California Press, 2000)

Neville-Hadley, Peter *Beijing* (London: Cadogan Guides, 2000)

The Peiping Chronicle *Guide to Peking* (Peiping: The Peiping Chronicle, 1935)

The Peiping Bookshop *A Guide to Peiping and its Environs* (Peiping: The Peiping Bookshop, 1946)

Putnam Weale, B.L. *Indiscreet Letters from Peking* (New York: Dodd, Mead, 1907)

Quennel, Peter. *A Superficial Journey Through Tokyo and Peking* (London: Faber & Faber, 1932; Oxford reprint, 1986)

Rennie, D.F. *Peking and the Pekinese* (London: John Murray, 1865)

Siren, Osvald. *The Gardens of China* (New York: Ronald Press, 1949)

Siren, Osvald. *The Imperial Palaces of Peking* (Paris: 1926, AMS reprint, 1976)

Sit, Victor F.S. *Beijing: The Nature and Planning of a Chinese Capital City* (Chichester and New York: John Wiley & Sons, 1995)

Sitwell, Osbert. *Escape with Me!* (London: Macmillan; Oxford reprint, 1983)

Smith, Graham. *Frommer's Beijing 4th Edition* (Hoboken, New Jersey: Wiley, 2006)

Trevor-Roper, Hugh. *Hermit of Peking* (New York: Alfred A Knopf, 1977)

Terzani, Tiziano. *The Forbidden Door* (Hong Kong: Asia 2000 Ltd, 1985)

Thomson, John. *Through China with a Camera* (London & New York: Harper & Brothers, 1899)

Warner, Marina. *The Dragon Empress: Life & Times of Tz'u-his 1835–1908* (London: Weidenfeld & Nicolson Ltd, 1972)

Wilhelm, Richard. *The Soul of China* (London: Harcourt Brace Jovanovich, 1928)

Willets, William. *Chinese Art, 2 vols.* (Harmondsworth: Penguin Books, 1958)

Wu Hong. *Remaking Beijing: Tiananmen Square and the Creation of a Political Space* (Chicago: University of Chicago Press, 2005)

Yao, Ming-le. *The Conspiracy and Murder of Mao's Heir* (London: Collins, 1983)

Zhou, Shachen. *Beijing Old and New* (Beijing: New World Press, 1984)

Yu, Zhaoyun, ed. *Palaces of the Forbidden City* (London: Allen Lane, 1984)

Drawn. by T. Allom.

"Jugglers exhibiting in the court of a Mandarin's Palace"
An engraving based upon a drawing by Thomas Allom

Engraved by T. A. Prior.

INDEX

The high-rise developments all around Beijing can seem relentless,
the tranquility of the palaces and parks are one sure respite summer or winter

*Splendid in the snow (inset) the Forbidden City in February;
consider an out-of-season visit to Beijing*

Dongbianmen, the Gate of the North-East Angle, houses four floors of museum space, including the Red Gate Gallery. Adjacent is the last remaining section of the

magnificent Ming dynasty city wall, the small park here is a nice place for a stroll either early or late in the day, beneath the very wall itself. Not one of our Six Walks but well worth visiting, perhaps before you embark on Walk 2
Insert: *Luggage label for the Grand Hotel de Pekin circa 1930*

As is frequently the case (at many other sights too) a visit early or late in the day is likely to be well rewarded with a sense of almost having the place to one's self. Out of season visits can be quieter still. Beihai Park, Walk Three

GENERAL SHAN.   THE LATE PRINCE CH'UN.   LI HUNG CHANG.
THREE GREAT MEN OF CHINA.

MIS/18/03

Recent reviews of other Odyssey titles...

"Thorough and beautifully illustrated, this book is a comprehensive—and fun—window into Afghan history, culture, and traditions. A must have for travel readers and a gripping read for anyone with even a passing interest in Afghanistan."
—Khaled Hosseini, author of *The Kite Runner*—

"...for coverage of Chongqing and the Gorges, and of the more placid and historically notable sites below Yichang and downriver to Shanghai, it is unrivalled... "
—*Simon Winchester*—

"It is one of those rare travel guides that is a joy to read whether or not you are planning a trip..."
—*The New York Times*—

"...Essential traveling equipment for anyone planning a journey of this kind..."
—*Asian Wall Street Journal*—

"If travel books came with warnings, the one for AFGHANISTAN: A COMPANION AND GUIDE would read, 'Caution: may inspire actual voyage.' But then, this lavishly produced guide couldn't help do otherwise—especially if you're partial to adventure."
—*TIME*, August 22nd 2005—

"Above all, it is authoritative and as well-informed as only extensive travels inside the country can make it. It is strong on the history. In particular the synopsis at the beginning is a masterly piece of compression."
—*The Spectator* (UK)—

"A gem of a book"
—*The Literary Review* (UK)—

"...Quite excellent. No one should visit Samarkand, Bukhara or Khiva without this meticulously researched guide..."
—*Peter Hopkirk, author of* The Great Game—

uide is terrific"
de Books—

utan guidebooks..."
 Leisure—

"   hat makes me long to go back to China..."
s Norwich—

urous travelers with a literary bent.
 Guide to where you're going, grab it..."
raphic Traveler—

Beijing Subway

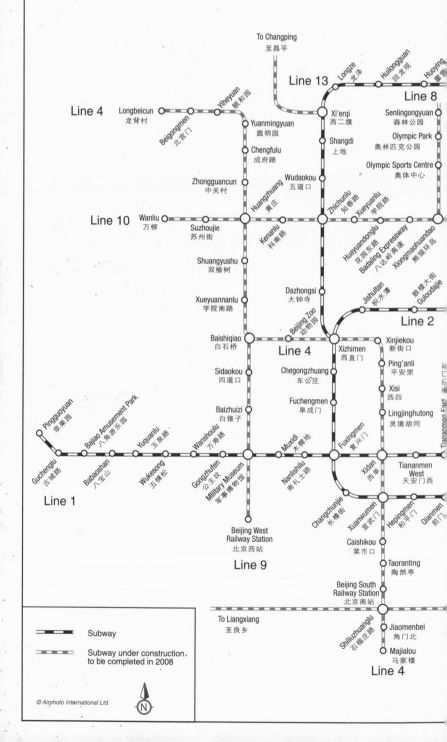

To Changping
至昌平

Line 13

Line 4

Line 10

Line 1

Line 9

Line 8

Line 2

Subway

Subway under construction, to be completed in 2008

© Airphoto International Ltd.